CREATIVE MANAGEMENT
A Strategic Paradigm for Digital-era

One of the contemporary puzzles in the world of business is how innovation, design thinking and creativity are linked, if at all, in the work place. Fragmented practice of innovations in processes pertaining to market sensing and fulfilment, creation and redefinition of business models, competencies and structures among others, leading to success are many in the business world. What this book does is crisply contextualize the intent and practice of these concepts with the help of case-lets. It is written in a non-jargonized style that helps practitioners as well as learners to create a roadmap in their own contexts based on the application based knowledge of creativity and its role in business.

A rewarding read this, from an author with impeccable credentials to guide us through the arcane universe of creativity and innovation.

Dr. Venkatesh Umashankar
Prof. of Marketing, Great Lakes Institute of Management, Gurgaon, India

Need for zero-based thinking towards our traditional management paradigm and case for considering creativity as the most critical business resource are very convincingly presented. The book should be read by everyone interested in the future of business and management.

Dr. Theresa Loo
Adjunct Faculty, New York University Shanghai
Ex-National Training Director, Ogilvy & Mather China

In this work, the author offers very useful strategy options and cases that can help us to reflect on and manage challenges of digital revolution and need for corporate transformation as well as imperative of innovation and creativity management. The book offers some systematic approaches to nurture and retain creativity within the organisation and effectively use it to meet digital era challenges – a skill that no organisation, new or old, wishing to survive in this century can afford to by-pass.

Dr. Felipe Villegas
Corporate Director IT/OPS, Strategy and Control
BBVA, Bancomer, Mexico

"There has never been a time when creativity has been so needed or important." In this most timely book, Prof. Saumya Sindhwani sets out a compelling case for building creativity in one's own organisation, and then sets out how to enhance creativity in the core business practices, including strategy development, innovation and management.

Prof. Saumya Sindhwani's book will help you and your organisation journey with success in this increasingly volatile world.

Simon McKenzie
Chief Operating Officer, Bridge Partnership

If you buy this book do not expect to read a list of do's and don'ts about creativity, or a formula for making an organisation more innovative and dynamic. Instead, you will read a series of ideas, anecdotes and case studies and be invited to reflect on them by answering questions as to what you would do in a given situation. There's no appendix with a list of 'right' answers either. You have to decide what might or might not work and while doing so you will improve your own abilities as a creative manager.

Both my children work in creative businesses, one in fashion, and the other in television. Sometimes I tease them by asking for an explanation as to why one of their new ideas will work. Normally they can't do so convincingly, as it's near impossible, for example, to justify what is not yet on the market. However, they both 'know' when a new product or program will sell. Why? Because they take their time, think their ideas through, discuss them, seek feedback and then move quickly to implement.

You cannot come up with new ways of doing things on demand, as creative management is not like pushing the right buttons on a coffee machine to get a different drink next time around. What works, as Saumya explains, is also a function of context. The thought processes she describes will help you reach a good solution. Try them and see.

Gary Davies
Professor of Strategy, Alliance Manchester Business School

CREATIVE MANAGEMENT
A Strategic Paradigm for Digital-era

Saumya Sindhwani

Foreword by
Prof. Rajendra Srivastava
Dean and Novartis Professor of
Marketing Strategy and Innovation
Indian School of Business, Hyderabad, India

Sterling Publishers (P) Ltd.
Regd. Office: A1/256 Safdarjung Enclave,
New Delhi-110029. CIN: U22110DL1964PTC211907
Tel: 26387070, 26386209; Fax: 91-11-26383788
E-mail: mail@sterlingpublishers.com
www.sterlingpublishers.com

Creative Management: A Strategic Paradigm for Digital-era
© 2017, Saumya Sindhwani
ISBN 978 81 207 9498 6

All rights are reserved.
No part of this publication may be reproduced, stored in a retrieval system or transmitted, in any form or by any means, mechanical, photocopying, recording or otherwise, without prior written permission of the original publisher.

Printed in India

Printed and Published by Sterling Publishers Pvt. Ltd.,
Plot No. 13, Ecotech-III, Greater Noida - 201306,
Uttar Pradesh, India

In the memory of Manoj

With immense love and gratitude to my parents

and

the love of my life Rishaan
(who likes to be called Dr Rishaan)

Foreword

As we transition from the industrial-era economics of land, labour and capital to the new knowledge-era economy driven by the power of thought, ideas and innovations, imperatives for new thinking become obvious. It is often said that managers are paid to solve problems. In this context Albert Einstein had observed—"we cannot solve our problems with the same thinking we used when we created them."

Digital technologies have revolutionised the world of business. Globalisation; new business models; near zero marginal cost business-economics; new organisational architecture; artificial intelligence and analytics embedded systems; without walls business offices, work-places with virtual work force; e-commerce options; any-time any-place work-places and shopping; new speed and scope of business operations; new human-human and human-machine relationships: new work-ways and work-place options have created new challenges as well as opportunities for business managers. New high-speed creative and strategic management thinking is essential to match with new business realities. To enhance business performance, managers and business leaders would have to create and blend appropriate creative intuitions in their management processes.

Most industrial-era organisations are in the process of finding ways to become knowledge-era fit. Business managers have to maintain contextual dynamic balance between change and continuity. Insightful understanding of customers, business processes, digital technologies and competitors is essential. Relationships between business organisations and their customers have been transformed by smart phones. Customers, the life-line for any business organisation have become information empowered. Shopping at-the-speed-of-thought is becoming the new normal. Also, empowered with mobile phones and social media, even one dissatisfied customer can create global impact. The multi-faceted challenges for business managers have increased many-fold. While making use of big-data high-speed analytics or advanced customer relationship management (CRM) technologies, managers cannot afford to neglect sentiments of individual customers.

New disruptive business models and ways of doing business have added many new complexities, uncertainties, ambiguities and instabilities for business organisations. Managers have to operate with many new unknowns and manage many complexities where a solution here creates a problem there. Initiating speedy creative solutions and approaches to problems is essential. To enhance participative management, managers would have to master the art of transforming problems into contextual creative challenges for their teams. In a complex fast changing business environment, to develop speedy response, knowledge of creative capabilities and competencies of their teams is critical for managers.

Digital technologies have become ubiquitous. For business organisations, knowledge-era socio-economic realities also include – globalisation with new global-local sensitivities; cross-cultural diversity; new geo-political and geo-economic interdependence; working in multinational real-virtual teams; managing cyberspace security issues; new speed of disruptive innovations and competition from unknown sources located in different parts of the world.

I am delighted to write the foreword for this book as, besides various other academic and management areas, the learning venture of Prof. Saumya Sindhwani has been multi-faceted and multi-disciplinary. Her ability to integrate insights across disciplines is a wonderful relief from narrow insights gained from single areas of study or discipline. By examining role of creativity in different business activities and contexts she has made her study comprehensive. In her own unique way, she has substantiated a strong relationship between creativity and commercial operations. She has explored ways to initiate and nurture contextual creativity in a disciplined and focused way to enhance business performance.

Foreword

Besides the concept of creative management, topics such as innovations and creativity dynamics; mapping business knowledge; economics of creativity; organisational learning paradigm; seeding and cultivating corporate creativity; designing integrated creative strategy would be of interest to business school faculty, working executives as well as students aspiring to be future managers.

With her own experience as start-up entrepreneur during her college days, the few interesting short case-lets developed by her are likely to generate lively discussions in corporate corridors as well as classrooms, and also encourage students to initiate their own digital ventures. In some ways the book seem to be a continuation of her earlier learning venture and book – Nurturing Business Leaders in which she developed the Zero-Based Proactive Learning Paradigm (ZBPLP).

Starting with her prologue, she has made a compelling case for the role of creativity in commercial ventures. She has narrated her simple and sophisticated approach to understanding the why, what, when, where and how of creativity in business operations.

Venturing to create future scenarios in an uncertain fast changing business environment is a hazardous task. As the epilogue of study suggests there are many new questions that need to be further examined. Saumya has invited readers to give their views and if they like be part of her continuous learning venture.

Perhaps the book can help create a small contextual community of people interested in creating creative spaces in business ventures and socio-economic development.

Prof. Rajendra Srivastava
Dean and Novartis Professor of
Marketing Strategy and Innovation,
Indian School of Business, Hyderabad, India

Prologue

During a coffee break discussion at one of the Executive Development Programmes, a perceptibly agitated participant said, "Doc., may I share some off-the-record personal observations about the programme? I know, all speakers are super specialists and international authorities on their subjects, but I have been feeling increasingly lost during most of the presentations. As an organiser of the programme, perhaps you would not agree, and please forgive me if you find my observations rude."

I smiled and said, "Please go on, say it. Feel free to express your observations in detail. I really want to know how you feel about the programme and why."

He responded, "I am an engineer and have been in the profession for over two decades, in various industries and in different countries. I may be wrong, but I feel that all the talk about digital knowledge-era and associated jargons, as well as need for creative and innovative mindsets as discussed here, are far from ground realities. These kinds of management education workshops on creativity and innovation are just buzzwords or jargons designed to show that one is in-trend or in-tune with topical hi-fashion management."

After a short pause to explain the need for high precision in industry, he went on to say, "At times, I feel that your approach may be harmful for some executives and some industries. Some of us need to focus on quality, through very high degree of standardisation and avoid disruptive innovations or creativity. It is doing-as-told and not fuzzy-disruptive-creative-thinking that is the critical success factor."

After another pause to explain his observations with some examples from his industrial manufacturing experience, he said, "To achieve day-to-day challenges of quality and performance, what we, as managers, need is more and more standardisation. In this age of six-sigma and consistent high quality expectations, what we really need is more focused, uninterrupted consistency and not abstract distraction from the so-called critical and creative thinking." His expressions indicated his disdain.

With a smile on his face he added, "As you know, the most coveted degree in business schools around the world is MBA—Master in Business *Administration*, not Master in Business *Management* or Master in Business *Leadership* or Master in Business *Creativity*. As far as I know, creativity is not a core subject in business schools. In real business situations, managers and leaders are expected to push or pull the existing structured cart of business and not create it."

After sharing some more workplace experiences, he went on to say, "As you already know, we are progressively replacing human workers by robots in our production lines. Automated or programmed machines are far more reliable than humans. This is happening in many industrialised and even some not-so-industrialised countries. All this requires standardisation."

Our conversation was abruptly interrupted by an announcement to return to the programme venue.

As we slowly walked back to the room, he said with a smile, "Doc., I feel your use of the term 'creative management' is an oxymoron—a self-contradicting statement like a serious-joke or juxtapose of management and mess."

He added, "I think of management as a science. A defined, structured, cold-blooded, target focused, result oriented, disciplined, activity. On the other hand, creativity, as I understand it, is unstructured, messy, fuzzy, free flowing imagination—emotional, random and undisciplined, as well as intuitive—an activity with undefined purpose."

He continued, "Doc., business realities are very different from what you assume them to be in your classrooms. I think academic institutions need to re-examine their assumptions about the real corporate world. I often tell my workers to leave their brains and heart at home when they come to work with me in the factory."

While the programme concluded with the customary mutual thanks, goodwill gestures and smiles, his observations stayed on with me. For me, his observations continued to be the topic of informal conversations with my colleagues, friends and managers in the world of commerce.

For days I wondered why such a highly qualified business manager had failed to see himself as a creative master craftsman while forging together a team of human beings as well as artificial intelligence embedded robots to achieve quality and quantity targets. How is the creative mixing and matching of human skills with artificial intelligence of machines to create efficient assembly line different from selecting and mixing of colours to create a painting on a canvas or producing musical notes to create a symphony?

In business, creativity is about exploring and evaluating alternate commercially viable value-adding options. Why do experienced international business executives often fail to see their own value-adding creativity? Complex commercial creative processes are an integral part of their cross-cultural global plans. Creativity contributes to their being nimble, agile and adaptive in local contexts. Also, use of creative diplomacy to design and negotiate win-win commercial partnerships is an integral part of cross-cultural global business activities. While being immersed in multi-faceted creative activities, why were they unaware of them?

I often wonder, what is so creative about the world of art—writing stories, composing music or colouring canvas—and so uncreative about the world of business management. Business managers creatively assemble talent, technology and other commercial resources to transform raw material into aesthetically designed products and sell them at affordable prices. They creatively display well designed products and attractively present them to create happy customers, corporations and communities.

How is a creatively created commercial product less creative than a sculpture? Both are in search of customers. Personally, I experienced many disconnects in my observations and thinking. In my own limited way, I adopted a zero-based approach to my enquiry as I had done for my earlier learning venture that resulted in the book, *Nurturing Business Leaders: Zero-based Proactive Learning Paradigm*.

This book is my story—experience and thought processes to find answers to the above, as well as related questions. It may also be seen as a collection of dialogues and musings. Besides the participant of the programme, who wants to remain anonymous, many people from different walks of life in different countries have been a source of my learning and this book. At the outset, I want to express my very grateful thanks to them all for sharing their knowledge and views.

Acknowledgements

With many questions in mind, while interacting with people from different industries, I felt that in this knowledge-era, with simultaneous high-speed on-line-off-line operations, new risks and scales, business management seemed to have evolved as the most creative of the creative arts. Digital technologies have introduced many complex challenges as well as created great opportunities. This book is an effort to understand these challenges, opportunities and possibilities.

Also, encouraged by the positive response from a diverse groups of readers—academic and industry—to my earlier book, *Nurturing Business Leaders: Zero-based Proactive Learning Paradigm*, with my university colleagues from China and Mexico, I felt encouraged to venture alone in this learning expedition. I am very grateful to Theresa and Guillerma for their support for my current venture.

People with experience, knowledge and insights of business operations in different parts of the world were my main source of learning. I am very grateful to them all. Since most wanted to remain anonymous, I have avoided linking views, observations and stories with names. Varied and disparate views are the result of the differences in the nature of industries, the position of the organisation in the industry, as well as the viewpoint of the individuals. Enquiries also came up while observing different business activities in my day-to-day life in different countries and industries.

Besides consulting various books and journals, to gain an overall understanding of the concept of creativity and management, I also sought views of people from different walks of life. One spiritual guru, who was also a visiting faculty at some business schools, while responding to my query said, "All living beings are creative at all times in all their actions. Organisations are created by people, for people and are managed by people. How can they survive without being creative?" After explaining a few related concepts, he went on to say, "Please remember the three facets of nature — *Brahma, Vishnu and Mahesh*. There is creativity and management in all three — creation, preservation and destruction."

Sourcing information, structuring and writing this book has been a humbling, learning and insightful experience for me. To gain suitable understanding of the concepts, as the readers will notice, I have limited the scope of enquiry to commercial operations. Also, as Zen masters tell us that the deepest insights are the most obvious, some readers may find this book a compilation of the obvious and common sense conclusions.

I owe a huge debt of gratitude to my family, friends and colleagues who encouraged me in my learning venture. My very special thanks, with love, to my late husband, who was always a source of inspiration. Thank you my dear Manoj, wherever you may be.

I am very grateful to my parents, Uma and Trilok Sindhwani, for their constant support and guidance. Without them nothing would have been possible. I can never thank them enough. My dear son Rishaan (now 4+), who likes to be addressed as Doctor Rishaan, for being the constant source of inspiration in my life. And for often excusing me from his classes of music, cooking and story-telling or travel in his "car" to different parts of the word for just two dollars. Thank you *nani-nanu* for attending his classes and keeping him busy so that I could work on this book. My very special grateful thanks to Ranvir and Adarsh Trehan for their encouragement and support in my various learning efforts.

My very grateful thanks to friends, who are more like family and mentors, Renoo Nirula, Divvya Nirula, Prof Umashanker Venkatesh, Prof Kamlesh Misra, Prof Gary Davis, Theresa Loo, Guillermo Alejandri, Flocy and Bonnie Joseph, Rajani Koduganti, Priyanka Mathur, Tithi Mathur, Shagun Singh, Irene Hoon, Frank Tan, Akemi Tahara, Rebecca Siow, Belle Chan, Ajay Kaul, Shweta Sharma, Vandana and Arush Barar, Subha Sheshan and Hemant Kedam.

Acknowledgements xvii

I would like to thank all my current and former colleagues and all the senior executives for their time and insightful thoughts on the topic. Particularly, I would like to thank Kwan Chee Wei, Catherine Mudford, Catherine McKenzie, Jerry Connor, Anupam Prakash, Neil Shastri, Havovi Joshi, Sarita Mathur, Ruth Chiang, Tan Suh Wen, Kenny Toh, Simon McKenzie and Lee Sears.

My very special thanks to Prof Philip Charles Zerrillo and Prof Howard Thomas for their constant encouragement, intellectual stimulus and support.

My very special grateful thanks to Prof Rajendra Srivastava, Dean and Noratis Professor of Marketing, Strategy and innovation, Indian School of Business, Hyderabad, India for his encouragement and accepting to write the foreword.

I am very grateful to Mr. S. K. Ghai, Chairman and Managing Director of Sterling Publishers for his valuable guidance and editor Sanjiv Sarin for his help in improving the readability and presentation of the subject matter.

The book represents views from many people and, once again, I am very grateful to all of them for sharing their insights. However, only I am responsible for the shortcomings of the book.

Saumya Sindhwani
Singapore Management University

Preface

Just as creativity transforms canvases into paintings and words into songs, it transforms innovative ideas into viable commercial propositions. Creativity is the prime mover as well as life blood of business processes. Creativity keeps organisations alive and ignited. It maps the future and creates a tomorrow for business units.

Each business activity is uniquely creative. Each business process is a complex mix of creative activities, be it sourcing raw materials; designing of products, services and strategies; manufacturing; controlling costs; generating sales or optimising profit margins. Overall, business is a creative value adding process, requiring creative management. Differences in the quantity and quality of creative skills—individual, teams and organisational, have always been the business differentiators. For competitiveness as well as for excellence, creativity is the required core competency.

Creative and innovative thinking helps entrepreneurs align the needs of customers, with technological feasibility and commercial viability. Critical thinking and creativity are intrinsic parts of business strategy designing process. Creative management approach helps in making business purpose more purposeful, relevant and sustainable for all stakeholders. Creative management is a people centric, digital technology supported and future focused management paradigm.

Quality of business is often used as a barometer for evaluating the levels of socio-economic development. Innovations—new, commercially viable ideas—have been the engines of commercial progress. Innovation and creative possibilities exist in every business activity, more so with digital technology options such as global connectivity, artificial intelligence, Internet-of-Things (IoT), virtual reality, robotics, 3-D printing and wearables. To identify and design products and services that meet customer expectations (or even create them), technical feasibility and commercial viability, business units often require iterative creative design-thinking experimentations.

Learning from mistakes, being aware of risks, speed and scale requirements are an integral part of creative management.

National as well as global commercial arenas are complex and risk infested. Operating simultaneously in the fast changing traditional physical and cyber environments, business managers have to maintain customer focus as well as counter new disruptive digital strategies of competitors. Integrative design-thinking is an essential part of creative management.

Globalisation and creative use of digital technologies have transformed the life-style as well as shopping behaviour of customers. Many radically new business models have evolved. Social interaction between people, as well as interdependence between workers and machines are changing fast. In many cases, the lines between work-places and personal-spaces are vanishing. Digital technologies are ubiquitous. Mobile global connectivity constantly creates new challenges for business managers in different industries. They are required to simultaneously operate in physical or real as well as cyber or virtual world, each having different attitudes, dynamics and cultures. Integrating diversity is a dynamic and creative challenge.

The constant changes require new thinking, new theories and new management paradigms. Managers need to constantly rethink their options and roles. Creativity requires a new creative agenda. Managers need a mindset that is customer focused, as well as aware of the dynamics, risks, complexities and uncertainties in the multi-cultural commercial arenas. They need a dynamic, multi-focused and creative design-thinking managerial mindset.

The paradigm shift has introduced many new known-unknowns as well as unknown-unknowns in the fast changing business arenas. Transitioning from *stand-alone* agro-industrial environment to *connected* agro-industrial-information environment, business has passed through the phase of creativity-on-the-move. Thus, there is a constant situation of facing ever-changing multi-faceted creative challenges by business managers.

Fast moving digital technology innovations have created volatility, uncertainties, complexities and ambiguities (VUCA) in the global business arenas. Waiting for disruptions to knock on the corporate doors and then *reactively* plan, organise and formulate policy to counter dynamic, undefined problems would be unproductive. To meet expectation of customers-on-the-move, managers need to simultaneously connect a number of moving dots. A proactive and creative management mindset is an imperative.

This book is an effort to understand the role of creativity, critical and creative design-thinking in the dynamic world of digital-business. A few caselets have been designed for readers and students to seed curiosity, initiate enquiry and provoke proactive learning, as well as to generate a sense of ownership over what they experience. Each caselet is expected to provide experience in ideas and thought sharing as well as collaborative problem-solving. Caselets, as well as the creative management role-play options at the end of each chapter, may be enacted by students individually or as a team. Each solution designing option provides enough creative space for them to clarify their assumptions, define and create their own platform and contextualise their role.

Most of the book has been written on-the-move. Inputs for the book also came while travelling to different countries and on different assignments. Readers may find some abrupt shifts in the thought process or some disconnects. It may also be seen as reflection of the complexities, uncertainties and fast changing nature of business environment. In my effort to make each chapter comprehensive, restatement of some concepts in different contexts was essential. I would be grateful for any observations and suggestions for improvement from the readers.

The Creative Management paradigm presented in this book has emerged from my efforts to understand the realities of the business arenas, visualise the challenges and opportunities that have emerged in the high-speed disruptive digital-era and understand the need for new human creativity oriented management thinking and theories. I would welcome suggestions from readers to improve the paradigm and make it more appropriate for the real world of business, practising managers, as well as for aspiring, future managers.

Saumya Sindhwani
Singapore Management University

Contents

	Foreword	vii
	Prologue	xi
	Acknowledgements	xv
	Preface	xix
1.	Creativity in the World of Commerce	2
2.	Creative Digital Disruptions	28
3.	Learning Organisations and Creativity	50
4.	Commercial Landscapes, Cyberscapes and Mindscapes	71
5.	Creativity Imperatives	100
6.	Context of Creativity	127
7.	Designing Integrated Creative Strategy	154
8.	Customers, Competition and Creativity	188
9.	Economics of Creativity in Commerce	215
10.	Creative Management	245
	Epilogue	278

1

Creativity involves breaking out of established patterns in order to look at things in a different way.

Edward de Bono

Creativity in the World of Commerce

To be creative is to be curious and question, be aware and think, explore and experiment with new ideas, observe, listen and learn, and much more. In every day parlance, a person is said to be creative or innovative when he or she can suggest some *new* appropriate contextual solutions.

In a commercial context, creative and innovative ideas are expected to be socially desirable, technically feasible and commercially viable. These ideas should enhance efficiencies of business processes or enrich customers' experience with products and services in more cost effective ways.

Critical and creative thinking is a process of exploring different options and possibilities. A creative work may also be defined as an assignment that requires a new contextual solution, use of imagination, intuition, new thinking and new inputs. In our daily lives, each new day brings in new and different sets of problems, new challenges, requiring new thinking and new sets of solutions. Creativity helps in designing appropriate value added solutions.

It is said that, by nature, we humans, like other beings, are creative individuals. Each one of us is the chief-executive officer (CEO) and full (100%) owner of his or her own Creativity.com or I.Inc. Also, as will be discussed in the chapters that follow, each individual in business operations is a unique source of creativity.

Creativity, Innovation and Design-thinking

Creativity, innovation and design-thinking are situation specific activities. From a business perspective, innovation may be a new idea or a new process of introducing new value for customers.

Or, it may be a new value added product or service—for a new segment of customers. Innovation need not be a brand-new product, service or business model. It may be an application of the traditional way of doing things in new contexts or in new ways. Or, it may just help in reducing systemic friction of business processes.

Be it in the virtual or cyberspace operations, or traditional business arenas, creativity, critical-thinking, as well as design-thinking are needed to make things simpler, cheaper, more efficient and more attractive for the customers. Design in business is about creating a satisfactory experience for the end users of products and services. For high-fashion and expensive luxury products, style and design are critical success factors.

Innovative ideas in business do not come up fully formed. As ideas travel through different corridors of business organisations, they undergo continual permutations, combinations, mutations and morphing. Many value adding innovations also happen as business managers address many different cross-cultural needs of customers in global business arenas, making products and services attractive, affordable as well as accessible in new cultural contexts.

Technology: machinery or process developed from scientific knowledge, by itself, would have little value. It is the contextual, creative and appropriate use of technology that gives it value. In business, design-thinking is also the process of matching technology with commercial objectives.

As will be discussed in later chapters, creativity or *rachnatmakta* is an integral part of every management *mantra*. Management is a creative process. Contextual and creative use of creativity creates more productive and value adding strategic options. A creative process includes critical perception of situations, processes, happenings and things around us.

Business: A Dynamic Creative Collage

Is commerce antithesis of creativity? Or, is creativity an integral part of commercial activity? These were frequently discussed topics.

In our day-to-day conversations, creativity is usually associated with fine arts such as poetry, music and painting, and innovation with science and technology. Business arenas are meeting grounds of both. As will be discussed in later chapters, throughout the business value chains, science and art mingle, mix and mimic each other.

Caselet 1.1

Management: A STEM Perspective

Even before he finished his post graduate degree, Rishu was recruited from his Ivy League campus by a well-known international management consultancy firm. He had demonstrated his commitment and exceptional competency in science, technology, engineering and technology (STEM) related subjects. The management consultancy firm was interested in expanding its consultancy operations in digital technology areas such as smart systems, use of artificial intelligence, self-driven cars, big data analytics, Internet-of-Things (IoT) and smart cities.

Soon after joining the company, Rishu's team was invited by a well-established business organisation to analyse and evaluate possibilities of improving competitive position of their brands as well as the organisation. The seventy years old organisation had a very favourable reputation for its high quality brands and customer services.

Recent industry performance data indicated increasing market share trends for new digital technology savvy organisations.

On returning from the meeting, the team held a short brain-storming session to develop their client strategy. Rishu, with two juniors to assist him, was given the responsibility to prepare the first draft of the strategic transformation plan presentation for the client.

With a firm belief in the virtues of self-sufficiency of logic, algorithms and artificial intelligence (AI), he, along with his two colleagues, presented their strategic plan for the reorganisation of their potential client organisation for consideration of their full team.

The key objective and suggestions included:

- The objective: To transform the industrial-era success story into a competitive and successful digital-era business organisation.
- Extensive use of the state-of-the-art digital technology in supply chain. Use of AI to automate inventory controls, placement of orders and expediting supplies to optimise through just-in-time approach. This was expected to result in significant cost savings.
- Also, to save cost and create seamless operations, it was suggested that the manufacturing operations of the company follow similar approach in automating and installing AI empowered monitoring and control systems.
- Following same logic, most advanced digital technology compatible systems were suggested for marketing, distribution, accounting, finance, human resource management as well as research and development departments.
- For effective overall coordination and management, advanced AI embedded comprehensive information systems were recommended. Based on the available business data, all known variables were to be factored in the network.
- Systematic processing of information, speedy and real time feedback network were recommended for performance monitoring and automatic corrective actions.
- To optimise the overall system, the management systems were designed as if they were playing a chess game with the operating system, reacting to data and developments.
- In the confidential note to the management, the transformation implementation strategy was to include:
    - As transformation would lead to redundancy of staff, it was recommended that the vast experience of the existing staff would be coded and captured in advanced AI systems.

- ○ As learning machines were to take over operations from staff and managers, systems design would be done by vendors and implementation of transformation should maintain "secret" or "confidential" status.
- ○ To minimise conflict situations, it was suggested that finer details of the transformation implementation strategy be confidentially worked out with nominated senior staff of the human resource department.

Some thoughts and questions:

- What are the basic assumptions in designing the business transformation?
- Are the assumptions appropriate and valid?
- Would artificial intelligence based systems and controls compete with:
  - ○ Human relationships and smiles, and
  - ○ Define future of business organisations?
- Will there be a meaningful role for human brain in management systems?
- What will be the future role of critical and creative thinking in business arenas?
- What would be the role of managers and business leaders in such an organisation?
- Your overall assessment of the recommended action plan?

Creativity has many *avatars;* many forms, colours and shades. To survive in an uncertain, ever changing, competitive environment, business organisations use a variety of creative talents. Depending on the nature and scope of business, each business unit creates its supply chain, operation, finance, skills management, marketing and sales activities. Each activity requires different sets of knowledge base and creative approach. Business process is a dynamic flow of knowledge, skills and creativity.

While sharing her views on creativity and innovation, a successful lady fashion designer, who is also a visiting faculty at NIFT (National Institute of Fashion Technology), said:

> English is not my first language. Creativity for me is an intuitive or instinctive act or process, while innovation for me is the end-product of creativity. It may be the end-product of a frugal engineering effort like a Nano car by Tata Motors. Or it may be a designer and customised bike with alligator skin saddle, frames decorated with 24-carat gold leaf costing more than a luxury car. Although, the must-have luxury item bikes have little in common with the more functional and utilitarian Nano cars, I think both are commercially successful innovations, full of creative inputs.

Innovation is an idea — a visualised end product or service. Creativity is the roadmap, process or strategy to transform an innovative idea into a commercially viable product or service. Creativity starts with an innovative idea. Creativity transforms an idea into a reality — be it colour on canvas, or a fashion item in a market place or an App in a smart phone. Thus, innovation may be perceived as the beginning, as well as the end of a creativity cycle.

To be commercially meaningful, creativity has to be contextual, appropriate and timely (CAT). The nature, scale and size of innovations vary from situation to situation, industry to industry, product to product and service to service.

Creativity and Entrepreneurship

Creativity is a synonym for entrepreneurship. Creativity and entrepreneurship have many common characteristics. Both include elements of imagination, originality, impulsiveness and proactive thinking. Both are solutions focused. Both want to add value. Just like creative artists, entrepreneurs visualise the end products and services. Also, like a creative artist, entrepreneurs go about assembling context specific resources to create their visualised products and services.

Proactive curiosity is the prime initiator of innovation, entrepreneurship and creativity. The differences are in the way different entrepreneurs evaluate and present their creations. Artists prepare their canvas to be displayed in art galleries. Football club owners assemble and present their teams in league playgrounds. Digital technology designers may launch their product-service mix or smart phones in an auditorium. Critical and creative design-thinking as well as insightful understanding of their customers' expectations are the key success factors for all.

A Narration

Past-Present-Future: A Creative Link

During a panel discussion, a very successful lady entrepreneur, who had created an international business in cosmetics, was asked to share her personal experiences in managing creativity and innovation. She said very humbly that she did not know much about the art and science of innovation.

> Elaborating on her own experience, she said that many of her products, which are very successful brands, are based on the information provided in the thousands of years old manuscripts — *the Vedas*. For her company, the *eureka* moment or the "innovation-of-product" was created by an old Sanskrit scholar and not by young technology or management experts.
>
> However, once the innovation or the core product was identified and defined, the responsibility of transforming more than five thousand years old innovation into a brand-new, modern, commercially viable product was creatively managed by experts from IITs and IIMs.
>
> It was a very complex, creative, expensive and time consuming process. A few over five thousand years old innovations had

to be made relevant to compete in the hyper competitive international business arenas and meet the global benchmarks of quality, presentation and customer acceptance.

Creativity, for her was an integral part of every technical and commercial activity.

*****

With the end product or service in mind, entrepreneurs proactively assimilate and focus on relevant creative energies. Their innovative products and services, and new entrepreneurial processes are the sum total of their creatively gathered creative skills from diverse sources. Each creative skill has a unique place in business process and organisational architecture. Creativity appears in many different forms in business operations.

Even if a new "product" is identified after extensive research and development (R & D), it would need to be transformed into a commercially viable proposition. Diverse creative inputs, ingenuity, imagination, creative design-thinking, along with creative cost control efforts, would go into packaging, pricing, and marketing of the new product.

Creativity and entrepreneurship are *proactive* value adding propositions. For a restaurant, an innovative recipe or dish must not just be appreciated but must also be bought by customers and generate profit for the organisation. The same would be true for professional painters, writers and musicians. For sustainable success in the market place, innovative ideas have to be creatively mass replicated, as well as creatively mass marketed.

Besides imagining, designing and creating a prototype of a new product, there is a lot of creativity and innovation in mass replication and mass marketing as well. Creativity in business may also be seen as the process of proactive zero-based contextual thinking to define problems and create solutions. Depending on the context, a zero-based approach usually gives a history-free future perspective to the creativity process.

Survival of commercial units depends on their continuous relevance and usefulness. Disruptive change is omnipresent and business units are in a continuous state of flux. In a fast changing business environment, entrepreneurs, business leaders and managers face numerous kinds of challenges to retain relevance of their products for their customers. Sustainability requires continuous creative inputs.

Business is a continuous multi-faceted and multi-dimensional open-ended creative process. To remain competitive and grow, managers look for new original ideas and innovative ways to add value to their products and services.

Creativity and Management

As stated earlier, creativity implies value addition. Besides other things, business managers have to evaluate and monitor value creation process. To plan, organise, direct and control, business managers need to have a clear understanding of the role of creativity in their own organisations as well as in the business arenas where they operate. Depending on the nature of the business, from the management perspective, nature and parameters of creativity in business organisations may include:

Context: As in other arts, creativity has to be specific and contextual in business. Activities such as sourcing of resources, operations, human resource management, finance, marketing, advertising or sales, are distinct but interconnected and interdependent activities. Each has its distinct knowledge-base, context and creativity options. Depending on the context, creative managers adopt different methods to synergise their business network. This will be discussed later in the book.

Customers: Customers are the life-line of all business organisations. Smart phones and other digital technologies are continuously adding new uncertainties, complexities and ambiguities in the shopping behaviour of customers.

Competition: Winning in the business arena requires multi-faceted creativity competencies. The nature and intensity of competition keeps changing with time. Thus, creativity itself has to be flexible as well as adaptive to keep pace with change and remain relevant.

Speed: Depending on the nature of the industry, global connectivity and globalisation have added new elements of speed in the competitive environment.

Security: Use of internet, cyberspace and social media have created many new issues of security for business organisations.

Complexity: Business organisations differ in diversity and complexity. Environmental factors such as globalisation, geo-politics, geo-economics and disruptive new business models have increased cross-cultural intricacies and complexity. Business organisations simultaneously operate in virtual cyberspace as well as real physical space, with diverse business cultures.

Chaos: Condition of disorder and confusion, along with many new unknowns, as well as volatility, uncertainty, complexity and ambiguity (VUCA) have become an integral parts of the new digital ecosystem.

Constraints: For sustainable operations, managers have to manage costs, as well as compete for revenues and resources. Business teams have to be creative within the prescribed budget constraints of time and resources.

Cost-benefit equation: Creativity is a business resource. As will be discussed in detail later in the book, like other business resources, creativity has its own cost-benefit equation.

It is often said that what cannot be measured cannot be managed. While creativity is invisible, in the business context, like other resources, it can be visualised, measured and evaluated. Depending on the nature and scope of business, each of the above factors have to be creatively managed individually as well as holistically in the context of overall business operations.

Creative Design Dynamics in Business

Creative challenges emerge in various different forms in business arenas. Global connectivity, global interdependence and creative use of digital technologies are adding new multicultural dynamics and diversities in business areas.

Digital technologies and globalisation are transforming business arenas, creating more disruptive and creative challenges. The world economy is becoming more integrated as well as more uncertain, complex and ambiguous. The nature of competition as well as relationships between business units, big and small, customers and governments, are becoming complex. Designs of products and services need continuous contextualisation. The stakeholders are more information empowered. Creative, critical and design-thinking are essential.

Change, digital technologies and creativity are omnipresent in the knowledge-era. Business managers are continuously required to navigate their operations, products and services through dynamic, cross-cultural, ambiguous, complex and often contradictory regulations. For successful implementation of their assignments, managers require proactive, analytical, critical as well as integrative creative thinking. As will be discussed later in the book, managers also need to master the art of creative business diplomacy as well as creative negotiations for creating value-added win-win situations.

Change implies situations needing solutions. Change creates need for creativity. Accelerated disruptive change is the norm in business arenas. Any change in business environment, customer relations or business process would be of concern to business managers. For effective management of transformation, managers would have to be aware of the reasons, that is, why, when, what, where, by whom and how (5W+H) of the transformation. As will be discussed later in the book, each element of 5W+H has its own set of creative challenges.

Managers have to take corrective action and find appropriate solutions to manage consequences or impact of transformation. Change creates new creative challenges, new risks as well as new strategic opportunities. For appropriate strategic results, speed of creativity must match the speed of change. Managing creativity in fast changing, unstable and highly unpredictable markets requires strategic and creative management skills.

To design their strategic framework, managers need to assess and evaluate their current position in the business arena and know where they are vis-à-vis their customers and competitors. Because of the various known and unknown sources of changes, internal as well as external, business organisation often need to evaluate their position in terms of strength, weakness, opportunity and threat (SWOT). Periodic SWOT analysis is essential to assess change and creativity requirements. These details will be discussed in later chapters.

Creative managers require a clear, focused mind. Disruptions, constraints, analysis, synthesis, discipline and focus are integral part of business operations. Whatever be the perceptions of creativity in different contexts, in business, Creativity is a process with a capital C – context, cost, customer, cash-flow, consumer, competition, compliance, communication, change, continuity and much, much more. These issues as well as why, how, what, when, where and by whom of creativity will be discussed in later chapters.

Notwithstanding the positive and desirable qualities associated with creativity and innovations, during conversations with experienced business players, a number of senior executives were ambiguous in their responses. It was evident that they would like to use creativity and innovation very cautiously and carefully in their day-to-day business operations. They were aware of the disruptions, risks, ambiguities and uncertainties associated with the two concepts. Creativity and innovations tend to disturb "standardised" and "well established" management comfort zones.

In some competitive business contexts, there seems to be an element of apprehension, even a sense of fear associated with the concepts of creativity and innovation. Change in product or service implies some readjustment and new uncertainties and ambiguities in brand-customer relationship. Even when newer digital technologies are disrupting existing strongholds, what, when, how, how much and by whom should the changes be made in well established brands, are complex questions to answer.

As one retired CEO said:

> No one wants to take ownership of a failed or a not-so-successful idea. Even when there is success in business and everyone wants to claim credit, one can never be sure of the real reasons for success or about its life span. In the real world of business, where success is linked with bonuses and failures with accountability, creative and innovative endeavours can become murky, messy and may often cause more overall damage than good.

During my discussions with experienced business players, at times it seemed that creativity and innovations are just buzzwords — nice "intellectual" subjects to talk about at seminars and in classrooms. It is in fashion to talk about the great creative and innovative things and services coming out of new evolving corporations such as Apple, Google, Facebook and Samsung. But how relevant are these to long established mature corporations? Some of these issues will be discussed in later chapters.

Creativity and Strategic Thinking

Creativity and strategy are future focused. Both require a problem solving mindset. In a multi-faceted, fast changing business environment, business managers have to face a variety of disruptions, uncertainties, ambiguities and complexities. Each business unit is a unique dynamic mix of diverse activities and specialised knowledge bases such as supply chains, operations, finance, human resource management, marketing, distribution, and sales. Business managers face many diverse kinds of creative challenges. Formulating effective creative solutions is a continuous necessity.

The dashboards of strategy planners and strategy implementers have many indicators, but few effective controls. In a disruptive, fast changing business environment, being aware and vigilant is essential. After each step towards the business target, strategy managers have to re-evaluate their situation. Each step would create a new situation requiring a more insightful, creative approach.

As will be discussed in the later chapters, evaluating the impact of change would include evaluation of changes in the internal value chain of the organisation, as well as changes in the external, political, economic, social, technological (PEST) factors. At times a zero-based analysis may be essential.

Depending on the nature of industry and their position in the industry, strategy managers may decide to be proactive or reactive. Proactive managers would need to develop early warning mechanisms to anticipate and evaluate change. Each change would require a unique contextual creative problem solving approach. Creativity is the versatile energy source.

In the world of commerce, creativity faces more intricate challenges in sensitive, complex and colourful multi-cultural environments. The multi-faceted globalisation and instant global connectivity have created many complexities, uncertainties and ambiguities for business organisations. Business organisations are legal entities. Each nation formulates its own legal framework for commercial activities. With more and more business units operating in more and more countries, business operations have become more multi-cultural and complex. The accelerated pace of change has added to the prevailing complexities and uncertainties.

Digital technologies have created various new forms of business organisations and business operations. Many industrial age business organisations have creatively adopted digital technology options to enhance their competitiveness. Some traditional business organisations have used digital technologies to deepen their traditional roots and fortify their traditional market position. Business arenas are full of diversity and multi-faceted dynamics.

Creative uses of digital technologies have created a variety of disruptive business models. With global connectivity, the scale-up from local to global can be very fast. In many countries, the legal framework is yet to be modified to be in sync with new commercial realities. This creates complexities and uncertainties as well as new creative challenges for creative business managers.

Speed considerations have also become an integral part of complex and sensitive cross-cultural strategic planning.

New situations create new creative challenges, warrant new managerial skills and mindsets. With the prevailing diversity in the commercial arenas, we need to see business and corporate events in their real-time contexts.

Creativity and innovative products are double edged swords. There are rewards as well as risks associated with each new idea. Creative business ideas need to be critically and holistically evaluated. As will be discussed in other chapters, creativity in business is a multi-faceted activity. While appearing to be very simple and attractive, if not appropriately managed it may silently bleed a business to death. Failures of many business leaders have many lessons for us. The shifts in the list of Fortune 500 global business leaders indicate risk dynamics of creativity in business operations.

Customers are ever-changing bundles of mixed emotions. With on-the-go impulsive shopping, business has becoming extremely challenging, competitive and uncertain. Understanding of contextual, dynamic, as well as customer focused creative strategic thinking is the new survival *mantra*.

Nurturing Corporate Creativity

Creativity is an integral part of business process. Search for innovative products, services and solutions in business are iterative experimental ventures. To be creative one has to be comfortable in uncomfortable situations. Creativity causes change as well as uncertainty.

Instinctively, we like to protect our comfort zone. Change causes discomfort—physical or emotional. This often makes people think, talk or work against the concepts of creativity, innovation or change. Unless effectively challenged by new creative strategic thinking, individual comfort zones or vested interests tend to reinforce themselves and generate their own defensive mechanisms. The boiling-frog syndrome is all pervasive.

At times, mental comfort zones, with their protective ego casings, can be very sensitive social and corporate landmines, even for well-meaning professionals and experts. Many professionals, with their own re-enforced comfort zones, would

Creativity in the World of Commerce

rather walk away from lucrative jobs than consider a change or "waste" a moment to reflect over an alternate thought process. Time and again, a complex mix of egos, pride, ideology, hubris, values and assumed virtues erupts on the local as well as national and international social, economic, political and commercial platforms. Change involves learning, unlearning and relearning. Unlearning is often much more difficult than new learning.

Discussing the challenges of accelerated change, creativity needs and associated risks, a senior executive of a MNC said:

> Please do not forget, individually, that we all have limited time horizons of careers and promotions. Who would want disruptions in his or her areas of operations? Who would think of disrupting a well-established process in a large organisation? Creativity and innovation sound good, but have many known and unknown risks associated with them and need to be isolated from day-to-day operations. Line operation managers have and need a different mindset from those in the idea-testing laboratories.

Different people have different ways to reason, create and protect their comfort zones.

Discussing the same topic, a Director of another MNC in the auto-industry said:

> Frankly, I do not really understand the concept of creativity and innovation in our business operations. As you know, we keep introducing new models. It is a *routine* and regular activity. I find it hard to say which activities in the overall process of introducing new models are creative and which are not. I do not know how to measure the 'intensity-of-creativity' or how to attribute 'creative-value' to any particular activity in our complex value-chain of visible and not-so-visible activities. What creates success? I do not know.
>
> Many creative and innovative activities in our organisation are incremental in nature. One individual or team may make some changes in power generation and another in its transmission systems. One team in one country may make changes in the packaging and maybe some minor changes in parts. The

overall product, with local adaptations, is usually presented to customers by another team, where the innovation or creativity-mix package encounters the moments-of-truth — it faces the customer. It is usually almost impossible to identify the causes of success or reasons for failure or evaluate the use of creativity.

It is a common observation that some models do well while others do not. Some do well in one market, others in another. Some are sold easily, while others require greater sales efforts. At times, there are many abrupt changes in sales trends. All this happens at times in most unpredictable ways. Even with years of experience, marketing experts cannot be sure of models, markets and customers. Sales are often managed on day-to-day basis and from showroom to showroom. Front line creativity is spontaneous. It changes with the situation and profile of individual customer. Like soldiers on the front lines, sales people have their individual creative way to define problems and generate contextual creative solutions.

As will be discussed in the later chapters, creativity has its own dynamics and speed of adaptability. Much invisible thinking happens before creativity gets expressed in words or drawings. At times it may occur in a moment of inspiration. At other times it is a prolonged iterative process of analysis and formulating strategic framework to transform an idea into a successful commercial product or service. Success in business is usually evaluated by the effectiveness and speed with which end products move towards customers and money from customers moves towards the company. Improved cash-flows are often critical success factors for business organisations.

Creativity is creativity only when it creates new value for customers and more profits for business units. Creative management may be seen as the invisible *extra* value adding ingredient in the complex, overall inter-dependent and inter-connected business equation.

In marketing, it is a common understanding that strong brands require stringent quality standards and controls. Variations in corporate, product and service brands impact customer acceptability, competitiveness as well as sustainability of business operations. To maintain customer confidence, managements often tend to opt for incremental changes rather than disruptive, creative and innovative options.

Discussing this topic, one senior business executive said:

> Once a product or service and associated processes have been accepted, one has to get on with disciplined implementation and standardisation. Time is money and opportunity. Search for creativity and related activities are very time consuming, with many associated risks. I may even say change is a taboo and tradition is an accepted norm — a virtue.
>
> I do not know whether you are aware, but many players, after a competitive win, do not change clothes, some even do not take bath as they fear their "good-luck" may be washed away. As a sportsman during my school days, I have experienced it.
>
> We all have lucky numbers and dresses. In our business, we even have lucky advertisements. We like to continue with same advertisements for years. Successful brands protect their "good-luck" by shielding themselves from change. Having been associated with this industry for many years in many countries, I feel this is a common approach towards brand management. Any suggestions of even small changes in the corporate systems, products and services are usually put aside or very carefully evaluated before being tested and incorporated.

Each industry has its own traditions and practices. As in different sports, different industries require different thinking, skills and strategies. Some industries attract customers by emphasising their traditions, while others by being modern, creative and innovative. Whatever the nature of the business, to survive and grow, it has to remain relevant, connected and useful for its customers. To be of value, creativity has to be contextual.

For survival and growth, even successful traditional industries and business organisations cannot ignore change or the changing life-style, preferences and expectations of customers or the changing competition policies of new and old competitors. To remain competitive in a fast changing business environment, business units have to be alert and agile to counter challenges on different fronts. Business processes and operations are complex interdependent systems. The policy changes require inputs from managers of different departments and activities. Thus, creative teamwork is essential in formulating contextual solutions. Creative managers have to manage creative teams from contextual as well as holistic perspectives.

Many business organisations spend vast amounts of money and do extensive research to keep products relevant for their customers. Notwithstanding the importance of critical thinking and sophisticated analytical tools used by business units, management is also a game of common sense and creative thinking. To remain competitive, companies have to find creative ways to reduce "traditional" costs and also creatively develop new revenue streams and increase profits. While evaluating creativity and innovation options, understanding of customer dynamics is essential.

A former CEO of a large MNC explained this:

> No doubt, many products and services are created and sustained by the product and service related creative activities. Please do not forget that markets are also graveyards of products and services that perished due to over enthusiastic use of creativity or addiction to innovation and technology. One has to understand situation and context.

> Please do not misunderstand me. I am not against the use of creativity and innovation in business. But perhaps we need to proceed as we do in the case of medicines — with a very clearly focused and disciplined approach. Also, like in the case of medicines, markets can be very unforgiving when creativity or innovations are used carelessly. Besides other things, creative managers would need to align and coordinate departmental creative initiatives.

The world of commerce is a very complex mix of delights, dreams and hard hitting realities; nightmares of debts; as well as the mirage of happiness packed products and services. In many industries or areas of business, corporations sell just egos, dreams and fantasies; some may even be harmful for customers. Some products are called "sin" products and some industries as "sin" industries.

Kautilya in his book *Arthashatra* (230 BCE) had also mentioned that we can create wealth through knowledge. However, it depends on us whether we create products and services that are *satwa* — socially useful, *rajas* — neutral or *Tama* — socially harmful. Sustainability of products and services also depends on their basic nature.

For business organisations, change depends on the perception of customers about the products or services. Understanding the context is critical for creative managers. Creativity is usually a problem focused multi-disciplinary teamwork. Cost-benefit dynamics of creativity and innovations keep changing with time, industry, markets and specific local context.

While discussing creativity, a lady entrepreneur said:

> I paint when I like. I also play music when I like. What is creative and uncreative about painting or music, I do not know. What is the difference between my children going out to play and my doing painting or playing piano? What is creative and what is not? What is more creative — designing a dress, being mother, cooking, teaching children, managing house, painting, playing piano or managing cash-flow of my business operations?
>
> If I paint a painting of a well-known artist, long dead and gone, I am accused of forgery. Why? I see an old tree and I paint it. I am an artist. So what wrong am I doing when I see an old painting and paint it? Why can't old paintings have modern versions? Just as I add my own colours to the image of the tree, I also add my colours and emotions to the old painting. I often add some new perception to items which were in fashion earlier.

As will be discussed in later chapters, in the world of commerce, creativity is a critical resource. It needs appropriate context. A purpose. A focus. And its value is evaluated by its commercial returns. In the present, fast changing competitive world, creative mindset is a critical need for survival of any business. For sustainable business, creative products and innovations also need creative and innovative marketing strategies. Overall business processes are dynamic and have to be creativity-balanced.

We experience commercial creativities through various products and services we purchase and consume. Our life-style is influenced by commercial products and services such as, fashion items, groceries, music, gifts, paintings, films, books, sports and games. For effective management of commercial process and creativity, managers have to be aware, passionate, concerned and committed as well as sensitive, to be contextually creative and meet ever changing expectations of customers.

Each and every activity in the business process requires creativity. As stated earlier, creativity is a critical resource. As will be discussed in later chapters, just as strategy is creativity intensive, creativity is a strategy intensive resource. By encouraging creative inputs from employees, work becomes exciting, interesting and invigorating. As in sports, so also in business, speed, teamwork and precision are essential. Creativity is a game of heart, head, data, insights and imagination. Integrative design-thinking is an integral part of creativity. Creative management is essential for optimisation of creative talents in business organisations. Business process is a never-ending stream of creative value adding challenges.

In the present context, readers may find that creativity and innovation have been described as linked and interdependent activities. There is a reason for that. Imagination, originality and proactive instincts are the common links between creativity and innovation. In business, innovation and creativity may be visualised as a *joint-venture*. Creativity helps make innovative ideas a reality. On the other hand, innovations are incarnations of creativity. As will be discussed in the next chapter, in the complex, disruptive, dynamic and risky business arenas, where speed is a critical success factor, innovations require focused and a disciplined creative mindset.

Creative Management: *An Overview*

Creativity has to be managed creatively. Each business unit is a unique mix of diverse creative inputs. In turbulent, multi-cultural, fast changing business environments, creative inputs keep changing. The nature, as well as the speed of creative activities, has to match the competitive challenges. Creative management includes seeding of curiosity and nurturing of creativity for competitive advantage in fast changing multi-cultural business arenas.

Each commercial unit has its own unique creativity map, value chain as well as creativity flow chart. Each company has its own unique knowledge and creativity centres. These may be procurement, operations, finance, marketing or talent management. The creativity centres have to be synergistically connected. Like a gear box in a car, in business operations, learning and creative energy of one gear must be creatively passed on to the other. An integrative design-thinking approach is essential.

Accelerated change often results in high obsolescence of knowledge bases and creative competencies. To be at par with change, at times use of Zero-Based Proactive Learning Paradigm (ZBPLP) becomes essential. Also, as will be discussed in later chapters, as knowledge and creativity have to be contextually relevant, it is useful to develop creativity nurturing initiatives and programmes in-house rather than outsource them.

The creative uses of digital technologies and instant global mobile connectivity have transformed the nature of commercial activities—be it mining or media. Different industries have been impacted differently. Different business activities and business units operate at different speeds. In some industries, creativity and innovations are survival imperatives as well as critical source of competitive advantages. In other industries, commercial organisations have to meet the challenges of impulsive decisions made by their on-the-go customers— customers who want instant gratifications of their decisions made at the speed-of-thought, at the click of their mobile button.

In almost all industries, the structure and grammar of management is being redesigned. Creative design-thinking enhances value. Notwithstanding the availability of high speed analytics and artificial intelligence, decisions are often based on intuition, imagination, instinct and experience. All these are critical elements of creativity.

As will be discussed in the book, creative management needs to have a comprehensive insightful understanding of their own business operations to assess the strategic needs of their organisation. As we move on to examine, discuss and understand the impact of creative digital disruptions and the role of creativity in the knowledge-era, it is important to remember that each business unit is unique and has unique creativity needs.

A Narration

Perceptions of a Creative Manager

Before moving on to next chapter, I would like to share a very short story with my readers. During my learning venture to understand creativity in the world of commerce, I interacted with an artist who also managed his art gallery as a commercial unit. He was a creative artist as well as successful entrepreneur. He was a one man creative management team — art creator, curator, entrepreneur and manager.

Right in the beginning of our discussions, he said:

May I share my views about creativity in the world commerce with a short story and an Urdu couplet? I hope I can recall it correctly.

A person was drinking wine in a mosque. Seeing him drinking, a priest told him not to drink in the house of God. To which the man replied:

> *Zaahid sharab peene de*
> *Masjid me baith kar*
> *Yaa wo jagah bata de*
> *Jahan Khuda na ho.*

[Believer in God, let me drink wine
In the Mosque
Or show me a place
Where there is no God.]

Creativity in the World of Commerce

God — by whatever name you may call him — and creativity go together. God does not repeat performance. Everything and every activity in nature is new, different and original. Time, days, dates and events do not repeat or come back. Each situation and context is new. The cloud formations, colours of each sunrise and sun set, each day are different. Show me an activity in nature, where there is no mystery, no originality and no creativity.

I feel creativity is a chain of short life-span activities. One may see it as a cycle or birth, death and re-birth — as, *Brahma, Vishnu* and *Mahesh*. Creativity is transitory. Creativity, as we know it or are cable of knowing it, ends to restart again. Life-spans vary. Poets create poems, musicians create musical compositions and entrepreneurs create organisations, products and services.

Simply stated, creativity for me is just a *problem-solving-process* for good or for bad. It may be done for constructive or destructive purpose. Each individual has his or her own perceptions of good and bad, right and wrong, as well as success and failures. As is well-known, many reputed global business organisations as well as banks have been involved in various anti-social activities.

I just create art to make a living. Sell it as a commercial product, to feed my family.

At times I think of trees as large reservoirs of creativity. They thrive on the limited resources available to them in their limited space. It is not uncommon to see a new sapling growing among old termite mounds. Creativity finds a way to recreate itself, at times in the most unexpected places and situations.

Creativity is creativity. You may view it as you like. I feel management is an amalgam of many creative arts. The quality of management practices in almost any industry impact the very essence of our life — mind, body and soul, our perception of life and living.

Creativity helps business organisations in discovering their future and also the future of societies where they operate.

*****

Creative Management: *A Role Play*

A new CEO has taken charge in your organisation. He is a man who thinks of business as a simple equation of revenue, cost and profit. He is bitten by the prevailing buzzwords — *creativity, innovation, design-thinking* and *creative management*.

a) To involve as many employees as possible, he has called a series of meetings with different groups with an objective to know his corporate team and also introduce creativity and innovation in the organisation.

b) After formal introductions and some informal interactions, he presents his plan in different meetings with few simple statements:

   i. Basically business operations consist of two streams — costs and revenues.

   ii. How to introduce creativity and innovation in the company to:
   1. Maximise revenue, and
   2. Minimise costs

He closed the meeting with simple statement, "Since all of you have been in the organisation longer than I have been, you would know how to go about it better than me. Please feel free to form your groups and formulate your strategies to introduce creativity, design-thinking and creative management in our organisation. I hope we can have the next meeting on the subject in four weeks."

As an aspiring business player, how would you go about creating your team and structuring your presentation? You are free to choose the organisation and make assumptions.

*****

2

The real danger is not that computers will begin to think like men, but that men (and women) will begin to think like computers.

Sydney J. Harris

Creative Digital Disruptions

Faced with the tsunami of digital disruptions, it may be advantageous to take a quick look at the path that has led us to it. It may also help us in better understanding of challenges, risks and opportunities in the fast changing digital environment.

Sharing and caring for one another, as members of a clan, is as old as humankind. The process of barter of goods and services to cater to the needs of fellow members became a common practice during early stages of human associations. Curiosity and creative learning have been vital factors in the survival, growth and development of humankind.

Demarcation of activities, such as livelihood ventures, household care and security of community also evolved during the early stages of human history. Thus, commercial activities evolved as creative solutions to meet the needs of communities. With expansion of societies, commercial endeavours grew in numbers, diversity and scope.

Today the global commercial landscape is full of diversity, ranging from patches of tribal, time-wrap, prehistoric activities to global, knowledge-era, digital operations. All commercial activities provide some socio-economic solutions for their customers. Employment opportunities as well as products and services created by commercial organisations are creative socio-economic solutions.

Like entrepreneurs, each commercial organisation is unique. Whatever their nature, customers are the life-line for business organisations. In response to their distinct environmental conditions, business units deepen their socio-economic roots, grow and diversify their commercial operations. Also, like other living organisms, when not in harmony with their environment, they weaken and often wither away.

Intertwined with the needs, desires and aspirations of humankind, the world of commerce is full of intricate interdependent diversity.

Commercial Collage: Diversity and Dynamics

Each business activity has a unique context, knowledge and creativity needs. A commercial organisation is a dynamic collage of diversity—knowledge, skills and creativity. Local as well as global commercial arenas are full of diversity in the nature of products and services as well as their operational reach. Socio-economic needs, desires and aspirations of individual consumers have been and continue to be the prime movers of commerce.

Over time, with the increase in population, knowledge, needs, greed and weapons, there have been wars for wealth, agricultural land, mineral resources, products and services. As people went beyond their shores in search of spices and riches, new continents were discovered. Explorations for treasures led to the creation of new nations and political empires.

With the advent of industrial-age, the agriculture based socio-economic world of land and labour was transformed by machines. Making use of new technologies, business organisations consolidated their market positions and also expanded their areas of operations. Many business units went beyond their national borders.

During the two world wars, many new technologies were created and tested. New geo-political and geo-economic systems evolved. New technologies transformed the nature of commerce, size and structures of business organisations and the nature of competition in global business arenas. Managers of business organisations and business schools adopted military terminologies and jargon. Product and service brands were used as bayonets, bullets and bombs to capture markets.

Besides various other factors, just as the use of energy provided by steam engines, electricity and petrochemical industries had transformed the agriculture based economy into an industrial economy, currently, the creative use of digital technologies is transforming the industrial economy into a knowledge economy.

The industrial-era created machines with physical force and power. The knowledge-era has made machines versatile with digital brain and artificial intelligence. Just as industrial age machines replaced farm workers, knowledge machines are replacing employees from more and more traditional factories and offices. The nature of work and ways of working are changing.

The global network created by industrial age commercial organisations is becoming extremely complex and interdependent. Knowledge-era instant global connectivity is impacting commercial operations in many different ways. The life-style of individuals, ways of communication, shopping and entertainment, nature of work and work places, as well as ways of national governance are being transformed.

Caselet 2.1

Optimising Information Usage

Meru, a second year undergraduate business student had taken special permission from her class teacher to use her class project time to share her "curiosity — unstructured views and thoughts" with the class.

During her high school, Meru had availed of the opportunities to work in some non-government organisations and travel with her parents. She had often heard and been involved in discussions on the topics such as virtues of being rich; why are poor, poor and rich-poor disparities.

As a student of economics, she was aware of some of the generally discussed causes of socio-economic disparities. What she could not understand was the reasons for waste creation — surplus capacities and production. Also, the wastage of waste. She wondered whether waste and perishable over-capacities could be commercially used. She was aware of the overflow and "wastage" of information. She wondered whether there was a business opportunity. Could there be a business model for utilising this?

Through her class presentation and discussions, she wanted to gain an understanding of her confusion and also of the waste phenomenon. She also wondered whether her concerns were valid, logical and made any sense. She was grateful to her teacher for giving her a chance to share her thoughts in the class in a formal manner.

To provide more time for class discussion, she made a short presentation. To initiate the discussion, she just presented some facts and general social and economic observations.

- During agriculture-era we produced surpluses of agriculture in some parts of the world and people starved in the other parts of the world.
  - Surpluses or waste was wasted and not used to save lives.
  - Humanity was shamed.
  - Some said there was some "economic-logic" in such anti-human policies.
- During industrial-era we produced industrial surpluses — excess capacities, products, services and weapons.
  - We produced lots of waste and weapons of mass destruction — enough weapons to destroy humankind many times over.
  - During the industrial-era the world was more connected.
  - But the disparities between the rich and the poor increased.
  - Even the rich, economically developed countries faced 1%-99% socio-economic syndromes in their socio-economic milieu.
- Now during our current knowledge-era, also referred to as information-era, we often hear of information overflow.
  - Every search by a search engine produces overload of surplus information and information waste.
  - The world is connected and interdependent *but* divided.
  - Cyberspace is a common meeting place for people from all nations, but people talk of future cyber wars.

- Cultural diversity has become an integral part of every society.
- The world is connected, but not united by values or concerns.

• Now some of my concerns and questions:
- What kind of world will the knowledge-era create?
- How much of data and information will be wasted in developing "meaningful" or "useful" knowledge?
- Digital technology operations such as sourcing of information, storage of information, replication of information, processing of information and transmission of information have near zero marginal cost. Why must interactive activities such as education and healthcare be so expensive?
- Is there an education-business opportunity for us—future managers and start-up entrepreneurs—to use surplus (wasted) information as business resource for developing simple, optimal, appropriate and relevant (SOAR) educational or training or healthcare framework for the world?
- Can we use the available information surplus to create purposeful business ventures that enhance global understanding and mutual happiness?
- Can the need for global cross-cultural understanding be used as a social and business opportunity?

• The connected, interdependent world is full of political, economic, social and political fault-lines. Weapons of mass destructions are spread around the world.
- I wonder, will the knowledge-era be more fair, understanding and just or will the 1%-99% syndrome move on to 0.1%-99.9%?

She requested her class colleagues for their views.

*****

The New Realities

Digital technologies and globalisation are impacting different industries in different ways. Global connectivity and social media are empowering customers, citizens and voters. Social, economic and political power is shifting. Creative use of digital technologies, artificial intelligence and analytics is providing more options for business organisations as well as national governance agencies. Business organisations have to operate in a more informed environment. In direct and indirect ways the rules of corporate citizenship are being redefined in different countries.

The boundaries between industries are becoming blurred. Today, business units function and operate in various different forms. Individual experts can provide uninterrupted consultancy services around the world. Some digital technology entrepreneurs are operating their commercial ventures as part-time hobbies. Even small e-commerce ventures, as in media, retail, finance and travel industries, are competing with global conglomerates. Many new digital business players are proving to be disruptive game changers in different industries.

Dynamic, multi-faceted local-global diversity is present in the business arenas. Besides various other factors, the nature, structure and size, as well as format of business models are being influenced by the creative ability of entrepreneurs and their teams. To a very large extent, global connectivity is reducing the importance of location for business organisations. Talent can be globally sourced. Production of products and services can be outsourced. Opacity in business is giving way to transparency. Smart phones and e-commerce still have high undiscovered disruptive potential.

The basic role of land, labour, capital and entrepreneurship in many commercial operations is changing. Global connectivity, creative use of digital technologies and globalisation are impacting operations of almost all industries around the world. Underestimating the synergistic power of the creative mind and the versatility of digital technologies can be fatal, even for established business leaders. This has been amply demonstrated by failure of many well-known and esteemed global business organisations and business leaders like Nokia, Yahoo, Kodak and Blackberry, to name a few.

In a fast changing competitive business environment, every business activity has to be a value adding link in the overall business process. Mindful of the fact that digital technologies have the potential to cause disruptions and provide more effective alternatives, business managers must conduct proactive skills and creativity-audit of each activity in their organisation.

Currently business units compete in creativity—creativity in listening and understanding expectations of information empowered customers and other stakeholders, creativity to create more effective business models to meet expectations of their customers, as well as manage disruptive challenges from competitors. Creativity is essential to fortify supply chains and distribution channels. Creativity is needed to design appropriate value-added products, services as well as effective delivery systems. In a globalised, fast changing, cross-cultural, business environment, along with creativity, speed is also a critical success factor.

The creative use of information technology is transforming the nature of competition. In some industries, the rules of the game are changing faster than the others. For most industries, the creative disruptive dynamics include:

Instant global connectivity: With instant flow of information around the world, customers, voters and workers, as well as organisations and national governance agencies, are information empowered. New global order and power structure has emerged

Geo-economics: Globalisation is a multi-faceted, disruptive process. It has created many VUCA situations—new challenges as well as opportunities for business organisations around the world.

Near zero marginal cost: Digital technology based operations have near zero marginal cost. This adds a new disruptive element in the competition.

Connect-disconnect dynamics: A new society with smart phone connectivity, connectedness as well as disconnect is evolving. At any public gathering, we can see individuals "connected" with "people" through screens and ear-plugs but disconnected with people around them. New lifestyles, social behaviours, values and relationships have evolved.

Social media: Social media has empowered individuals. Personal whispers can get spread at the speed-of-light in the new global-village. Social media can also be a medium for anti-social activities at the speed-of-thought.

New lifestyles and work-methods: The changes in lifestyles, social communication patterns and work-methods are changing the very nature of business operations. Automation and robots are transforming work places and the nature of work.

Information empowered customers and other stakeholders: Whatever the nature of business, customers are able to instantly compare value propositions of business units. Better informed stakeholders expect more purposeful, socially responsible and sustainable business policies.

Click-shopping unknowns: Notwithstanding the extensive big data analysis, marketing executives are yet to completely understand the thinking and on-the-go click-shopping behaviour of customers.

Re-establishing brand bonds: The strength of brands depends on the nature of their bonds with their customers. The digital business models are disrupting the old established communication ways between business units and their customers.

Reconsidering product design and services: With the change in the lifestyle and shopping behaviour of customers, products and services need to be contextualised for e-commerce requirements; speed, virtual or web presentation and delivery systems.

Future market landscape: The future business landscape is unclear. Globalisation and creative use of digital technologies have introduced many kinds of volatilities, uncertainties, complexities and ambiguities in the business environment.

Changing nature of competition, conflicts, contestants and weaponry: Business units face many known and unknown competitors located in different parts of the world. Creative use of digital technologies is changing the nature of competition and conflicts as well as business and marketing weaponry being used by corporations.

Diversity management: With transnational, cross-cultural, commercial operations, business managers are expected to be diversity sensitive. Not only are business managers required to cope with enhanced elements of diversity within their organisations, but also in the competitive business arenas.

Business diplomacy: Business managers have to often navigate business operations through local political and cultural passions—complex, uncertain, ambiguous and potentially volatile situations. Global business arenas can be full of contradictions and regulatory uncertainties. Creative business diplomacy and negotiation skills to create win-win situations have become an integral part of transnational creative management processes.

Geo-economic shifts: Cross-cultural and transnational commercial operations as well as geo-political and geo-economic shifts are creating complex, uncertain and potentially volatile conditions for business organisations.

The two "global-villages": Currently we have two global-villages—one in the physical world and the other in cyberspace. Both have distinct socio-economic, operational characteristics. Most business organisations operate in the both spaces—real or physical and cyber or virtual. This creates new complex, creative challenges for business organisations.

Given the multi-faceted, fast changing business environment, there is a need for business managers to constantly redefine their roles. New commercial situations require new contextual, creative business and strategic thinking. For survival and growth, business organisations would have to respond to the new realities promptly. For some organisations, zero-based critical thinking and creative approach may be essential.

Whatever the quantities, nature, diversity or range of business activities, appropriate creativity helps in evolving effective structure and sinews of operations. Corporations, like individuals, learn by trial and error.

Digital disruptions impact each organisation differently. Like individuals, organisations differ in size, structures, skills, nature and range of their products and services, as well as their relationships with other organisations and societies at large. Also, like individuals, corporations operate at different speeds and with different cultural values. With all the complexities and dynamics of business environments, it is critical for commercial organisations to remain relevant to local societies and customers. Understanding the nature and dynamics of creativity in their areas of operation is critical for business managers.

Business units are a network of diverse talents and skills. Complexities, uncertainties and ambiguities are an integral part of organisations. After all, a corporation is the sum total of its people, with their individual cultural and professional diversities, as well as group dynamics. Digital technologies are an integral part of corporate processes, whether through automation or information processing options and impact corporate cultures. Already in industries, new software and hardware have redefined corporate structures, processes, jobs, risks and relationships.

To manage change, managers and their business organisations have to be aware of change, understand the nature and speed of change in their industries, understand the dynamics of customer as well as competitors and how the change and creative use of digital technologies by competitors may impact their customers and their business operations.

Given the above dynamic business framework, creative thinking of business managers has to be multi-focal. Digital technologies and change impacts different corporate activities differently. The managers have to be contextual and futuristic, as well as customer and competitor focused. To be effective, every grand global strategy of business units has to be locally relevant. All business is local. Global business walks on local legs. Dynamic and creative strategic thinking is essential.

New Disruptive Business Models

Start-ups have created very disruptive situations in many industries. Digital technology has global reach and near zero marginal costs. This disrupts economics of established organisations. Disruptions — internal as well as external — seem to be the new norm for most industries.

Mobile connectivity, artificial intelligence and big-data analytics embedded systems have recreated industrial-era landscape and organisational architecture. Business organisations have to restructure themselves to integrate their *real* physical world operations with *virtual* cyber world activities. They have to realign themselves with the evolving lifestyle of their customers. Speed has emerged as a critical success factor. Competing against time has become the new normal. Faster and enhanced value adding, creative management thinking has become essential. Managers have to think creatively and become creative managers.

For business managers to be in sync with the spirit of the knowledge-era is an imperative. As will be discussed in later chapters, managers need to be aware of the creative potential of digital technologies to cause multi-dimensional — internal as well as external — disruptions in their industries.

The digital technologies have also disrupted the earlier demarcations between industries. The present industrial landscape is evolving at an accelerated pace. Competitors from different industries may appear as black-swans.

With machines becoming increasing more versatile in processing various kinds of data, business managers have to move up the learning curve. They need to acquire higher levels of critical thinking and new skills to navigate their products through sensitive, cultural diversities. Situation specific, design-thinking approach is essential.

Products — Internet-of-Things (IoT) — are becoming connected and smart. Fast developing and changing digital technologies impact customer life-styles as well as their shopping behaviour. Digital technologies also offer many alternate, creative ways to redesign business processes and stay connected with customers. Managers have to balance gains from scale with strengthening bonds with local customers. For business leaders, the new creativity challenges are dynamic, multi-faceted as well as multi-dimensional. All this requires new contextual creative design-thinking.

Even simple products and services may incorporate many inputs from different international sources. This creates uncertainties as well as complexities for the supply chain and operations managers. Smartphone empowered customers demand instant gratification. Thus, the whole business process is impacted by many known and unknown techno-economic forces. Managers not only have to learn continuously but also unlearn at a faster pace. Contextual creativity is critical.

Given the digital options, covert and overt competition and commercial wars have become more intense and sophisticated. Business managers need to be more aware, analytics savvy, as well as imaginative and creative to cope with new challenges.

Critical Life-Line Disruptions

Product-service-customer (PSC) relationship is the life-line for every business organisation. Digital technologies have created major disruptions in this relationship for many industries. Mobile phones have transformed the shopping behaviour of customers. Smartphones are becoming smarter. Customers can compare offerings from competitors before deciding.

Digital technologies introduce various disruptive business models. Many digital start-ups are working on different facets of e-commerce. Information empowered customers are in a dynamic multi-faceted and multi-directional flux. As customers experience new products and services, the levels of their expectations, experiences and outlook changes. Internet and social media enhance uncertainties for many industries such as retail, transport, hospitality and real estate.

Whether a business unit is market-driven or technology-driven, it has to be customer focused. Depending on their situation, to be in sync with changing life and shopping style of their customers, business units would have to continuously reconsider the utility, design, packaging, communication, pricing, positioning and the services mix of their offerings. Periodic 360 degree zero-based analysis may be essential for some organisations.

As a senior executive in the shoe industry said:

> We do have a number of "repeat-customers", but there is nothing constant about them. One may tend to think that people get set in their consumption patterns, but how new information impacts their expectations is very difficult to know. During their repeat visits, they almost always tend to ask for new features and have new expectations. It is our job to creatively match and "fit" their "new" expectations with our "available" products. Customer expectations based sensitive interactions are critical. The challenge for us is to be instantly and contextually creative. Most important, in the prevailing competitive business environment, I feel, taking customers for granted is the biggest sin a business manager can commit.

Caselet 2.2

Mapping Business Knowledge

Having heard discussions on learning organisations and dynamics of the knowledge-era, Rishu was keen to get answers to many questions:

- Is "learning organisations" just another management jargon?
- How does one assess organisational learning needs? That is: Why, what, who, where, when (Ws) and how of organisational learning.
- How would one decide creative learning objectives for an organisation?

- How would one introduce design-thinking approach and culture?
- How to initiate and prioritise learning and coaching activities, etc.

Business organisations from his perspective consisted of:

- Business purpose
- Business process — people, machines, systems, management, etc.
- Products and services that connect business organisations and their customers.

To clarify his fuzzy concepts, he presented his views as a class project. From his perspective, survival and sustainability of business depended on:

- Its ability to generate profits.
- Profit is essential for survival and growth of business organisations:
  - The source of revenue is the customer.
  - Cost management is critical.

Thus, from his understanding, his hypothesis was that:

- The most critical learning for any business organisation is:
  - Understanding of customer needs:
    - It is the understanding of the customer that gives rise to the purpose of a business organisation
    - The purpose of business determines the appropriateness of the business process — marketing operations, finance, supply chain, etc.
- Thus, from his perspective, the basic mantra of organisational learning is:
  - Know thy customer
  - Not just numbers and data, but also the human side of customers: heart, mind, values and aspirations of customers

- ○ Reason and purpose of business or the *why* of business
- ○ Rest — *what, when, where, how* and by *whom* just follow.
- His assertion was that critical learning and knowledge was in knowing customer:
  - ○ Maximising revenue and minimising cost.
- Customers and business objectives are best served by a learning, creative and design-thinking organisational approach.

As he presented his thoughts in the class, there was a silence for few seconds and then many hands went up for questions and discussions.

He wondered, was he right?

What is your perception of Rishu's dilemma?

*****

Learning, Unlearning and Relearning Imperatives

Curiosity, questions and ideas are the prime movers of the knowledge-era. Effective learning starts with proactive curiosity and questioning. Given the fast changing business environment, the need for awareness and proactive learning, unlearning as well as relearning cannot be overstated. Unlearning and being contextual is critical. While navigating through turbulent, fast changing terrain, looking in the rear-view mirror tends to enhance risk. In a fast changing environment, new experiences have to be constantly revalidated and strategies contextualised.

As will be discussed later in the book, internet and digital technologies provide many new opportunities. By making appropriate use of creative energies, local business units have options of global reach. On the other hand, corporations located in distant places may be able to cater to the needs of customers located in remote places. Thus, global competitors using creative business models and strategies can present themselves in various markets and directly reach customers, in many visible and invisible, known and unknown ways. This makes business arenas more uncertain, complex and ambiguous.

Being aware is essential. Making creative use of mobility and connectivity, known and unknown competitors may unexpectedly add new dimensions in business arenas. Creative use of global connectivity and digital technologies gives business players new strategic options, almost at the speed-of-thought. Also, global business players have the option of various creative forms of strategic alliances and partnerships.

Explaining his dilemma, a global business player said:

> Local as well as global business game is changing fast. Even when you see many entrenched brands in many business areas, there are many visible and invisible undercurrents impacting them. Managers of some well-known global brands are having very stressful times. One has to be aware of the various divergent as well as convergent currents of change. Also, business managers need to have the skills to quickly identify and define problems, as well as find some effective creative solutions.

In the evolving knowledge-era, innovation and creative business skills should be seen as capabilities and competencies to define problems and find quick appropriate solutions while remaining customer focused. For example, if we think of the situations in the World Cup games, each player has a dynamic context. In every situation, players try to be more creative as well as innovative than the competitor. They are goal focused — whether one is hitting a penalty shot or defending as a goal keeper.

Business: A Perpetual Quest for Creative Solutions

Business units, through their products and services, provide solutions for personal and social problems. Commercial units operate in a dynamic environment. There is a need to keep a constant watch on the effectiveness and validity of solutions provided by the business units to their customers. A business solution is an effective business solution only when customers value it—accept it, purchase it, use it and come back for more.

By developing and offering new business models, digital technologies are creating many kinds of disruptions in the traditional world of business. The relationships between business organisations and their workers as well as customers are being transformed. In many cases, it is not just the business game but even the rules of game that are changing.

To manage relevance of business solutions — products and services — for customers, managers need a holistic approach. Comparable offerings originating from competitors need to be evaluated in entirety. Also, information inflows that impact expectations of customers and their decision making need to be critically analysed and understood. Business is as much a game of data and analytics as it is of emotions and sensitivities — a dynamic mix of art and science. Customer relationships need to be well thought-out from all perspectives. In a way we are all customers and connected by business.

Creativity and methods used by competitors to win over trust of consumers have to be countered. Depending on the nature and size of a commercial unit, new technologies may have to be incorporated, new skills mastered and new ways found to enhance the value of solutions provided by the organisation.

In a fast changing environment, speed is of the essence, whether it is to define a problem or creatively design and implement a solution. As it will be discussed in later chapters, the challenge many business units face is to make their team players and managers more contextual, creative and critical thinkers. Managers need to be high-speed, creative, value-adding design-thinkers.

Corporations: Creativity Platforms

As stated earlier in a different context, digital technologies and start-ups have created a variety of internal as well as external disruptions for established corporations. Corporations, in their various sizes and structures, are the major business players around the world. As commercial units, corporations are designers and producers of socially useful creative products and services. As economic units, some are larger than many nations. Some recently started knowledge-era corporations have acquired global reach.

Corporations are living, legal organisms. Corporations were designed to serve various national and international commercial requirements of societies and nations. Over the years, as societies grew in size, sophistication and organisational abilities, the need for larger commercial organisations to serve the needs and aspirations of societies also grew.

Multinational corporations (MNCs) are the leading movers of global commerce. Around the world, there are various forms of corporations, with different ownership patterns, business models, as well as range of products and services.

Faced with disruptive innovations of digital technologies, industrial-era corporations have gone through a transformation. In many cases, human talent has given way to learning machines. Vast amounts of data, high-speed analytics and artificial intelligence embedded systems are routinely used to enhance the reliability of management decision support systems. With increase in speed and complexities in designing appropriate products, services and business models, need for imaginative thinking and innovative solutions has increased manifold.

Notwithstanding their social and economic usefulness, corporations face many new issues. While by creative use of information technologies and systems, as well as robotics and outsourcing options, corporations have managed to remain globally competitive, this has often gone against the aspirations of local job seekers. Policies followed by MNC managers often hurt the interests of local communities. Conflict management as well as dealing with various disruptive forces is an integral part of the job of business managers. With increasing uncertainties, managers need to be more proactive, creative and imaginative in managing cross-cultural human relations.

MNCs have many stakeholders with diverse interests. There are different stakeholders that makeup the "body" of corporations. Then there are different interest groups that facilitate its operations. Different constituents have their own unique roles and power bases. Global information flows have empowered individuals as well as groups, thus creating new dynamics for corporations. As will be discussed in later chapters, integrative design-thinking must be an integral part of creative management.

For effective performance and to meet the challenges of competition, corporations need to be internally strong, resilient and nimble. All this makes up a continuous, multi-faceted creative challenge for corporate management and managers responsible for performance of individual activities. With information empowered stakeholders, corporate managers have to simultaneously manage internal conflicts as well as external competition.

As in various other competitive games, some management gurus, borrowing the war situation terminology, have also suggested that to be competitive, in the existing hyper-competitive and disruptive business environment, corporations need to be lean with a "mean" competitive mindset. But being "mean" in an environment where stakeholders are information empowered and have global connectivity, may not be very sustainable. For sustainability, business units, more so global business organisations, need to be more contextually purposeful as well as overall purpose focused.

Today, *virtual* cyberspace shopping platforms are used to display and sell goods as well as services. Markets have become very dynamic, multi-layered, muddled and messy. Customers have become more unpredictable, creating new challenges for marketing managers. Like consumers, markets are also on the move and the movement is multi-directional at multiple speeds. New technology-driver socio-technical order has emerged. The use of 3D prints, Internet-of-Things (IoT), artificial intelligence empowered equipments, big-data analytics and use of interactive technologies has become widespread in various industries. New, more contextual and more creative thinking is essential. As will be discussed in the next chapter, individual learning must become shared departmental team learning and then overall organisational learning. Business units must evolve appropriate learning-individuals and teams, team-to-team learning systems and network-of-teams oriented organisational architecture.

The future corporate work places may look like scenes from science fiction. Perhaps an office would look like a large floor areas where teams of engineers and technicians may be designing, coordinating, upgrading, optimising and standardising production operations with a variety of robots, experts teaching workers skills to communicate and work with robots and, overall work being coordinated by real-virtual global teams. Neither workers nor robots would be able to reach their productive potential without creative understanding of one another. Corporate learning must facilitate evolution of corporate-brain. Various corporate learning options would be discussed in the following chapter.

*****

Creative Management: *A Role Play*

After taking charge of the business organisation, Rishi wanted to gain an understanding of its operations and assess its competitive position in the business arena. The organisation chart was in front of him. Boxes and white spaces clearly indicated roles and responsibilities.

He individually met all department heads. However, he was unable to get a comprehensive understanding of the nature of business challenges the company was facing. No department head had thorough, insightful understanding of the challenges faced by the company as a whole. Each one had his or her own perspective.

He realised that boxes in the organisation chart had become fortified silos. Department heads had used white spaces to demarcate their fiefdoms.

To gain an insightful understanding of the challenges faced by his company, he engaged services of a team of well-known industry consultants. The terms of references given to consultants were:

- Study the external business challenges faced by the company.
- Do a SWOT analysis of the company.
- Develop a talent inventory of the organisation.
- Suggest ways to give the company a sustainable competitive edge.
- *Most important* — the research or fact finding was to be a low key operation and findings would *only* be known to Rishi.

The key findings of the consultants were:

- The company is talent rich.
- Not too long ago, it was one of the industry leaders. But it is losing its market share.

- The company has become bureaucratic and system oriented.
- The corporate team is unaware of market realities.

The consultants recommended that:

- The company must be transformed into a customer-focused learning organisation.
  - Departmental silos need to be demolished.
  - Learning and shared-learning culture must be introduced.
- Introduce participative customer-focused corporate creativity culture.
- Each employee should be an integral part of the corporate creativity team.
- Each employee must be aware of the potential role of digital technology in his or her work. They should be technology savvy.

Now Rishi is faced with the "change and creativity" dilemma — how to introduce change, customer-focus, flexibility, learning and creativity in a structured organisation?

He wants creativity and design-thinking to *evolve* in the company. He wants his corporate team to take *proactive* ownership of the change and solution creating process. He is keen that each member of the corporate team *proactively* design his or her learning agenda.

Assuming yourself to be CEO (Rishi), how would you attempt to initiate the *evolution* of a *customer-focused* learning culture in the company? You are free to choose any company. Give your selected company the above profile and formulate your approach. Present it before the class.

*****

3

An organisation's ability to learn, and translate that learning into action rapidly, is the ultimate competitive advantage.

Jack Welch

Learning Organisations and Creativity

A business organisation is a network of diverse skills, talents and competencies. As discussed in earlier chapters, business teams consist of people and machines. Through their product and services, business units compete for share of their customers' wallet – their current and future purchasing power.

Business units usually consist of teams handling a supply chain of raw materials including data and information; operations to transform raw materials into finished products and services; finance, human resource management and marketing to present products and services to customers. Each activity in the business process is interdependent. Each activity has a role in determining efficiency, effectiveness and competitiveness of the organisation.

The entire organisation can be, and should be, involved in the change and organisational design process that requires continuous shared learning. It helps to enhance a sense of commitment and ownership in the organisation's team members. As will be discussed later in this chapter, besides aligning organisation structure with purpose and strategy, effectiveness of organisation design needs to be evaluated and monitored on a continuous basis. Awareness and appropriate new contextual knowledge is essential.

Organisational Learning Imperatives

Business organisations are value chains. Each activity in the value chain has a specific value adding role. Each encounters unique context-specific challenges. New challenges arise due to external and internal changes. Change is omnipresent, continuously creating new problems that require new thinking and learning.

Learning is the process of acquiring *new* knowledge, skills and competencies. Creativity is the art and science of using imagination to find *contextual value adding solutions*. For meaningful and effective learning, managers have to be mindful of the why, what, when, where, whom and how (5W+H) of learning in the organisational network.

Business value chains comprise a variety of activities and expertise. Depending on the nature, range and scope of business operations, each activity team would have its own unique learning requirements. The challenge for managers is to make individual and team learning synergistic and holistic from the organisational perspective. Creative managers also add value while managing their creative operations.

Peter M. Senge in his book *The Fifth Discipline* explains that a "learning organisation" is an organisation that is continually expanding its capacity to create its future. And defines "generative learning" as learning that enhances our capacity to create.

In turbulent VUCA business environment, to remain contextual and relevant for customers with changing expectations, learning, unlearning and relearning is essential for managers as well as business units.

Caselet 3.1

Using Zero-Based Proactive Learning Paradigm (ZBPLP)

Rishi had recently read about Zero-Based Proactive Learning Paradigm (ZBPLP). He was aware that in a fast changing, volatile, uncertain, complex and ambiguous (VUCA) environment being contextual was critical — contextual in knowledge, thinking and action. Accelerated learning and unlearning was essential. He was also convinced that Zero Based Thinking (ZBT) and ZBPLP provided appropriate options for business organisations.

As a student of business administration, he was keen to know the views of other students on the subject. He wanted to test his concepts and thoughts. He sought permission from his faculty to present and discuss appropriateness of ZBT and ZBPLP for business managers in class, as a class project.

Summarising the definitions, the points he presented were:

Zero-based thinking in the business context implies zeroing-out the past to have a clear picture of the present possibilities. Tradition, history and emotion free thinking. Perceived future opportunities need to be evaluated on the bases of current realities and overall trends.

Being proactive, is being aware, anticipatory and being in control of the prevailing situation. Being pre-emptive is making things happen rather than just responding to events after they happen.

ZBT and ZBPLP are essential in a fast changing business environment. Both are any-time, any-where options and help enhance future value of products and services, as well as appropriateness of business models.

The prevailing realities for business organisations include information empowered, globally connected, impulsive customers, with their changing lifestyles. Their ever active smartphones are the source of uncertainties and ambiguities. Purchasing at the speed to thought, impulsive "buy" clicks of the mobile phone by on-the-go customers' decides the fate of many products and services.

Markets are dynamic, complex and uncertain. Competitors are creative, technology savvy and unpredictable. Global connectivity and global interdependence are constantly introducing new diversity and complexities in the business arenas. With global connectivity, customers have global information. Competitors from remote parts of the world have access to connected markets. Making creative use of digital technologies, new entrepreneurs are introducing disruptive innovations as well as new business models.

Business managers and business leaders are faced with very fast changing volatile, uncertain, complex and ambiguous (VUCA) situations. Science, technology, engineering and

Learning Organisations and Creativity 53

mathematical (STEM) based manufacturing logic seems to be in conflict with emotional, impulsive and dynamic (EID) behaviour of markets. Optimising trade-offs is a *continuous* challenge for business leaders.

Given the above dynamics, is there a meaningful role for ZBPLP in the world of business? Or, for business managers and leaders? Rishi went on to ask the class:

- Would being proactive tend to be *more* or *less* risky?
    - Would it make managers operate in *more* or *less* uncertain environment?
- In a fast changing environment, does rear-view mirror lose its relevance?
    - Does history become less relevant?
    - Can history be misleading? Can it be a hindrance?
- Would zero-based situation analysis create a *disconnect* with the past?
    - Would it provide more realistic strategic growth options?
- Would zero-based analysis help in making an organisation stronger or weaker?
    - For marketing operations?
    - For manufacturing operations?
    - For overall business organisation? How?
- Would ZBPLP provide more timely, appropriate and insightful understanding of business situations to managers and business leaders?
    - How should business managers and leaders make optimal use of ZBPLP for themselves and their organisations?
- Would ZBPLP provide a time and cost saving option for organisational learning and strategy designing?
- Would ZBPLP facilitate evolution and nurturing of creative design-thinking culture in the organisation?

- Rishi summed up his presentation with the statement:
  - The best time and place to start our journey towards the future is *now*.
  - *Not* yesterday.

Ending his presentation, he requested other students to share their views.

*****

An Approach to Organisational Learning

Each individual in an organisation has a specific role. Learning is done by individuals. The challenge is to initiate and nurture contextual individual learning. Also, to translate and transform that individual learning into organisational learning.

Since each individual has a specific role in the organisation, the organisational learning efforts have to be specific as well as general, contextual as well as connected. Every employee does not have to learn everything about the business. Besides other considerations, cost-benefit evaluation is an integral part of business operations. Thus, focus, appropriateness and effectiveness of learning are essential.

To be useful, learning must be relevant, contextual as well as comprehensive. Depending on the nature of business operations, the learning journey may start from the job and move on to geo-economics or from general to specific. The overall methodology adopted for organisational learning would have to be organisation specific. It may start with participative and shared organisational awareness. The organisational learning process may be designed as:

> *Being Aware*: This involves making organisation members aware of the general geo-economic and geo-political nature of the global business environment. This would help to bring all employees on the same page. This may further be divided into:
>
> *Industry awareness*: Although boundaries between industries are becoming blurred, each business unit operates in a fairly well demarcated and defined industry. Understanding the nature of the prevailing industry dynamics would be useful.

Local business arena: Even if business operations are global, sales are local. Local customers define the life-line of business. Global business walks on local legs. Understanding the local business culture, local legal business regulatory framework, lifestyle and shopping behaviour of local customers, the nature of competition and strategic thinking of competitors, is critical.

Being aware of overall business operations: A comprehensive and holistic understanding of business operations and its stakeholders is essential. This should include understanding of the social-fit of business purpose as well as its operations.

Major business activity areas: Depending on the nature of business, these may include supply chain or inflow of resources, operations or processing of resources, marketing of finished products and services, accounting and finance, human resource and talent management.

Activity teams: Each business activity would have its own unique learning needs. Each activity, such as supply chain, would have its own activity partners. Suppliers also have suppliers. The study and adaptation of best practices would require departmental as well as overall business perspective.

Subsets of activity teams: Depending on the nature, diversity and spread of business, some teams, such as marketing, operations and finance, may have specialised sub-sets. Digital technologies have created new engagement options for customers and business organisations. Business units need to constantly re-evaluate effectiveness of their communication strategies.

Overall Political, Economic, Social and Technology (PEST) analysis: Globalisation and creative use of digital technology have introduced many complex elements of diversity, uncertainty, complexity and ambiguity in the business environment.

Overall Strengths, Weakness, Opportunities and Threats (SWOT) analysis: This may also start with organisation vis-à-vis competitors and then move on to individual departments.

Evolving strategic perspective: With the above information and perspective, through dialogue and discussions, the corporate team can reach a common understanding on:

Where they are: Have a fairly good idea of their position in the market vis-à-vis their competitors and their customers.

Where they would like to be: In a fast changing competitive business environment, it may be difficult to create a realistic well defined vision. However, one can have a fairly good idea of the direction in which one should go, or define the purposeful pursuit for excellence.

How to get there: An organisation is a team consisting of various departmental teams. This may be seen as a football team in a perpetual, never ending match, that is, the organisation team moving together as a team-of-teams, towards a predetermined goal or direction.

Enhancing learning and knowledge flow: As stated earlier, individuals in the organisations do the learning. They share their ideas with their department or activity team members. Effective organisation learning happens when knowledge flows between activity teams and transforms into sustainable competitive advantage for the organisation as a unit. This will be discussed in detail in later chapters.

Purposeful and customer focused learning: Business purpose creates the bonds between customers and organisation. Each individual and department from their perspective or vantage point must try to acquire skills and knowledge with the objective to enhance overall organisational purposefulness and enhance value for customers. Customers value overall experience with organisations through their products and services.

Sustainable "excellence" learning culture: Most business organisations are facing accelerated, multi-faceted change situations. Pursuit of excellence here may be seen as an organisation trying to achieve its best. It means continuous proactive learning to make business purpose more purposeful for customers. As will be discussed in later chapters, continuous nurturing of curiosity is essential to promote questioning and proactive learning.

Integrated corporate communication network: For a business organisation to evolve as a learning team, it is essential to have a comprehensive integrated corporate communication network.

A business organisation may be said to be moving up its learning curve when its new learnings are valued by its customers. This can be evaluated by its overall business performance or by individual indicators such as organisational networks show more effective communications, more coordinated processes and systems demonstrate more customer friendly services, feedbacks show more satisfied and loyal customers, repeat sales, reduced costs and increased revenues and overall happy customers, more committed employees and future-fit organisation.

A Narration

Curiosity, Learning and Creativity

While discussing the topic *Learning Organisation and Creativity* with an international business consultant, she said:

> I do not have a specific answer to your question, but let me share my experience on the subject with you. Once I asked a spiritual guru: What is the best way to learn? How would I know that what I am learning is what I should be learning or is it a waste of time? A waste of life (as time is life)?
>
> The gist of what my guru said was: Who am *I* to tell you what *you* should or should not be learning? It is for *you* to decide. Let the curiosity of your own head and compassion of your own heart show you the way. Each one of us has to decide his or her own life journey. Remember, in Mahabharata, each one selected his or her own path. Krishna, the great strategist and guru, only indicated options. He just ignited curiosity to make them aware of their situation and options before

them. Even by narrating Gita, he only made Arjun aware of his situation and the options before him. He asked Arjun to decide for himself.

As I recall, his main guidance was, first become curious. Meditate. Think. Become *aware* of who you are and where you are — *now*. Understand your present — *now*. Understand your *present* reality, context and situation. Critically evaluate the options before you. Think and decide your action plan. Like life itself, let your curiosity, learning and creativity evolve.

I guess what he said would be good guidance for organisations also. Learning organisations need to be curious to know where they are *now*. Be aware of their context and situation. In other words, be aware of their customers, their purpose and their competitors. Awareness of their situation and change around them will germinate curiosity, questioning and creativity.

It is important to keep in mind that to be in tune with change, corporations and managers will have to change. Change will move on in its own unpredictable ways. The creative managers can creatively seed curiosity, plant questions, help in evolution of the learning process and creatively guide and mentor the learning process of their organisations.

I do not know whether I have confused you or replied to your question.

*****

Organisations: *A Solution Perspective*

Commercial as well as non-commercial organisations are channels for social solutions. Organisations come into existence when two or more individuals come together to take action to solve a community, country or global problem.

Thus all organisations, like commercial corporations, have external objectives and internal systems to achieve their identified goals. Organisations are created to serve a social purpose. Whatever the size or structure of organisations, the purpose is to provide some service or solution to the community in which they operate.

Organisations may have one or more objectives. They may be designed to serve only their members, a section of society or the society at large. Business organisations are customer focused with commercial objectives. To be self-sustaining, profit is essential.

Business organisations define their functions, areas of operations, products or services they will deal in, processes they will follow to meet their objectives or the set of people they will serve. Organisations may be simple or complex, formal or informal. The objective is same — a social solution through products and services.

Organisations: *As Socio-Economic Systems*

As stated earlier, organisations may also be seen as processes or systems — as dynamic solution-focused systems or processes of men, women and machines, with a context and objective. Like individuals, each organisation is unique in its origins, context, structure, values, culture, way-of-working and objectives.

Over time, depending on the thinking and policies of their organisers and managers, as well as their need and abilities to remain relevant, organisations change, evolve and grow or wither away. Each organisation has its own unique set of stakeholders and beneficiaries.

Organisations may also be seen as a dynamic network of relationships or a talent-technology network of individuals and activities working towards a common goal. Depending on the size and scope of the social problems being addressed, organisations create their own networks and cooperatively work to solve common problems. Organisations use technology to support human efforts. New levels of productivity and effectiveness are achieved by appropriate use of machines and systems. Digital technologies have created a variety of disruptions and also added new support systems.

Socio-economic problems are often complex. They need to be divided into manageable components and also given a local context. Given the social diversities, to arrive at appropriate solutions, the proposed solutions have to be examined and need to pass through appropriate filtering processes. Design-thinking helps in designing inclusive and integrated solutions. Each individual in the organisational activity may constitute a subset of the overall solution process. Working as a seamless, overall system, each activity unit enhances the quality of solution, speed of solution and appropriateness, as well as relevance of the final solution.

Keeping in view its unique context, each organisation designs its own unique organisational as well as management structure and process. Each organisation has its own requirements of managerial approach, skills and mindsets. For departmental, divisional, as well as overall performance evaluation, managers devise key performance indices (KPI) for their organisation.

Organisations: *As Living Organisms*

Organisations are created by people, for people and are managed by people. Organisations are living organisms. All living beings are born with the instinct for survival. Also, management may be seen as an embedded, instinctive, mind process that helps organisations in their survival.

As one senior manager said:

> Organisations, like individuals, survive or grow based on their ability to generate and sustain curiosity, learn, self-manage and use creative managerial energies. Digital technologies provide unlimited learning opportunities.

Discussing this matter, a spiritual gurus said:

> Plants and trees are perhaps the most creative managers on earth. They are usually able to gather resources for survival from the limited spaces available to them, wherever they are planted or their seeds germinate. I feel germination of a seed and growth of a plant is perhaps one of the greatest examples of creativity in nature. Without moving from their place, the plants and trees survive all forms of attacks from animals as well as humans, and still manage to grow. Many of them live for hundreds of years.

Learning, creativity and management are not monopolies of human beings. Just look around and see the wonders of nature exhibiting creativity and management. At times, I feel management is creativity in action.

What would management be without creativity?

Many formal and informal, new and old organisations operate in societies. Some may be hundreds of years old. Whatever the size or structure of organisations, their growth and sustainability rests on their ability to serve the purpose for which they were created and their learning ability to remain relevant to the society in which they operate. For business organisations, remaining relevant for customers is critical.

Organisations: *As Legal and Individual Entities*

Organisations are legal entities. Like individuals, each organisation has a unique persona, learning needs, capabilities and value system, a culture, as well as a survival instinct of its own. As international business organisations, complex international legal systems influence their operations.

Each organisation has unique internal processes to manage its operations to meet its survival and growth objectives. Also, like individuals, each organisation interacts in its own unique way with its different stakeholders, as well as at each social interface point or its customers. As a part of society, we experience this every day.

Like individuals, organisations have some common as well as unique distinctive traits due to their origins, ownership, objectives, structures, values, philosophies and contexts.

Organisations: *Purpose, Objectives and Values*

Besides various other factors, organisations may be grouped or classified on the basis of their purpose, objectives or values — commercial or non-commercial. Vision, objectives and values are the prime movers of organisations. Values influence standards of behaviour of people working in the organisation and also usefulness of organisations to societies where they operate. As with other living organisms, to survive, organisations need to change with time and circumstances.

A promoter of a non-government organisation said:

> When I started my organisation, it was dedicated to education, but due to various circumstances and changes in local social needs, our current activity is mainly old age healthcare. Over time, there has been a need based step-by-step transformation of our purpose, thinking, objectives and values.
>
> To stay alive, organisations have to remain socially relevant and change as social needs change. Our financial resources come from society. So our services have to have value for society in which we operate.

Organisations: *Ownership and Management*

Organisations are created, operated and owned by individuals or groups of people. Ownership patterns of organisations and their objectives are an often discussed subject. There are many ideological perceptions and management theories on ownership of organisations, such as by private individuals, joint-ventures, cooperatives, trusts, limited liability ownership and general public.

Management practices and policies also tend to differ with ownership patterns. Private organisations with personal and individual ownerships are driven by self-interest, while publicly owned organisations are meant to serve the interests of the general public. Each requires a unique, purpose focused management approach. Multinational organisations encounter multinational challenges.

Keeping in mind the ownership differences, to meet the different organisation objectives, managers need different sets of knowledge-bases, systems, processes and key performance measuring indices. It is the appropriateness of the management policies and practices, as well as performance evaluation criteria that often determines the success or failures of organisations.

There are different objectives for which different organisations are created. The problems are defined differently by organisations. Social cultures or communities in which they operate are different. Thus, the approaches to solutions are different. Keeping in mind the contextual uniqueness of each organisation, search for appropriate management framework for each organisation needs a suitable zero-based approach.

It may not be wrong to say that context and purpose of an organisation determines the nature as well as the parameters for its learning, creativity and innovations. Each organisation has its own unique creative management needs.

Continuous Proactive Alignment with Strategy

In a disruptive, high-velocity VUCA business environment, organisation systems need to be in continuous alignment with its strategy. Even a short duration mismatch may create serious disconnects with customers. Being aware, with an observing, learning and listening attitude is essential.

Managers manage organisations. Creative managers manage creatively. Besides various other differences, their attitude towards problems may be seen as a distinctive factor. Some managers try to be proactively aware of the potential problem areas or issues. They try to pre-empt and minimise occurrence of complications, while others tend to react only after the problems are reported to them.

Change creates multi-faceted disruptions. Just as doctors examine each patient individually, managers also have to examine each problem in its unique context. Here, proactive attitude may be seen as a mindset to visualise the side-effects, as well as the future consequences of present disruptions. A quick proactive contextual visualisation of past, present and future is required.

Discussing the topic, a senior vice-president of a multinational organisation said:

> Attitude towards problems is a very critical and distinctive factor in classification of managers. Problems define our roles in an organisation. I expect managers to enjoy dealing and playing with the problems as they search to identify a few possible alternate solutions, like a World Cup football player searching for the most appropriate option before he kicks the football.

Notwithstanding all the talks about big data management and analytics, I feel management is a very creative as well as instinctive game. Making sense out of massive complex data requires very perceptive and creative inputs. Most business activities are creative and instinctive. I look at artists, musicians and also football players as people who are searching for ways to improve their decision making skills. Be it for a football player or an artist, it is the creative, instinctive skill in problem solving that makes them distinctive. I look for that trait in my management team players.

Organisational learning starts with individuals. From the creative management perspective, individual team-players may often be seen as walking on a tight rope. Creative forces impel them to move forward towards their individual goals and their management skills help them in maintaining their balance. As will be discussed later in the book, organisational learning and creativity are cooperative ventures. For success, it is essential to maintain coordination as well as balance between individual, creative efforts and organisational needs.

Like the power of an atom, societies often underestimate the power of an individual, at their own risk. Today, individuals are connected with local as well as global communities. Besides the time-flow, human history may also be seen as a story of ideas and individuals—individuals who created their own national and trans-national space and followings.

Caselet 3.2

Creating Learning, Sharing and Caring Circles

While in Bhutan on their business school learning trip, Rishi's class attended a seminar where they discussed the concept of "Happiness Index" for nations and communities. After this, Rishi wondered whether he could use the available digital technology to create "small self-learning, sharing and caring, happy communities" in a large, cosmopolitan city. He was keen to explore this idea.

He was concerned about the isolation and lack of connectivity between individuals in his city. As he perceived it, internet and mobile phones had created more isolation rather than connectivity and the spirit of camaraderie between people living in the same high-rise buildings was severely lacking. Even the exchange of informal social greetings and smiles were often missing. Smartphones, with their numerous options—global connectivity, entertainment, news, messaging, music and shopping opportunities—created barriers rather than bridges between neighbours. These problems of individual isolation were enhanced due to addictive nature of digital technologies.

While he had often heard the phrase "global-village", he found increasing isolation among people around him. The spirit of *vasudheva-kutumbhakam*—the world is a family—was sorely missing.

He wondered whether the available digital technology options could be used to link up people with common interests, hobbies and social concerns to create small "one-mile sharing and caring circles". He wondered if he could create a network of *little-villages* with heart and soul.

He visualised various kinds of mini socio-economic creative opportunities. He felt people had many kinds of dormant and unexplored capacities, ideas, hobbies, competencies and knowledge-bases which could be used for mutual benefit, building and bonding communities and forming small creative social ventures. He wondered whether he could create a platform where senior citizens could also share their skills and wisdom, as well as explore their unfulfilled dreams with the help of others.

He also wanted to discuss the possibilities of using a similar approach in organisational learning. He made a small presentation to discuss his ideas and views in the class with other students.

- To start with, he proposed development of a friendly "know-thy-neighbour" platform or a website.

- Besides experimenting himself, he also wanted to be an enabling-catalyst for small, neighbourhood, social enterprises:
  - Know-thy-neighbour — profiles, hobbies, interests, etc.
  - A collaborative platform for mutual-learning, caring and sharing.
  - A participative and evolving platform.
- He wanted to make use of easily available, low-cost, simple, workable digital technology options.
- He wanted to create and promote a network of websites such as JustSmile, SayHi, etc., which would be used by people:
  - As first step to introduce themselves.
  - In case of any help for home maintenance they may need.
  - *First* social support option.
- He wanted the platform to be a place where people would:
  - Get to know their neighbourhood and residents
  - Share hobbies, knowledge and aspirations
- Neighbours could exchange ideas, aspirations and enrich the cultural life of one another — children, families and senior citizens:
  - Cooperate to enhance social and cultural lives.
  - Create a "little friendly village".
- Hobbies such as cooking, music, yoga, games, teaching, etc., could evolve into small, social ventures.
- To transform their "day-dreams" into dream-for-day ventures. To actualise their aspirations and dreams into reality by creating dream-for-the-day ventures by doing it and sharing it. Experiment and test their dreams — cooking, backing, coaching, teaching, etc.

- To start with, business model could be to let the user determine the price. A part of the income could be contributed to the organisation fund.
- To keep the group small and neighbourly, the membership would be limited to a one mile radius.
  - Next mile, next *village*.

He was keen to know the views of his classmates and about the different ways he could initiate his venture, with minimal investment and maximum neighbourhood participation.

*****

Organisational Learning Imperatives

Change creates multi-faceted disruptions. Disruptions distort alignments. They create frictions and distort workflows. In the fast changing business environment, business organisations have to compete against time. New problems require new solutions, new thinking and new skills. For sustainable competitiveness, continuous and contextual learning, unlearning and relearning are essential.

Whatever the nature or goal of an organisation, with customers, communities and nations in a state of flux, organisation need to be aware of the changes around them. As will be discussed in the next chapter, global connectivity and digital technology options are changing the way people think, shop, relate with each other and work. The commercial landscape, as well as mindscape, is changing. Internet and cyberspace operations are creating various kinds of disruptions. Volatility, uncertainty, complexity and ambiguity (VUCA) have become an integral part of business environment.

Digital technologies are becoming ubiquitous as well as inextricably intertwined with every part of commercial operations. New digital business models continuously transform the game of business. To keep pace with the accelerated change, business organisations as well as managers have to do high speed learning as well as unlearning.

Globalisation and popularity of ecommerce has reduced the lifecycle of products and services. Given the newer and newer digital options, managers need to rethink their assumptions about the structures, processes and roles of different organisations in solving their current and future socio-economic problems. Just as the industrial revolution changed the lifestyles and work culture, thinking and management practices of the agriculture-era, there is need for new thinking and creative management to make optimal use of digital technology options.

Already some social as well as commercial organisations are facing discontinuities and uncertainties. Managers of organisations need to be aware of currently evolving challenges as well as be aware of possible future realities. Also, managers need to question their own mindsets, thinking, assumptions and wisdom in the context of emerging new disruptive challenges.

Given the information empowerment of all stakeholders, it is time to re-think and revaluate management thinking in its current operational contexts. Business organisations have to operate in an environment of disruptive innovations. Creative uses of digital technologies have empowered individuals and transformed structures as well as processes of business organisations. To keep pace with change, we need to understand the nature of change. The power shift between business organisations and customers is continuously in progress.

With increasing pace of change and imperatives of future focus, appropriate use of imagination in management is critical. Many experts feel that management is the most creative of the creative arts. This point is discussed in detail in later chapters.

New situations require new thinking. Peter Drucker observes, "The greatest danger in times of turbulence is not the turbulence, it is to act with yesterday's logic." This is of special significance in the present context.

Individual and organisational learning helps in winning challenges of the marketplace. For appropriate matching of operations and technology, it would be advantageous to take a critical look at the landscapes and mindscapes of commercial arenas, as is done in the next chapter.

*****

Creative Management: *A Role Play*

1. Identify an industry of your choice.
2. Develop a short business activity profile of a medium sized company in that industry.
3. Appoint yourself as its CEO.
4. Your assignment is to transform your organisation into a proactive, learning organisation.
    a. Decide organisational learning objectives.
    b. Design your approach to initiating organisational learning.
    c. Design a feedback, evaluation and course correction mechanism.
5. How would you make it a sustainable, continuous, organisational learning process?

*****

4

If there is one thing that's certain in business, it's uncertainty.

Stephen Covey

Commercial Landscapes, Cyberscapes and Mindscapes

While the digital technologies have transformed agriculture-era as well as industrial-era commercial practices, a new cyberspace with its own unique social and commercial framework has emerged. Cyberspace is a global computer network space where people from different parts of the world interact through their computers or devices like smartphones. Cyberspace has evolved a world of its own with its own unique cyber culture. It is a space with global dimensions, instant connectivity, diversity and its own cultural dynamics. It has its own unique set of challenges, opportunities and risks.

Cyberspace is a space where people from different part of the world interact for various socio-economic activities such as to exchange ideas, conduct business, play games or create political or social movements. It is also a space for global friendship, cooperation as well as cyber-wars. Commercial models and commercial rules have evolved for cyberspace operations.

When digital technologies became an integral part of commercial operations, many questions arose. How will the overall commercial landscape change? Digital technologies are omnipresent. With more intensive and extensive use of information technologies, how will the overall business mindscape be transformed? How will the use of automation and artificial intelligence impact corporate business processes and management thinking? What will be the future corporate human-machine job-mix? How will the overall architecture of corporations change? These were some of the questions asked.

Many other questions were also being asked: How will internet and Internet-of-Things (IoT) change the landscape of the evolving global-village? How smart will be the smart driverless cars? How smart will be the smart cities? How smart will the organisations be? What role would the artificial intelligence empowered learning machines play in corporate management? What will be the future global-local mix in different industries? How will the increased use of global connectivity impact corporate-customer and customer-product relationships? Will the future markets be vertically or horizontally divided by customer purchasing power? What will be the structure of "cloudy" global marketing communities? What will be the new *normal* in knowledge-era business arenas?

In my efforts to understand the world of commerce, many such questions cropped up as I interacted with people from different industries and professions. While providing some understanding, each interaction also gave rise to new questions. Each day brings in new data, trends and alternate scenarios.

Commercial Landscape Dynamics

Business scenario is continuously in a state of flux. The entire business scenario seems to be under transformation as the creative use of digital technology provides instant options for customers, corporations and business partners. With the help of mobile technologies, markets as well as work-places are moving with people — customers and talent. There is a continuous need for new thinking, theories and paradigms to effectively manage changes being introduced by global connectivity, social media and other creative options being brought about by digital technologies.

Making creative use of digital technology, whose use can be extremely addictive for customers, many business units aggressively and creatively try to lock-in current and future purchasing powers of their customers.

With global connectivity and global interdependence, geo-politics and geo-economics have become integral parts of business environment. The global commercial arena has massive trans-national corporate structures as well as stretches of quicksands where big and small business units struggle to remain afloat. Also, there are many opportunities for new creative and innovative start-ups. New start-ups create uncertain situations for traditional organisations. The kaleidoscopic commercial scenarios keep changing unexpectedly.

Caselet 4.1

Wondering in the Wonderland of Business

Meru had been silent ever since she came out from her first class. After her remarkable achievements in her high school, along with a few friends, she had opted for this prestigious business school. Her friends were concerned about her silence. They had enjoyed their first day classes at the university.

On their way back home, her friends asked her reason for silence. She just smiled and said that there was no specific reason, she was just confused.

Alone at home, she recalled her experience in the class. The teacher had asked all the students to introduce themselves and also share their reason for selecting "business" as a career. He had asked them all to say a few words about *why* they had opted for business education and *what* role they were planning to play in the world of business.

Like most other students, she had also introduced herself and made a general statement about her future career in business. In the class she had replied in general terms. However, it was at that time that she realised that she had *zero* knowledge about business. She had a lot to catch up and learn. She also had to discover satisfactory answers to *why* and *what* for herself. She had to understand the mysterious world of products, services, costs, revenue and profit.

As a sportsperson, she knew that the only way to learn a game was to play it. She discussed her dilemma with her friends. After discussions, she decided that the best way to learn the game of business, too, was by playing it.

Along with two friends, she decided to explore the digital technology start-ups arena. They worked as a close-knit team. Even though she had *zero* business experience, Meru was designated as the CEO of their proposed venture.

In class they had often heard that, notwithstanding the need for extensive computing and various other skills, business is a game of common sense. The basic ideas behind most leading business organisations were simple, common sense ideas. As a team, they wanted to play with ideas and use their common sense. For them, this was a risk-free game with unrestricted learning opportunities, a game to be played with curiosity and questions. For team learning, they opted for Zero-Based Proactive Learning Paradigm (ZBPLP) approach.

During their meetings, whenever they would go astray from their main subject, someone would laughingly say — *laksha sadhoo* — call from the *guru* Dronacharya, in Indian mythology Mahabharata to his *shishya* Arjun, to focus on his target. With their limited knowledge of information technology and business operations, they targeted education and healthcare for their selected customer segments.

- Their basic raw material — information — was available free of cost. They did not factor in their own efforts.
- The business process consisted of creating credible "information and knowledge packages".

Their business model was simple:

- To start with, they wanted to create an *interactive* platform to provide reliable, confidence building information in the areas of education and healthcare.
- They named their venture: you-me.com
- They wanted to create *contextual credible* information packages or banks for
  - Students
  - People requiring healthcare services
- Users would evaluate the value of information and pay according to their *valuation* of services.

- Customers were considered as *active* business partners. They were requested to share their experiences with the services providers and suggest improvements.
- Simplicity was going to be their core strategic competency — simplicity in designing services, communication and in structuring their business operations.
- They wanted to start their venture as a small seed of *peepal* tree and grow slowly by simply asking, listening and testing (SALT) feedback from their customers. As for their organisational structure, their approach was contextual, appropriate, research and technology (CART) oriented.

They requested permission from their teacher to present their business project in class to source ideas from their class colleagues and share their experiences.

- Does this kind of simple, zero-based proactive learning approach make any sense in the hyper competitive world of business?
  - Why?
  - Why not?
- What would be the strength, weakness, opportunity and threat (SWOT) profile of you-me.com?
- Is this approach of learning-by-experimenting appropriate for future business players?
- What could be alternate approaches to:
  - Learning about the game of business?
  - Experiencing *reality* of the business game?
  - Initiating a career in the world of business?

They requested their colleagues for feedback.

*****

Commercial Cyberscape Dynamics

Cyberspace is a digital technology space. Besides transforming agriculture-era and industrial-era commercial landscapes, digital technologies have created cyberspace. The cyberspace is a world with its own codes of communication, social and commercial relationships. It facilitates global strategic alliances, partnerships and competition, as well as cyber warfare. It has its own rules of aesthetics and economics. Like the industrial-era corporations, some cyberspace communities are larger than traditional nation-states. Cyberspace has its own *cyber communities* with their own culture, identities and codes. Some cyber communities have memberships in millions.

Whether we visualise cyberspace as flat, uneven, spherical or cloudy, a complex commercial cyberscape has evolved. Millions of entrepreneurs from around the world are exploring new ways to create social, commercial and political platforms in the cyberspace. It is a dynamic multi-cultural space with its own unique commercial and social culture. Some of the unique features of commercial cyberscape include:

Global reach: Cyberspace is global in reach. Directly or indirectly more than half of the world population — and these numbers are growing rapidly every day — makes use of it for activities such as communication, business, entertainment, information search, shopping, etc.

Global social media: Interactive social media is a very important part of cyberspace. It is a multi-functional social platform where individuals exchange ideas; create teams, groups and communities, as well as commercial platforms.

Global community: Cyberspace users may be seen as a global community. Various digital technologies have created a new global community with its own local-global options. New multinational and multi-cultural communities with their own values and interests are continuously evolving in the cyberspace.

Multi-ability diversity: Smartphone users have a variety of choices in selecting apps for their phones. This has created a new form of multi-ability diversity in the commercial cyberspace. This diversity is increasing almost on daily basis. New convergence and divergence dynamics is developing.

Multi-cultural diversity: Cyberspace is a collage of multi-cultural, multi-lingual, and multinational diversity. Technology savvy people from any part of the world can use it and create their own groups and communities.

New areas of conflict and cooperation: New forms of cyber-politics and cyber-economics are evolving in the cyberspace. A new dynamic socio-economic-political order is emerging in the cyberspace.

Uncertain, dynamic, disruptive environment: Cyberspace is characterised by unexpected dynamic disruptive commercial events. Speed, mobility, complexity and ambiguity are integral part of cyberspace business environment. It is an environment of fleeting opportunities.

New economics and commerce: Economic and commercial transactions in the digital technology driven global cyberspace happen instantaneously. Distance, computing and marginal costs have little significance. Talent and ideas are the critical resources.

Product and service development: Products and services created and developed by digital technologies for use in cyberspace or traditional industries are mostly "technology" or process oriented. Creative use of information technology is used to make agriculture-era and industrial-era operations more efficient and productive.

New customers: Be it business-to-business (B2B) or business-to-customers (B2C) or customer-to-customer (C2C), in the cyberspace all actors are information empowered and technology savvy. Their life-style, expectations and shopping behaviour are different from those of previous industrial-era actors.

New technology-emotional mix: Mobile phones are the new "agents" between business organisations and their customers. Phones act as the new "purchase assistants" for customers. Phones also act as "sales agents" for business organisations. Trust and transactional bonds between business organisations and their customers are based on new dynamic techno-emotional mix. Each business organisation has to do its own homework to understand the shifts and changing trends.

Marketing challenges: Just as customers are information empowered, business organisations can empower themselves with information about their customers. Business units have the means to know history and profile data of their customers. They can get real-time feedback about their shopping behaviour through high-speed analytics. Appropriate use of information technology, artificial intelligence and big-data are part of the new creative management challenges.

Customer relations: Digital technologies can be creatively used to gain an insightful understanding of the shopping behaviour of customers. Preferences of customers as well as their decision making triggers can be identified. Creative use of digital technologies can help in crafting effective bonds between business organisations and their customers.

Competition: Global connectivity creates an environment of global competition from many known and unknown sources. Entry barriers to most industries have been reduced by digital technologies. New business models are creating various kinds of disruptions in established industries. Business organisations need to continuously re-evaluate their competitiveness positions.

Business intelligence and strategic designs: To acquire contextual business intelligence and formulate effective strategic designs requires new digital skills. Managers have to learn to make creative use of high-speed data collection, big-data analytics and imagination. Depending on the scale of operations, artificial intelligence, computing, automation and robotics may also be required. Global business strategic designs also include various forms of trans-national business and strategic alliances, partnerships, acquisitions, mergers and joint-ventures.

New customer-centric business models: Being connected through technology, customers have become more integrated in the overall business process. Instant feedback, extensive data collection and data analysis gives business units more opportunities to consider customers as co-creators of products and services.

Business process and organisational architecture: Human talent, critical and creative thinking and technology constitute the main resource of cyberspace business units. Business process is a solution focused, prototyping-testing-learning-adapting-iterating creative chain. Global connectivity provided options for global interactive teams. Depending on the nature of the business, the future organisation architecture will consist of mobile, modular, technology platforms that incorporate contextual flexibility for dynamic alignment of talent needs.

Creative management and business leadership: Innovation and creativity are the prime movers as well as disruptive agents of the knowledge-era. Business leaders are expected to initiate, nudge and nurture solution focused creative energies of their organisations. With more self-managed teams, managers would be required to do more coaching and co-ordination rather than planning and directing.

Power games, conflicts and cyber-wars: Individuals, organisations and nations have developed their own creative ways to express their anger and disagreements. Global connectivity offers many ways to hack and counter hack opponents. Cyber-attacks, cyber-terrorism and cyber-wars are often discussed topics.

Future scenarios: Cyberspace is in a state of flux. With its global reach, the future depends on the common interests, concerns, values and willingness to collaborate among the cyberspace users.

Internet and social media provide opportunities for individuals as well as organisations to create social and commercial platforms. It provides opportunities for individuals to create their own global communities — for social, commercial or political purposes. Possibilities are limited by their own imagination and capabilities.

Caselet 4.2

Developing an E-Brand: A Business Adventure

Rishu had read and heard many industrial-era stories of people who started with almost no material resources but went on to create vast business and political empires. Brainpower was their only socio-economic resource. He had also read the life stories of Kautilya, Karan and Eklavya, as well as Bill Gates and Steve Jobs.

He was aware of the fact that e-commerce was a competitive game. He would have to create a new contextually appropriate value and trust base. He also had to understand the relationship between smartphone screens and his potential customers. He would have to be part of it. He was aware that he would be entering a crowded competitive arena. He was focused on finding ways to know:

- How to create a pleasant and enriching purchasing process for his potential customers?
- How to create a neighbourhood shopping community bonding?
- How and where to start?

As a digital-era student of business administration, he wondered what kind of business venture he could create with his own creative abilities, his mobile and his computer.

He defined the terms for his business adventure:

- He would continue his studies and put in his best possible performance.
- Studies would remain his first priority.
- He would devote only two hours of his time every day on the venture.
- He would not take any financial help from his family or friends.

After a few months of efforts, he was pleasantly surprised by his success and his friends were surprised by his confidence. They requested him to share his experience and future plans with the class. Rishu agreed. He prepared few slides for the class presentation.

- His first slide stated:
  - Please do not ignore simplicity.
  - Simplicity and honesty can be a very effective business strategies.
- His assumption and beliefs:
  - Business is a game of relationship and mutual trust.
  - Service with a genuine smile, humble gratitude and personal touch is a valuable competitive advantage.
  - Digital technology helps building, sustaining and reinforcing real relationships.
  - Some important actions:
    - Monitoring customer relations
    - Appropriate, concerned and respectful feedback mechanism
    - Proactive listening and learning
    - Winning back lost customers with new learnings
    - Persistence and resilience are critical
    - Some failures and setbacks are part of the game
- He initiated his business by making "cold calls" to seek orders for delivery of products.
  - During his calls he introduced himself with humility and honesty.
  - He told his potential customers that:
    - He was a student of business administration.
    - Had adopted this venture as an experimental-learning and exploring real business opportunities.

- As a keen observer as well as an active listener he found that customers were insightful business teachers.
* He was encouraged by the support and enthusiasm he received from many of his customers.
* One of his suppliers even agreed to let him use his delivery van.
* He consolidated his customer-relations through phone calls and e-mails.
  - Developed a feeling of "family" or "customer community"
  - Honesty and integrity were his bonding factors.
* Sources of his business growth impetus were:
  - Satisfied customers and repeat orders
  - Honesty of purpose – his cherished competitive advantage.
  - Making the purchase process simple and customer friendly
    - A customers' inspired web-site
  - Word of mouth expansion of customer base
  - New product and service demand from satisfied customers
  - Cost awareness and control
  - He generated enough profits to expand his operations.
* His learning and experience sharing:
  - Start small, even very small, if you have to.
    - The sky is the limit. Limits are in our own head. Test your limits.
    - Enjoy the business adventure.

The class got into animated discussion as he had ignited curiosity, creative thinking and the spirit of entrepreneurship. Some students requested his partnership in their own ventures.

*****

Commercial Mindscape Dynamics

New situations, new challenges and creative disruptions initiated by competitors require new thinking and new mindsets. Overall commercial mindscape constantly experiences dynamic kaleidoscopic shifts.

In a fast changing environment, to remain relevant and competitive, managers have to learn and change, at least, at the speed of change. Global software industry, commercial operations and mindscape scenarios are changing fast. Internet and digital technologies have ushered in the new knowledge-era and have transformed the commercial environment, skills and talent, as well as the job scenario.

The free flow of information has impacted the commercial mindscape in many different ways. Business organisations have to constantly re-think their business processes and their relationships with their customers as well as business partners. Technology has become the new disruptive agent.

With a fast changing business environment, even well established brands may need to re-evaluate their value propositions. Considering the extensive use of smartphones and changes in shopping behaviour of customers, old products may be in need of being redesigned, re-packed and re-positioned.

Management thinking has to keep pace with the change in business environment as well as thinking of customers. Globalisation has introduced multi-cultural diversities in the business environment. Keeping in view the nature of their businesses and their contexts, also given the fast, uncertain multi-dimensional, multi-directional change, it is essential for corporate managers to proactively initiate their learning efforts.

Giving his views on the subject, the CEO of a medium sized software business unit said:

> Given the global learning options, managers need to proactively create their own contextual learning agendas. It would be in their own interest to proactively do their own periodic zero-based evaluation. Given the uncertain and risk flooded market situations, it is in their own interest to sharpen their creativity and multi-tasking skills. For effective management, managers will have to constantly enhance their

business knowledge and move up the creative value chain in their managerial functions as well as their relationship with their customers.

As the business environment is changing fast, managements have to learn, unlearn and relearn fast. Unlearning is often more difficult than learning. To move ahead in a fast changing environment, managements have to seize the present opportunities and comprehend new realities to design their future.

Digital technologies and global connectivity that is empowering customers and stakeholders must be effectively used by corporate managers to keep pace with changes in the markets and in the minds of customers. To appropriately serve customers with an effective smile, it is essential to understand their aspirations as well as emotional composition.

Discussing this point, a senior marketing executive said:

> Creating a compelling value proposition for current and prospective customers requires timely, insightful, focused and critical, as well as creative thinking. Along with that, one needs a creative combination of multi-cultural sensitivities, marketing talents, as well as contextual strategic thinking. In many commercial areas, hiding behind traditional management jargons and slogans is no longer an option.

The innovative uses of digital technologies also provide alternate ways for corporations to meet the challenges of reducing costs and enhancing their connectivity with consumers as well as business partners. Keeping in mind the global connectivity and global interdependence, the dynamic diversity of markets, brands require micro as well as macro analysis. Along with the political, economic, social and technical (PEST), the strength, weakness, opportunities and strengths (SWOT) parameters can change unexpectedly.

Digital technologies, give individuals opportunities to select their associations globally. It is not uncommon to walk into a crowded area where people are connected with someone far away from those present around them. A new globally-connected and locally-disconnected society has emerged.

Various "cloud-societies" have been formed. Each business unit has to make its own assessment of the impact of changes on their business operations.

New Commercial Players

Along with information empowered customers, digital technologies have introduced many disruptive innovations and new commercial players in business arenas around the world. Customers create their own space and enact their own scripts on the commercial landscape. New digital technologies have created various new entrepreneurial opportunities. Business arenas have become very unstable, complex and uncertain.

Quick emergence of some knowledge-era giants has stunned leaders of many conventional industries. Many industries are yet to wake up to the realities of new commercial arena and realise how the digital algorithms and new technologies may impact their own conventional cosy business zones.

New technology moguls, using their connectivity as well as knowledge of consumers, are encroaching on the business territories of various industries in many diverse ways. Creative use of artificial intelligence in areas such as self-driven cars, drones, Internet-of-Things (IoT) is creating smart cities and new management options for managers and business leaders.

Knowingly and unknowingly, the new technology titans have amassed immense data and information about the customers and consumers. Some digital technology corporations are data-mining and creatively exploring possibilities of providing products and services more conveniently to the consumers.

Commerce, as discussed earlier, is a game of making customers reach for their wallets or credit-cards and generate cash flow for the business organisations. Digital technology savvy business organisations are finding new ways to interact with technology connected customers.

Smartphones generate immense data. The concept of "privacy" for individuals and organisations is likely to go through some major changes. There are many visible and invisible undercurrents in the local-global dynamics. With creative mix of real and virtual business options, individual entrepreneurs can create new commercial platforms and systems. The 3D printing options may create a new mix of customised and standardised product-service mix. Creative entrepreneurs may be able to test and try new innovative products and set up fast robotic assembly lines to capture local and distant markets.

As citizens and consumers become more and more digital technology and information savvy, we are likely to see more transparent, participative and responsive corporations and national governance systems. This will directly impact the business environment. By effectively using social media, even a single dissatisfied customer can instantly communicate his experience with many existing and potential customers and concerned authorities. Thus commercial units would have to be extra vigilant in designing and marketing their products and services. Known and unknown competitors may be very creative, swift, stealthy and customer focused.

Caselet 4.3

Matching the Big League Players

Somu's family had a well-known traditional sweet shop. After her graduation, she went to Canada for studies. Cooking and baking were her hobbies. While doing her business studies, she also found time to learn about baking and making local sweets, including chocolates.

On return, besides taking up job at the local bank, she would spend some time at her parents' shop. Being exposed to business, she was bitten by the business bug. Along with her friend, she started a small scale chocolate making unit in the local industrial area.

Their chocolates were well received in the market. The price was reasonable and the quality was appreciated by different customer segments.

As their business operations expanded, Somu's high quality chocolates were seen as an irritant by the sales staff of a multinational organisation (MNC). They started creating many kinds of obstructions in her distribution and retail operations. However, Somu and her friend overcame the obstacles without much problem. Their business was on growth curve.

One day, some representatives from the MNC came to meet Somu and her friend in their office. After some general discussions, they expressed their organisation's interest in purchasing their operations. Somu and her friend said that they were not interested in selling their business. As they were walking out, one of the representatives of the MNC rudely said to them, "You may regret your decision soon!"

The business tactics of the MNC staff became more aggressive. To meet their targets, the staff of MNC became unusually offensive. In spite of the irritations, Somu and her friend wanted to continue their operations. However, a few months later Somu's friend got married and left the city. Somu wanted to continue her business venture and meet the business challenges, but she, too got married and her marriage took her to another city.

About seven years later, while visiting her parents, Somu went to see the industrial area where she had once created her business. She stood at a distance and just gazed at the plot of land that was now just a warehouse.

During the seven years, she had read *Panchtantra*, Kautilya and Sun Tzu, often discussed nitty-gritty of her business venture with her friends and often paused, meditated and reflected on her business experiences. She had often bought and consumed products of her former competitors to get a better understanding of their products, distribution policies and customer relations. With the backdrop of her past experiences, she visualised some interesting current and future creative business challenges for herself. She experienced a strong desire to re-create her business venture.

She was aware that it would require significant adjustment and reorganisation for her family. She wanted it to be a family venture with full family support.

After some discussions with her family and friends, she formalised plans to restart her old business with new options. She had full support from her family and friends. She felt confident that she would be able to create an aware, learning, committed and creative team.

Learning from her past experiences, she wanted to be as realistic, data-based and digital technology savvy as possible. She used zero-based approach in analysing and prioritising her strategy options. Based on her past experiences, she knew the hurdles that established MNCs could create for her. However, she became more confident as she did her strengths, weakness, opportunities and threats (SWOT) analysis vis-à-vis her potential competitors. To avoid overconfidence, she often re-checked her options. She also interacted with some of her old friends, people from the industry, as well as start-up entrepreneurs to discuss her overall plans.

In the strength of her competitors, she saw traditional well-known brands and deep pockets. However, she felt that although they had trans-national reach, the operations of MNCs were based on weak local social and cultural foundations. She visualised their international well established competing brands as almost fixed targets or sitting ducks for a smart innovator — perhaps the way David might have visualised the big structure of Goliath that made it easy for him to fight with him. She felt confident that she would be able to match the money power of competitors with learning and creative mind power of her team.

Also, while her competitors were trapped in their histories, brand images and global practices, she felt that she was free to demarcate her own opportunity zones and design appropriate strategic framework. With cooperation of her creative team and feedback from her customers, she wanted to use the threats, uncertainties, complexities and ambiguities to her advantage. She wanted her organisation to be simple, nimble and speedy.

For her new venture, she managed to get a plot near her old location. As a strategy, she wanted her operation to be of a low profile. The end product was packed in small, well designed, attractive, reusable packets. She carefully added colours and features of local culture and aspirations on the packets.

Although a chocolate product, it was not sold as chocolate but as a traditional sweet with added nutritional value. With a phased strategy, it was decided that in the initial phase, the product would be distributed and sold through various school canteen shops with contextual and appropriate promotional schemes. The products were promoted as "good-health" products.

As a basic component of her business strategy design, along with customers, business associates, such as suppliers and distributors, were considered an integral part of the business. Future product developments were to be inclusive and participative ventures.

To implement the strategy of minimal direct confrontation with any of the established players, identified unused distribution channels were used to reach customers. Retailers were personally informed about the health benefits of the products, as well as customer feedback mechanisms.

As an integral part of strategic design for the business, strong business and social relations were nurtured with the distributors, retailers and customers. Her company policy was to be simple, honest and communicative, to build strong purposeful bonds of trust with all stakeholders. Digital technology provided effective support systems.

Although her company tried to maintain low, non-confrontational stance, her rapid growth and success did not remain unnoticed by the competitors. As luck would have it, the first direct business confrontation was with the same MNC.

She instructed her team to follow normal business practices, rules of competition and avoid direct confrontation. She and her team tried to use their business diplomacy skills to arrive at some alternate mutual win-win solutions. But, she realised that the business arrogance of MNC and found their policies monopoly focused. She had experienced that earlier, too. However, this time her team decided that they would be ready to meet their competitive challenges in a well thought out, creative way.

She had a series of meetings with her team. Besides the traditional distributions channels, her company had created an e-commerce platform. She had also created some export business. With a reasonably secure cash flow, she was ready for some creative provocations and strategic experimentation with the MNC, her major competitor.

She asked her team to create mild, planned provocations, such as aggressive product displays of their products at the common retail outlets. A few, selected members of her staff were instructed to make discreet audio and video recordings of the reactions of the MNC staff at the distribution and retail centres.

In office, her team evaluated their own acts as well as reactions of the competitor, almost like a game of chess. She tried to use happenings in the market place to provoke creative inputs from her team. Later, with senior members of her team, she discussed possibilities of further planned, strategic and controlled provocations for the MNC's sales staff in the market place.

Aware of the criticality of approaching festivals, she, along with her team, repeatedly did their SWOT analysis vis-a-vis their competitor. To get a larger perspective and examine more creative options, they occasionally took zero-base stance.

Somu was enjoying the creative management game and playing with confident mindset. Time was in her favour. She could challenge her competitors at the place and time of her choosing. And she knew the mighty MNC had to be hit at the most vulnerable business spot and at the most opportune time. In her spare time, she read some international business history books and chapters from Mahabharata to understand war strategies of Shakuni and Krishna. She also re-read tales of *Panchtantra*, as well as chapters from Kautilya's *Arthshastra* and Sun Tzu's *Art of War* to know their views on how small armies can defeat much larger armies.

As a student of geo-politics and geo-economics, she knew that global corporations had global concerns. She was also aware that appropriate strategic use of social media could provide her effective global reach. She had to design a well thought out effective local-global strategy.

Analysing the various reactions of her MNC competitor, which were almost casual repeat acts, she planned her main act after collecting as much relevant information as she could.

She knew the MNC staff operated on their fixed rounds and for assigned targets. A few days before the festivals, she arranged a major business provocation for the MNC staff at the main market place outlet. It was a well-planned act. A few people from the local media were also taken into confidence.

Coverage by local media, which was followed by national media, gave her business enormous publicity. Making creative and strategic use of social media, Somu won local, regional as well as global sympathy.

Discreetly, the issues of local employment, entrepreneurship, fair competition, public health, well-being of small scale industries and national pride were also introduced. This prolonged the life of the controversy and gave Somu extra publicity.

From her perspective, the strategy was successful. However, reflecting, analysing and considering the above events from general business perspective, many questions came to her mind.

- In the above caselet, is there an issue of:
  - Business ethics?
  - Fair play?
  - Business war?
  - Fair competition?
  - Customers' perspective on business ethics and competition?
- Was appropriate use made of:
  - Organisational learning and creative management?
  - Creative strategic design, strategic framework and implementation?

- Should business be conducted as a:
  - Game?
  - War?
  - Social and economic venture?

She was keen to know views of her friends, other business players and business students.

*****

Besides various other socio-economic transformations, globalisation creates new demand for self-identity — for nations as well as individual citizens. A new local-global socio-economic mix has evolved. The local-global mindscape is more informed, sensitive, effectively connected and in search for its own values.

Slowly and sometimes not so slowly, we are moving towards a new and different world — a well-informed, perhaps more participative world with new social, political, economic and commercial values and concerns. Be it local commerce or global geo-politics, there are multi-directional changes happening. Along with a new landscape and mindscape of a "global-village", a new world of "global-cyber-communities" has evolved. At the same time, there are pulls and pressures against globalisation.

The "global-village" is experiencing multi-directional drifts. At times, it seems that the world is moving apart with extended fault-lines and at other times it seems to be getting glued together. It seems like a kaleidoscope of hope, despair, break-ups, re-connects, challenges and opportunities.

Industrial-era organisations face a variety of challenges from digital-era entrepreneurs. For their survival, older generation managers have to become aware of realities and have to creatively design competitive strategies. Challenges, options and opportunities will be discussed in the subsequent chapters.

Caselet 4.4

Synergising Traditions and Cyberspace Options

Dr. Rishi is a highly respected doctor with goodwill and reputation. Having successfully worked in a renowned hospital for few years, he is keen to explore possibilities of starting his own practice with the larger social good as the objective.

- He wants to serve a larger number of people at a lower cost.
- He is keen to make effective use of digital technologies to reach a larger number of people.
- His main concerns are:
  - How to provide credible, reliable and customised service in the neighbourhood.
  - Whether digital technologies can create credible, reliable and customised platform for delivery of medical services to distantly located patients?
  - Can the physical-world medical services be effectively provided and delivered in the virtual-world?
  - Can the physical-world and virtual-world operations be synergistically integrated?

  He has approached you for your views and guidance.

*****

Cyberspace offers many new creative opportunities for entrepreneurs. Creative use of new technologies and innovative use of old systems also offer many new challenges as well as opportunities for the established commercial organisations. New entrepreneurs making creative us of digital technologies are exploring different ways to reach their customers more effectively. A new commercial life-style has emerged. Keeping this in view, managers have to be aware of the changing trends in their areas of operations. Business units need to be more aware, mindful, creative and technology savvy in understanding and serving their customers.

Notwithstanding all the turmoil being created by the digital technologies in the world of business, business will continue to be a customer focused game of products and services. Whatever the real-virtual mix, business will continue to be a game of controlling costs and generating cash-flows. Thus, the creativity and innovation context will continue to be similar, but with new dynamics.

Given the new flow of information about customers and the storage of this information in large data banks, businesses units will have to make new, creative use of their thinking, imagination and intuition, as well as knowledge of their customers and consumer behaviours. As the technology savvy, creative business players keep experimenting and developing new products and services for new generations of customers in different parts of the world, the rules of the local and global business games will continue to change substantially.

Explaining changes in business, a senior business executive said:

> The game of cricket has changed from five day international test matches to one day, fifty over, internationals and then to twenty-twenty games. So also the formats and rules of business have changed. Now the business also operates at the speed-of-thought or the click of a mobile phone button.

New platforms to market and new marketing processes will develop to cater to the needs and aspirations of the technology savvy consumers. The innovative business players would continue to write the new business game rules, be it in the areas of business-to-business (B2B) or business-to-consumer (B2C) or consumer-to-consumer (C2C).

Commercial Creativity Quotient

From a commercial perspective, awareness, curiosity and questioning (ACQ) may be seen as the prime movers of the creativity quotient (CQ). It is ACQ that leads to creation of new products and services. Creativity, as discussed earlier, is the ability to use imaginative ideas to create something commercially meaningful. In the commercial context, creativity is creativity only when it creates products or services that pass the market test. In business, creativity has to earn the approval of its final customers.

Notwithstanding all the local-global digital technology generated turmoil, for sustainable growth, commercial units will have to continue to be focused on providing new, creative, socio-economic solutions and create happy customers. The success of all creative efforts in developing the new varieties of products and services will ultimately depend on response of the customers or customer happiness.

Given the global reach of digital technologies, business managers have to be more responsive and faster in more creative ways to anticipate the needs and aspirations of their customers. Depending on their situation and nature of their business, mangers have to master the art of faster creative and innovative responses than their competitors and also keep a careful watch on the life-style trends of their customers, at times trying to test new products and services for leading customers to the next levels. Commercial creativity may also be seen as the *survival instinct* of commercial units.

In an uncertain competitive business environment, the commercial CQ may be seen as a determinant of the health as well as the growth potential of commercial units. Intellectual capital — an aggregate of employee awareness of overall business operations and contextual creativity focus, would be a critical success factor.

Keeping in view of the local-global connectivity and continuous, incremental as well as disruptive changes happening in the business arenas, to enhance their CQ, proactive learning, unlearning and relearning have to be an integral part of organisational learning. Continuous knowledge renewal, as well as sharpening of contextual creativity skills by business managers, are essential. Also, design-thinking and multi-cultural diversity management have to be integral part of day-to-day management operations.

There are many multi-dimensional paradigm shifts, some incremental, some disruptive. The challenges and opportunities in the globally connected, information intensive, knowledge based, intellectual social and economic framework will be discussed in detail in the following chapter.

Brands: Need to Rethink and Reconnect

Besides content, design and packaging, a brand also has a unique personality and a soul. In a competitive environment, many social, economic and emotional factors go into making of the "glue" that binds products and customers together. These bindings and bonds create brands.

Creating and developing meaningful brand-customer bonding requires careful nurturing with head and heart. Very often, brand managers have to rely on their intuition. This is a critical function, as bonds between products and customers define the life-line of business organisations.

Discussing the shifts and risks in brand management, a senior brand manager said:

> I would say that right now it is both the best of times as well as the worst to times for brand managers — a dynamic mix of creative challenges and business opportunities. New realities are emerging. With digital technology options, the mind of a customer is in exploratory stage. I feel some aspects of social media are still in development stages. Some organisations are yet to firm up their business and revenue propositions. Business units need to be customer focused and creative in communicating with customers.

The dynamics of branding and corporate communications are changing with extensive use of globally connected communication technologies and social media. To develop credible communication strategy, brand managers need to clearly understand the information sources and media consumption patterns of their customers. Given the diversity in media, for effective corporate communication, the message and the medium have to be creatively harmonised. Mobile phone screens are one of the most important medium. They are complex, crowded and very competitive.

It is a well-known observation that nothing kills well-established brands faster than erosion of trust. New situations call for new credible, innovative and creative thinking.

Dynamic, Uncertain, Fuzzy Scenarios

Dynamic fuzzy scenarios require more focused as well as more flexible approach. Enhanced perceptive curiosity and more frequent insightful questioning have become integral part of management philosophy. As will be discussed in the later chapters, analysis, synthesis and integrative design-thinking are an integral part of creative management.

To cope with overflow of information, every corporate team member must be made aware of the contextual and relevant corporate information needs. Use of unreliable and irrelevant information would be detrimental to business. Data and information gathering, as well as information filtering and processing systems, have to be constantly updated.

As increasing use of digital technology and globalisation enhance volatility, uncertainty, complexities and ambiguity (VUCA) in the business environment. Business units have to keep a closer watch on their relationship with their customers. To make sense from the sundry and ambiguous information overflows, corporations need to be more watchful and selective. Use of inappropriate information and out of context creativity can be as harmful as wrong medicine. The next chapter will discuss creativity options in various business activities in detail.

*****

Creative Management: *A Role Play*

The multi-product manufacturing company where you have been a department head for a few years has been losing its market share. The Board of Directors has inducted a new CEO. Aware of the multi-faceted digital technology challenges faced by the company, the new CEO wants the company to become

an *aware, learning, creative* and *competitive* company.
- He wants the organisation to adopt a *proactive* learning approach.
- Each employee and department to develop its learning programme.
- He wants employees to identify their knowledge-gaps and develop learning plans.
- He also wants employees and departments to identify alternate options to enhance competitiveness.
- The department heads are also expected to take an *overall organisational perspective.*
- Department heads are also expected to develop plans to synergise *inter* as well as *intra* department learning efforts.

The CEO called this exercise as the first-phase of organisational learning.

1. As a department head, what would be your approach to this?
2. What would be your proactive approach to developing strategies to transform the organisation into an *aware, learning, creative* and *competitive* organisation?

For this exercise you are free to choose your industry, nature and size of the company and your department. To enhance learning, try it out with different industries and departments.

*****

5

There is no doubt that creativity is the most important human resource of all. Without creativity, there would be no progress, and we would be forever repeating the same patterns.

Edward de Bono

Creativity Imperatives

By its very nature, creativity is contextual, futuristic and solution focused. Customer focused creative solutions are essential for sustainable competitiveness as well as to save distressed business organisations. Nurturing creativity and creative problem solving competencies as core-competencies are the new survival *mantra* as well as mandate for business organisations.

Life-lines of many business organisations are being disrupted, distorted and even being disconnected by changes in the life-style and shopping behaviour of their customers. Mobile connectivity, e-commerce and information empowerment have transformed preferences and priorities of customers. A large number of business organisations face life threatening situations that require urgent, creative and corrective actions.

Notwithstanding the above observations, creativity, in the business context, is not a complex, rocket science. It is a simple and natural activity. In many situations, it is just about contextual common sense, proactive curiosity and questioning. At times it is just simply asking and exploring why or why not? It is being aware and getting interested, engaged and excited about the business activities.

To cope with the fast changing business environment, corporations need to often ask themselves if they have appropriate talent-pool as well as creativity capacities. Business units need capabilities and competencies to deal with uncertainties, change and challenges from competitors.

In the continuously evolving digital business scenario, competitive advantages often emerge from the creative capabilities and competencies of people in the organisation — talent, with ability to use imagination and ingenuity to find unique next level value adding solutions. To increase productivity and growth, creative inputs are essential.

Caselet 5.1

Seeding and Cultivating Corporate Creativity

It was only after taking over charge of the Friendly Department Store (FDS) that Shweta realised that the well-known store had been experiencing steady downward trend in sales as well as profits. A few months before her joining, a leading advertising agency was appointed to attract customers. However, the results were short lived.

Shweta discussed her dilemma with her friend — a teaching faculty at the local business school. After detailed discussions they jointly worked out a plan to try and make her organisation a learning, creative and competitive organisation. Design-thinking culture had to be initiated and nurtured.

FDS had a staff of about fifty people. As it was a good place to work, most employees had substantial working experience in the organisation. Over time, the organisation had become *well-structured* and jobs had become well *segmented*. All seemed to know their job boundaries and what to do or *not* to do. The team spirit was missing.

They wanted seeding and nurturing of curiosity, creativity and design-thinking to be evolutionary. Shweta and her friend quietly wanted to introduce curiosity, questioning, team-spirit and the spirit of experimentation. They wanted their plan to be introduced and implemented as a learning experiment. The learning and creative process was to be participative, with regular feedback and evaluations, with flexible learning paths and personal monitoring.

The plan was designed as an experiment in creative management. The plan entailed:

- Two postgraduate business students with a good understanding of retail operations were inducted into the team. They were enthusiastic learners.
  - The students would use their experience and learning as their class project.

- The students were introduced to the organisation and their presence was explained as their pursuance of a class research project. All employees were requested to cooperate and provide full support to them in their research endeavours.
- They were free to interact with all employees and ask any questions. The students selected had a very pleasant and friendly persona.
- To gain appropriate understanding of the problem, students were asked to interact with some old employees as well as study start-up ventures related to the industry.
- The first-phase of the plan consisted of *seeding* curiosity and questions. The students were asked to raise contextual questions to provoke thinking and generate awareness. They would casually and informally ask employees questions such as:
  - *Their* perception of *their* job and responsibilities.
  - *Why* they were doing, *whatever* they were doing?
  - How did *their* job relate to the *overall business operations* of the store?
  - Instances and stories of *competition, creativity* and *change* in general.
- The objective was to *seed* the elements of *curiosity, questioning* and *change imperatives* in the mind to employees.
- The second-phase consisted of Shweta *informally* interacting with two or three employees from *different* departments and enquiring about their interactions with the students. She would also enquire from them their views on improving quality of service to customers, need for change in policies, "ways" of doing things or overall work culture. She would be an active listener and *not* share her own views.
- Through her personal, informal interactions with different employees in different combinations, she wanted to know and assess:

- Customer focus of employees.
- Their understanding of the overall organisation process.
- Their understanding of the nature of competition.
- Their understanding of the role of digital technologies in retail operations.
- Attitude of employees towards proactive learnings, creativity, change, use of digital technology and transformation of organisation.
- She also wanted to identify thought, creative, and change leaders, for the next phase of her plan.

- In conformity with her informal approach, Shweta arranged an informal dinner meet with a short *brainstorming* session. She also invited the students and her faculty friend as observers. Since it was to be an informal dinner gathering, all employees were asked to share or give their ideas on how to make FDS:
  - A better place to work — more friendly for employees
  - More friendly and service oriented for customers
  - More competitive, creative and innovative as well as sustainable or profitable
  - All ideas from everyone were projected on the screen, without any discussions or evaluation of ideas.

- The informal *brainstorming* session was to be used as a launch pad for formal introduction of creativity and design-thinking culture in the organisation.

- Shweta wanted FDS to be a customer-focused creative team.

After the brainstorming session, Shweta, her friend and students had a meeting to review and evaluate the outcome, as well as their own learnings from their planned actions and consider next phase of operation. The issues they were grappling with included:

- How should they evaluate success of the each phase of their operation?

- How should they utilise the organisation's creative energies?
What are your observations on their approach? How should they proceed with their plans?

*****

Business: An Innovation-Creativity Mix

Entrepreneurs are innovators — very creative creators. Entrepreneurs create new products, services and social institutions. In a commercial context, for an action to be termed as innovation, the innovative idea must add new value for customers and enhance revenue as well as profitability of the business units.

Creativity transforms ideas into viable commercial propositions. While transforming innovative ideas into commercial products or services, creativity managers creatively contextualise the original idea to meet customer needs and local market requirements. To manage creativity, managers also have to be creative and add value as they manage. Management process itself must also be creative.

While creativity is an abstract concept, in business it has a context, purpose and an objective. Creativity is an energy form. Like other economic resources, creative energy can be extracted from the minds of employees. Creativity can be creatively mined, managed and channelled. It has a time cost. It has manpower cost. It has knowledge-cost. It has mind-power cost. Creativity is a rare, nurtured resource. If mined and managed creatively, creativity becomes a critical competitive resource for business organisations.

In a disruptive, fast changing business environment, creativity may also be viewed as a very perishable, high opportunity, cost resource. As in case of other perishable resources, for optimal results, creativity must be nurtured creatively and used in an opportune way. Creative talent, along with creative management, helps organisations design and navigate their future.

Notwithstanding the fact that abstract imagination is an integral part of creativity and commercial operations happen in the real world, creativity is a critical commercial resource. Creativity is the life-blood of an interdependent business process. Creative managers shape and package imagination in their products and services and then link them with the dreams and aspirations of their customers.

Business problems are real. Markets are unforgiving. The solutions have to be real and contextual. When creative imagination is creatively managed to define as well as solve specific commercial problems, it has the potential to yield high value for customers as well as business units. Entrepreneurs, employees, managers and customers are all linked by creative bonds.

To appropriately define a commercial problem, one has to be a creative listener of various market languages. Each market is unique. To provide alternate solutions, one has to have a comprehensive understanding of business processes as well as shopping behaviour and expectations of customers. Customers also value creativity in their purchases.

Sharing his views on creativity in business, a senior management consultant said:

> Creativity *talks*. To understand creativity, *talk* to creativity. Yes, creativity *talks*. Look at the brand carefully. Close your eyes. Think. Meditate before *the brand* of product you see or use. Brands *talk*. Listen to them. Brands speak in many different languages. As you use them, feel their commercial creativity in action.

> It may sound simple, but in business operations, creativity is a complex, multi-discipline and multi-talent team work, requiring a contextual creative management mindset. It is not linear. It is an experimental and iterative venture, often with very high failure possibilities and enormous direct and indirect costs.

Each industry, each business unit and each manager is faced with unique creativity requirements and challenges.

Caselet 5.2

Learning from Failures

Rishi was aware that almost all banks had large amounts of non-performing assets, mainly because of failed ventures. For his class project assignment, Rishi, along with his team, took permission to study and present a case of a non-performing business unit.

Coconut Plastics Limited (CPL) was once a much esteemed name in the plastic industry. It had state-of-the-art technology to make a variety of well-designed, high quality plastic toys and useful furniture such as tables, chairs and book racks for children.

Products of the company were well received in the market. Investors were happy with its performance in the stock market. Bankers were happy to have CPL as their client. It was a good place to work and the management team enjoyed professional respect.

However, during the past few years, CPL shares were not doing well in the stock market. Its products were not preferred by distributors and retailers. As it was unable to meet its financial commitments, the banks had declared CPL a "sick" business unit.

When Rishi and his team visited the CPL office and interacted with the corporate management team, they found them very cooperative and helpful. The team provided them most of the information they sought. They also answered most of their questions. It did not take much time for them to realise that CPL was out of touch with its business realities.

Rishi and his team presented following facts before the class:

- CPL, soon after starting its business operations:
    - It was market leader in its areas of operations.
    - It had the most advanced and cost effective technology.
    - It had appropriate business data collection systems.
    - It was a preferred work place.

- Over the years, CPL had developed its business and organisation culture that became a mix of:
  - Structures, divisions, silos, systems and bureaucracy.
  - CPL work culture indicated *reactive problem solving approach* — no need to fix it, if it is not broken.
  - No one was ready to own the problems or "mistakes".
  - Operating as a "silo", each department wanted to "push-out" problems from their "silo".

After presenting above observations about CPL, they said:
- They felt that CPL was suffering from the boiling-frog syndrome.
- In their view, CPL had become "over" structured and managers had become too protective of their position and administrative space.
- Managers seemed to be in hurry to "pass-on" the problem than to "solve" the problems.

They asked the class for ideas and ways to improve the commercial health of CPL:
- What was *missing* in the management process?
- How to revive CPL?
  - How to "awaken" the organisation?
  - How to get CPL out of the boiling-frog syndrome?
  - How to introduce proactive learning and a creative design-thinking culture?

*****

Change, Black Swans and Creativity Imperatives

Change is integral to life and living. As change flows, it changes everything. Unexpected events happen. Black-swans appear. Change challenges established relationships, practices and norms. Like change, commerce is a perpetual, ongoing activity.

Change transforms things, situations and relationships; it creates gaps. From business and management perspective, change may either be foreseen, probable or unexpected. Business managers may be proactive or reactive to change. Whatever may be the perspective of management, gaps and distortions created by the flow of change would need to be corrected.

Business may be seen as a process, a network of economic value-adding relationships or an interdependent chain of commercial activities. Whether business is viewed as a mathematical equation, a complex financial system or just a simple activity to transform customer purchasing power into profit, change impacts all factors, all activities and all relationships. Thus, business managers constantly need to adjust, realign or recreate their business linkages.

Creativity, as discussed earlier, is the art and science of using new ideas to find new value, adding solutions, bridging the gaps and solving problems, improving efficiency and effectiveness of systems. Thus change and *need-for-creativity* move in tandem.

Like living beings, business organisations, too, are impacted by change. Interactions with various business leaders and management consultants indicates that depending on the nature of business and business leadership approach, the change-impact and creativity-need (CICN) analysis should include consideration of following factors:

Change and business vulnerability: Change changes relevance of existing technologies, business practices and relationship with customers — the life-lines of business units. As business is an inter-dependent operation, every activity in the business process gets impacted by change.

External change-impact: The overall political, economic, social and technology (PEST) environment is impacted by change. Managers need to be aware of these changes.

Internal change-impact: Creative use of digital technologies can impact any individual activity in the business network. Business leaders must be aware of the changes in technology options.

Change-impact on customer relationships: Mobile phones are emerging as greatest disrupters of relationships between business organisations and their customers. New digital applications can transform relationships with the click of button. For business organisations, need to remain customer focused cannot be overstated.

Machines as "customers": Customers are using smartphones to assist them in shopping. Artificial intelligence (AI) empowered machines are being used as sales as well as corporate purchase support systems. Even human resource managers make use of AI systems in sorting out applications. Machine-to-machine (M2M) data and information exchange is an integral part of business environment.

Overall cost analysis: Costs of business organisations get impacted in many different direct and indirect ways.

Revenue stream analysis: Depending on the management perspective, some business leaders may be focused on revenue or market share.

New situation analysis: Some business organisations may wish to evaluate change-impact by the traditional

- SWOT: strengths, weaknesses, opportunities and threats analysis or
- PEST: political, economic, social and technical change analysis.

Zero-based analysis: To get a future-focused, history-free perspective, some organisations adopt zero-based analysis of change. Each change situation is reviewed afresh — history free and assumptions free.

New strategy options analysis: With change, organisations need to re-examine their strategy. Some strategy centric organisations analyse impact of change from the perspective of its impact of their strategic options. New situations require new strategic thinking, new evaluation of options and redesigning of strategy.

Business process analysis: Change impacts relevance of business purpose, business process, as well as relevance of products and services. Depending on the nature of business, some business units may view change in terms of how it impacts the market position of their products and services.

Competition and market share: Digital technologies have shifted many industrial boundaries, yet many companies continue to measure change in terms of market share of their products and services vis-à-vis competitors. A holistic analysis may be more appropriate.

Technology shifts: Technology centric organisations must evaluate change from the perspective of technology shifts. They may see change as the increase or decrease in the gaps between cutting-edge technologies and their position.

Creativity and innovation: Depending on the nature of business, some organisations may perceive change from the perspective of trend-shifts in innovation and creativity, business operations or talent and creativity competency. This may also be seen as efficiency-gaps analysis. Managers must review the learning and knowledge base of their organisations.

Organisation teams and attitude: Change gives managers a chance to evaluate the attitude of their teams towards challenges. Change impacts team spirit and attitudes of individual team players. Business leaders need to keep track of such changes.

No matter how managers or business leaders perceive change, change impacts all aspects of business operations. To be in tune with change and visualise new options and opportunities, managers have to be aware of the nature of change and accept its multi-dimensional implications.

Continuous, disruptive, multi-faceted change necessitates continuous, multi-disciplinary, purpose-focused, creative energies. Also, these creative energies need to be managed creatively by creative management.

Creativity in Business: New Multi-faceted Challenges

Business units operate in a digitally disrupted world. Digitisation is changing the boundaries of industries and the nature of markets. Critical and creative thinking are the new imperatives. Business units do not need creativity just to transform innovative ideas into commercial propositions. Given the multi-dimensional market dynamics, spontaneous and intuitive creative applications are also needed during the so called "routine" day-to-day management operations.

Being aware, with a creative and constructive attitude, generates competitive advantages. Every customer interaction, be it business-to-business (B2B) or business-to-customer (B2C) is unique and ever changing. Automation and outsourcing business processes only shift creativity zones. In a multi-cultural business environment, smartphones empowered customers with various apps are uncertain, complex and often ambiguous disruptive agents.

Creativity may be creatively used to simplify and streamline work processes. This would help in enhancing efficiency and effectiveness of business processes. Simplicity may also be used as an overall business strategy.

Given the customer activism and the power of social media, commercial units have to be vigilant in nurturing their customer relations. Brand-customer bonding is the lifeline of every business unit. Digital technologies are adding many new variables in the lifestyle and shopping behaviour of customers, thus disrupting brand-customer bonds.

Discussing the use of creativity in different business operations, a senior business executive said:

> Show me a business activity that does not require creativity. For me, creativity includes a creative and constructive attitude. Just as we require creativity to convert innovative ideas into a new products or services, we also need creativity to maintain relevance of old, established brands. We need creativity to reduce cost and simplify our business processes.

Discussing on similar lines, a senior international business manager said:

> Creativity has many *avatars*. In international business operations, we need to be careful and creative at every step. Small, cross-cultural errors can cause major disruptions in otherwise smooth business operations. English is considered to be the normal business language, but one has to be careful in selection of appropriate English words even when interacting with people from different parts of United Kingdom. Do you know how many kinds of English is spoken in London or New York?
>
> One has to be creatively correct in selection of words, dress code and expressions. It is important to remember the dictum — medium is the message. We need to be aware and creative in managing international communications. Trust and confidence, the foundations of commerce, depend on creative communication skills. For me, creativity in business includes creative business diplomacy.

Business units not only have to create new products, but effectively communicate with customers about the "value" of their new products. Given the inter-related dynamics as well as complexities of conventional and new digital media, one has to think creatively in designing messages. Business managers have to understand the language and nuances of social media and smartphones. Cyberspace has its own code of conduct and culture. Differences in the nature of business in cyberspace and the traditional physical world have added new complexities.

Discussing the role of creativity in business, a senior executive said:

> In the fashion industry, we act on the basis of our expectations of the future happenings. Also, our acts influence our future. Creative thoughts flow throughout our organisation. Every little detail is critical. Given the fast shifting business environment, it is prudent to think and act more analytically, imaginatively, mindfully, meditatively and creatively. In our business context, at times creativity is spontaneous, while at other times it requires prolonged thinking and meditation.

You may not like it, but I feel, in the business world, creativity is often discussed in amateurish and uncreative ways. We only see creativity in the success and money generating power of products. We often fail to see and value creativity as an iterative activity. Failures and successes are intrinsically intertwined in creative operations.

Along with business insights, creativity teams and creative managers need to have high customer empathy quotient. Products and services are presented to customers as packaged items. Business units have to creatively pack hopes and happiness of customers in their packages.

Many other factors, such as the nature of competition, strategic thinking and policies of competitors, price as well as positioning, have to be harmoniously aligned. Product and service design and packaging are critical channels of customer communication for brands. Unique pursuit of hope and happiness is associated with purchase of every product and service. To effectively design a product, one needs to understand consumer behaviour and their aspirations associated with the product and its specific brand. Brands are also used by customers to create their own identities.

Commercial activities need to be customer focused. Commercial processes are multi-faceted and require multi-disciplinary inputs. Business arenas are competitive, dynamic, uncertain, complex and ever changing. To cope with diverse changes, business managers require a constant flow of creative energies.

Creating Innovation-Fit Teams

Being innovation-fit implies being competent to creatively transform innovative ideas into effective commercial propositions and being able to counter marketing challenges from competitors with value adding solutions for customers. Keeping in view their unique requirements, commercial units need to nurture their creativity needs. Future is uncertain and may be unforgiving for those caught napping in the market place.

Every industry has its own unique operational complexities. Within the industry, each business unit functions with its own unique competitive environment and uncertainties. Each business organisation presents its own unique value propositions — products and services — to its customers. To meet new challenges, business organisations need multi-talented creative teams and design-thinking culture.

To remain motivated, employees as well as managers need a feeling of involvement and a sense of their future. They need to be aware of their current context and future directions. Creative business thinking provides the glue for team-work and emotional commitment to workers in their work life.

Caselet 5.3

Proactive Learning and Creativity Paradigm

As her Creative Management class project, Shagun decided to present her start-up venture ideas in the class. She discussed this with her venture team and took approval from her professor.

The basic assumption on which Shagun and her team had based their coaching and learning venture MoveOn.com was that people are keen to learn but they do not have *convincing* reasons or purpose to learn. Simply stated, their approach was:

- You tell us where you are.
  - O This would nudge curiosity and questioning
- We will tell you the options open for you.
- You select your option.
- We will offer you proactive learning roadmap to get you to your destination.
- Curiosity, questioning and creativity were basic ingredients of their proactive learning paradigm.

Creativity Imperatives

While the above framework was for general people wanting to become job-fit, they also wanted to design similar programmes for business units. They wanted to design proactive "move-up-the-ladder" (MUL) learning and coaching programmes for business units. The outline of their approach was:

- They would translate overall business process into creative value-adding chain.
  - For each department
  - For overall organisation
- Each activity or set-of-activities would be defined in terms of (ASK):
  - Attitude or approach
  - Skill-sets required to perform the activity
  - Knowledge-base, capacity and competency required
- The employees would know the requirements to move-up-the ladder
  - This would be co-created with the organisation
- MoveOn.com would provide the proactive learning and coaching opportunities.

Shagun and her team were keen to give their venture a structure and also create an appropriate business model to make it commercially viable.

Simply stated, their question was — is it possible to take zero-based proactive learning paradigm (ZBPLP) to the next level? Appropriate questions based ZBPLP can provide any-time, any-where learning option for everyone. They wanted to explore possibilities of developing a zero-based proactive learning and creativity paradigm (ZBPLCP).

The questions they often asked themselves and wanted to share with their class were:

- Were they moving toward a useful value proposition?
- Did they miss out on any useful alternate value adding idea?

- Given the uncertain, fast changing commercial landscape and mindscape, how could they create realistic future business scenarios?
  - By creative use of artificial intelligence and education technology, would it be possible to create future business and work place scenarios?
    - Create job-profiles based corporate ladders?
- How should they design their business model?

*****

Creativity: In Every Activity at Every Level

Business is a complex, interdependent operation. Every activity in the business process and network involves some creative and design-thinking. In a dynamic, changing, business environment, interdependent business operations need continuous alignment. Every business activity has to be appropriately and creatively contextualised as well as connected.

Every business unit is a network of diverse activities such as procurement, manufacturing, quality control, accounting, marketing, finance, human resource management, import, export, corporate communications and public relations. With change of context, the focus and nature of creative management thinking changes. Managers require different contextual insights and creativity orientation.

Just as the nature of creativity changes with each piece of art and art form, so also in business. The nature of creativity, its quality, quantity and focus changes with each commercial activity. Each activity has a different context, input and output goals Employees at different positions have different contexts and concerns for value adding, cost and quality. This is true in every form of business, be it manufacturing, service marketing, talent, entertainment or event management.

Business processes may also be complex, inter-related, input-output chains. Each activity in the chain has its own value adding creative requirements. Also, each activity must be seamlessly, harmoniously and synergistically linked with the preceding as well as succeeding link. This can be a daunting challenge for any manager.

Manufacturing a product involves an enormous variety of creative inputs of skills and talent. Introducing a product in the market would require different sets of creative skills. For aware and creative managers, the contextual micro as well as overall macro concerns keep changing. All this requires a variety of creative inputs.

Business Innovation-Creativity Wars

At times, business is a competitive, war-like, zero-sum game. One wins at the cost of others. As in war, business arenas are full of complex, unforgiving uncertainties. These arenas are becoming fuzzier. Competition is getting more intense. Creativity is evolving as the essential core competency, as well as a critical success factor (CSF) for most business units. In an uncertain, fast changing business environment, businesses need to develop proactive, high-speed, cutting edge, creative design-thinking capabilities.

In the evolving knowledge-era, as commerce becomes more knowledge intensive, it would be advantageous for commercial units to develop their own knowledge-bases, as well as business intelligence systems. Insightful understanding of customers and monitoring their shopping behaviour is essential. Why, how, when and where does the product or service meet and interact with its consumer? Real-time, proactive understanding of the landscapes of markets and mindscapes of customers is essential.

The success in corporate wars will depend on the creative versatility of employees, managers and business leaders. To reinforce their strategic arsenal, business units are hunting for talent. Organisations require proactive, creative thinkers in every business area. Organisations need talented people who have the ability to comprehend contextual needs and design appropriate creative strategies. Every segment of business is in state of flux.

Change is an integral part of life. From the business perspective, it is multi-faceted. Digital technologies can simultaneously impact almost every area of business operations. Analysing implications of these impacts and identifying alternate solutions becomes more complex because of the speed at which events happen. Simply stated, there is a constant change in business models, products, services and customer behaviour.

As business operations become more knowledge intensive, customers become more technology savvy and markets become more mobile, contextualised and focused creativity will become the main weapon for business wars. As will be discussed in the next chapter, organisations need critical, contextual and creative design-thinking.

In an uncertain, fast shifting, competitive, socio-economic environment, where products and services have to match changing requirements of on-the-go, globally connected customers, need for contextual creative thinking cannot be overstated. The context would include the knowledge of customer needs, customer behaviour, competitive offers as well as the decision making patterns of customers, assisted by their smartphones.

Digital technologies are interlocking markets, products, services and customers. The boundaries between industries, markets and customer segments have become fuzzy. In a fast changing business environment, any kind of data, information, critical and creative thinking have very limited life-spans. Relevance and economic relationships keep changing. As will be discussed in the next chapter, for some business organisations, it is essential to review and re-calibrate context and strategies at every step.

Creativity is also finding new ways to add value to existing brands, business relations and business operations. To effectively add value, managers need to know the nature of value as well as why, where, when, by whom and how much value needs to be added. Thus, it is critical to have an insightful understanding of the value system of the people who will evaluate the value—the customers. Value has value only when the person (customer) evaluating the value knows and appreciates the value of the value.

It is critical to be aware that segmenting a market is no longer similar to slicing bread or cake. Today, with all the turbulence and turmoil in the market places, it is more like trying to carve out a "slice-of-water" from a flowing river. At times a river may be in flood fury. Market dynamics as well as acts of competitors can be abrupt and very disruptive. In such unpredictable situations, creativity — the appropriate solutions generating ability — may also be seen as an ability to remain connected with consumers. In some situations, creativity has to compete against time.

Notwithstanding globalisation and global connectivity, given the any-time any-where connectivity, customers expect individualised services. And the expectations of customers keep shifting with changes in their information base, inflows of information, perspectives and contexts. Creativity may also be seen as exploring possibilities of enhancing customer bonding in such chaotic market situations. In business arenas, managers often face ambiguous, complex and undefined challenges. Defining problems is an integral part of creative process. As will be discussed later in the book, contextual and creative use of digital technologies can provide alternate options for meeting customer expectations.

A Story

Creativity: The Soul of Commerce

While discussing the role of creativity in her business process, a lady CEO of an international business organisation said:

> My tryst with creativity started in an unexpected way. I would like to discuss it from my personal experience. I did my graduation in non-medical science — physics, chemistry and mathematics. I had no knowledge of business or economics. Through competitive exams, I was selected in a reputed business school. On the very first day, in the very first class on management, a middle-aged professor entered the class.

After formalities of mutual introductions, which were done in a very informal, warm, friendly way, the professor asked the class, "Do you have any questions to ask?"

There was a pin-drop silence in the class. Slowly, he looked at each one of us. He asked us again: "Does anyone have any question to ask?' No one asked any question. After a short pause, in a very firm tone he said: "Learning starts with questions. Twice, I offered you a learning opportunity. Since you have no questions, I feel there can be no learning. Your attendance is marked and so is mine. You all have earned your attendance and I have earned my remuneration. So let's not waste time."

You will not believe it. He picked up his file from the table and walked out of the class. We were all shocked. There was an eerie silence in class. We all looked at each other in disbelief — *ye kya ho gaya* (What has happened)?

We were about sixty students. Almost all were either engineering or science graduates. We were all surprised. Some went out to meet the professor and invite him back to class. He was not to be found. Some students went to meet the Director of the institute. He explained that that was his style of teaching. He was one of the best faculty they had. The subject would continue, but the class-time was over for the day. The Director suggested that we all should prepare questions for his next class.

The next class was one of the most fascinating management class I have ever attended. All of us could feel the learning curiosity and energy. The Professor walked in with a smile. He looked at us and said, "I know you have questions. I do not promise you answers. *We* all will try and explore answers *together*. For some questions, there may be no definite answers. Some questions may remain questions throughout your life. You will have to learn to enjoy the mysteries of your questions, as well as those of others. Enjoy the joys of learning, unlearning and relearning. Try and make it a lifelong exploration."

Throughout the duration of his classes, he often stated, "Your learning must start after the class ends. I want you to walk out with more questions than the questions you had in your mind, when you walked into the class."

The Professor stressed the point, "Please do not think you do not have business or management experience. Each of you has more than twenty years of experience, as CEO of You.Inc. Please relate *your* questions to *your* own experience. Over the years, please ask yourself — how creatively have *you* defined the *purpose* of your life, *planned* your activities, *organised* your various options, *managed* your studies and career path? How you would *evaluate* your performance so far? How many *big* mistakes you have made so far? How did you celebrate your successes? What did you learn from your failures?"

I am elaborating my experience because I feel it was in that class that *I discovered the creative spirit and the soul of the entrepreneur in me.* I discovered myself. Learned to enquire, observe, be aware, actively listen to the complaints of my customers, learnt to be my own customer, know what my customers wanted. Apologise to them and proceed to create better products and services for them. I learnt to be curious and remain focused on my business purpose and customers. For me, experiencing the value of questions and creativity was the most valuable by-product of that subject, in fact of the total MBA programme.

This narration has been incorporated here because creativity is often seen as a by-product of listening to customers. Actually, curiosity and questions initiate creativity in business.

*****

The pace of economic change is constantly accelerating. In a volatile, uncertain, complex and ambiguous (VUCA) business environment, it is essential for organisations to have real-time business intelligence updates. Organisations have to keep themselves informed, nimble, resilient and flexible. As discussed earlier in the book, a culture of proactive learning, knowledge-sharing and collaboration is essential for sustaining creativity in a business organisation.

Change is multi-faceted and multi-dimensional. Thus, creativity would have to be contextual as well as customer and competition focused. Unless creativity is institutionalised and employees are made a part of the corporate creativity team, organisations would run the risk of aging and rusting of their competitive edge.

The need for proactive awareness in the fast changing, uncertain times is obvious. For appropriate action, managers have to be aware, as well as understand the realities of the situation. Being unaware can lead to very costly mistakes. Such mistakes have proved fatal for many organisations. In the evolving era of information overflows from many sources, managers have to be discerning and perceptive business players. Decisions need to be contextual, relevant and insightful.

In the creative digital age with massive data bases, where more and more organisations know more and more about customers, being unaware of the thinking and acts of direct and indirect competitors can be very risky. Appropriate proactive learning systems are essential to select, digest and act on the basis of appropriate information.

As one senior business intelligence expert said:

> Paradoxically, with more and more information available, we often do not know what we do not know. I often feel that the uncertainties and "don't know" spaces are increasing. At times, information overflows create mental blackouts.

Global connectivity works at the speed-of-thought. In a multi-faceted, fast moving environment, with a high rate of information obsolescence, it is essential for business organisations to design appropriate information sourcing, filtering and management systems. Managers have to be data and information savvy. Business managers also must have capability and competence to creatively channel appropriate information into relevant knowledge management processes.

Being aware includes anticipation of new knowledge products. Knowledge has to be matched with superior knowledge — more valuable knowledge and useful knowledge that helps in understanding competition, competitors or the market position of the product, services and customers. Being aware also means being aware of knowledge that would help in adding value for the existing and potential customers. In other words, knowledge to understand knowledge needs is essential.

Effective awareness helps business units understand their own strengths, weaknesses, opportunities and threats (SWOT) vis-à-vis their competitors on a continuous basis. In an uncertain, dynamic, fast changing business environment, the awareness has to be continuous and uninterrupted. Also, the information providing awareness has to be reliable and relevant. Knowledge of data sources is also essential.

Just as every part of the human body is equipped to sense danger to the body, so also every person in organisation should be sensitised to send warning signals to the corporate knowledge management centre. As will be discussed in the next chapter, each corporate member can be made to act like the eyes and ears of the business unit.

Institutionalising Creativity

Digital technologies are ubiquitous and have become inextricably intertwined with our personal and professional lives. Each interaction, be it machine-to-machine (M2M), business-to-business (B2B), machine-to-customer (M2C), business-to-consumer (B2C) or customer-to-customer (C2C), generates data. Creative, contextual and relevant data generation and management is are integral parts of business management operations. Many innovative options may emerge, if data is creatively managed and analysed.

Institutionalisation implies becoming an integral part of organisational systems and culture. Multi-faceted change and creativity imperatives require that creativity be institutionalised in business organisations. With speedy creative developments in the digital technology usage, all business activity units have to be on a constant watch for any disruptive impacts on their business activities. Even short lapses can have very serious and difficult to retrieve repercussions. Continuous, proactive watch is essential.

For appropriate, swift and creative action, awareness, competitiveness and response systems need to be synergistically synchronised. In the past, many well established industry giants have suffered serious, unrecoverable damage because of their failure to understand market trends and challenges created by competitors. Awareness and speed are critical success factors in many industries. Corporations cannot afford to take even short naps in the hyper-competitive business arena.

Business units need to make all their employees aware of the overall challenges faced by the organisation. Creativity has to be an inclusive, overall, cooperative, corporate venture. To nurture the culture of creativity and innovation, appropriate processes need to be instituted to receive, acknowledge and process value adding ideas, as well as suggestions from all sources — internal as well as external to the organisation.

Multi-cultural commercial arenas are full of uncertainties, complexities and ambiguities as well as volatile disruptive innovations. From the perspectives of large national or transnational corporations, it may be advantageous to appropriately divide and contextualise their business knowledge as well as business creativity centres into broad business groups.

To compete with innovations, one has to be innovative as well as creative. Given the uncertain, risk infested, fast changing business environment, the strategic importance of creativity and innovation for a business organisation is obvious. Corporations need to think of ways to enhance their capacities, skills and systems to think creatively and find ways to innovate. Failure to match industry creativity speed requirements can be unforgiving for individual business units. As in the case of individuals, the real strength of organisations often comes from their undiscovered internal knowledge sources. Critical, contextual, knowledge sources are often overlooked. Contextual understanding of events is critical.

In a fast changing environment, past experiences or successes should not be mistaken as expertise on future. The future may be very different from the past in many new ways. Unlearning and relearning have to be continuous processes. Believing that we know things, which in fact we do not know, can be a very costly, at times fatal, mistake in the fast changing world. As will be discussed in the next chapter, creativity helps business organisations to contextualise and design their future.

*****

Creative Management: *A Team Role Play*

Select any large business unit of your choice. As the CEO of that organisation, ask your department heads to list out potential disruptions which can happen due to creative use of digital technologies by *competitors, new start-ups* and *cyber-attacks*. Consider departments such as:

- Procurement — national and international, etc.
- Operations — manufacturing, information and control systems, etc.
- Marketing — competition, distribution, sales, customer relations, advertising, etc.
- Finance — loans, cash-flows, etc.
- International business operations
- Human resource management — talent needs, organisational dynamics, etc.
- Overall organisation structure.

Each department has its own context, agenda and technology (CAT) requirements. As the CEO of the organisation, how would you proceed to:

- Minimise impact of potential disruptions?
- Make each department competition fit?
- Make your organisation information-era fit?

While you are free to select any organisation from any industry and make any assumptions you like, please state all your assumptions clearly. Give your strategy to make your organisation:

- Technology savvy.
- Creative, knowledge and customer focused.
- Please suggest appropriate organisational architecture for your organisation.

*****

6

Sometimes your greatest strength can emerge as a weakness if the context changes.

Harsha Bhogle

Context of Creativity

For a meaningful understanding of a statement, act, event or any happening, we need to understand its context. Context is the circumstances, conditions or set of facts that form the background for an event, statement or an idea.

To understand the role and significance of creativity, we must understand its context, purpose and objective. In business, creativity has many shapes, forms, colours and shades. Creativity and design-thinking happen under contextual constraints. On the business front, the creative process must match the real-time dynamics. Creativity also needs coaching as well as mentoring and monitoring.

Creativity, knowledge and technology may have little value if not used appropriately and contextually. A rocket scientist may be of little value in a football match. To be useful, knowledge would have to be contextual. Although creativity and management are synergistic, for contextual suitability, creative inputs must be evaluated from the perspectives of why, what, when, where, who and how (5W+H).

Creativity in business is a means to an end. Creativity may also be perceived as a strategic activity a creative process from context to objective. The creative process is a dynamic mix of ideas and execution. Innovative ideas are often the initiators, prime movers as well as consumers of creativity. Innovative ideas create contexts for creativity. In business, creativity is useful only when it takes us towards a predetermined innovative idea — usually an improvement in system or commercially viable product or service.

Business managers think in terms of contextual resources, markets and people. Be it in the agriculture-era, industrial-era or the present digital-era, business has been an entrepreneurial game of customers, products, services, and business models.

Business and management theories become useful for managers only when contextualised. Context demarcates value of management operations. Even grand global business strategies need to be creatively adjusted to local contexts.

Understanding of context, having creative energy, and being technology savvy are the essential core competencies for any strategic business operations in the prevailing disruptive environment. Creativity also needs contextual seeding and nurturing as well as coaching, mentoring and monitoring.

Contextual Intelligence, Knowledge and Wisdom

Context is a given reality in which business operates. Customers are the *why* — the prime reason for creation of the business. Insightful understanding of customers is essential. *Why* also defines the purpose of business organisations.

With intelligence and information about context and customers, based on the decision *what* products and services would be created for the identified customers, entrepreneurs move on to decide *how* the products and services would be created. This leads to structuring of their organisation.

Nature of skills, know-how and technology used by entrepreneurs determines work-culture and information flow in the organisation. Like other living organisms, for survival and growth, organisations change with change. Change impacts relevance of business organisations, their products and services. With change, products and services as well as organisations need to be re-contextualised. To keep pace with change, survive and grow, organisations have to be learning, creative and adaptive organisations.

Business organisations operate in a competitive environment. Managers design strategies to link context with their customers through their products and services. Strategies are creatively designed to create bonds of trust between customers and business organisations. Observing and listening to customers is an integral part of developing relevant business intelligence. It creates contextual, creative energies in employees, managers and organisations.

In a connected world, depending on the design of business model, organisations may incorporate flexibility in their business operations to decide *where, when* and by *whom* the products or services will be produced. Dynamics of context, customers and strategies will also be discussed in more detail in other chapters of this book.

Business units use resources or raw materials to produce products and services for customers. To transform the resources or raw materials into useful products and services for customers, business organisations have to use various kinds of knowledge, talents and technologies. In designing and operating the transformation process, business organisations as well as business managers have to conform to the legal, social, commercial and political norms of the country where they operate.

In a fast changing environment, nothing in business can be static. Success of business units depends on their ability to meet changing expectations of customers. For sustainability, business units not only have to meet changing expectations of customers, but also generate profits for their organisation. Commercial process starts and ends with customers. Besides other factors, the role of mobile phones in the shopping process of customers also defines context for the business.

Neither customers not business units exist in a vacuum. Each activity in the business value chain has its own context. In order to understand the context of any business unit, it is essential to take a micro as well as macro view of the business process. An interdependent business process is as strong as its weakest link. Each link has a different role and a different context. In a fast changing business environment, continuous, insightful understanding of the overall business context is essential.

Context of each business activity, no matter how simple or complex, has a multi-dimensional as well as dynamic profile. Business units often operate in a diversified multi-cultural environment. Context, in the current commercial framework, is the reality that defines relevance, or why, what, when, where, how and by whom of activities in the business process.

For their sustainability, business organisations have to be contextual. The need to have a local face, emotions and cultural connectivity. Context is the reality with which employees, managers and business leaders have to work. Context is also the take-off point or base for creativity as well as strategy. Context defines the current position of business organisations, that is, where they are.

Each context has its own dynamics. For example, in sports, different games have different contexts as well as objectives. Grounds and stadiums where the game is played is of significance for competing teams. Each game requires different skills, capabilities, as well as competencies for competitiveness in different contexts. Business has similar situations.

Each business activity is impacted differently by change. Context is multi-faceted, multi-variable, as well as multi-directional. In a multinational business organisation, it has its own internal-external, local-global, geo-political and geo-economic dynamics. For successful and sustainable operations, business managers need to acquire intelligence as well as insightful understanding of the context of their operations, individual activities and overall value chain.

Creativity, as discussed in earlier chapters, is the proactive use of imagination to design a value adding solution. Historically, some industries such as music, fashion and entertainment are considered more creative. It may not be wrong to say that there are no rules in creativity. Creativity may be seen as a dynamic process between the context and objective. Each business process defines its unique context and objective for creativity. In a fast moving environment, both context and objectives may be dynamic as well as fuzzy.

Defining context often becomes difficult and complex as business units simultaneously operate in cyberspace as well as physical space. The cyber culture is different from physical culture. Cyber links operate at the speed-of-thought. The real-virtual dynamics create numerous kinds of uncertainties, complexities and ambiguities for managers.

Besides contextual relevance, creativity, to be commercially meaningful, must be focused, disciplined and time-bound. It has to operate within specified cost constraints. In business, for creativity to be useful, it must be measurable for managers, valuable for customers and profitable for the business organisation.

In business, innovations are just ideas or ideas in a given and defined context. Innovative ideas have to be creatively unwrapped and then more creatively repacked as commercially viable products or services. All this has to be done in a dynamic context. Change keeps changing; dynamic design-thinking is essential.

As discussed earlier, in the commercial context, creativity may also be seen as an intellectual curiosity within a context. Creativity is a means to an end, not an end itself. It is a form of energy. It is a know-how with contextual knowledge, imagination and solution searching attitude. For a creative business designer, understanding of contextual dynamics is critical.

In a commercial environment, creativity has no objective of its own. It is just an abstract energy with diverse possibilities. To achieve an objective, it has to adapt to a given context. The creative process is a situational mix of ideas in action and objective oriented accomplishment. The wheels of creativity help business units move towards their targets. Business objectives, strategic roadmaps and pace of movement are decided by creative managers. Creative managers synergise diverse creative activities in the business process. Each has a unique context but common overall objective.

Caselet 6.1

Creative Balancing of Global-Local and Local-Global Dynamics

Soon after taking charge as Country Head of a fast moving consumer goods (FMCG) multinational corporation (MNC), Rishi discovered many emotional as well as operational disconnects in the overall working of his company – the country unit.

The nearly eighty years old MNC operated in more than fifty countries. International operations contributed more than sixty percent of revenue and eighty percent of profits. International operations were critical for the growth of the company. However, comparative growth trends of Rishi's country unit indicated that the performance was below the global average.

Rishi discussed his concern with heads of marketing and human resource management. The HR head was more forthright in expressing his views. He said that while the company was a good pay master, employees did not feel *committed* to organisation. The marketing head also observed that while his staff was *apparently pushing* company's products in the market, he had observed some of them using products of *local* competitors themselves.

Rishi critically analysed his information and also informally discussed his concerns with some former employees of the organisation, local business persons, as well as business school faculty members. He was keen to understand global-local perspectives of the business.

Some of his advisors observed that notwithstanding the revolutionary changes brought about by digital technologies and globalisation, head-offices (HOs) of many MNCs continued to follow traditional ways of administrating their global operations. Impacts of globalisation, social media and information empowerment of local customers were generally ignored by HOs of MNCs. Most Country Heads had adopted do-as-told-by-HO approach in managing their country operations.

Summing up his observations and learnings, he identified the following factors for low performance of his own country unit:

- The MNC was not locally grounded. HO of the MNC generally had us-them approach towards international business operations. The foreign operations were treated as global with little, if any, concern for individual and unique local sentiments or for global-local perspective. Local contexts in global operations were missing.

- HO issued *instructions* for Country Heads. Besides sending performance reports, HO interactions or consultations were mainly on local legal and compliance issues.
- Globalisation had given rise to need for local identities, aspirations and local socio-economic concerns. This had created *local-global gaps*. This was almost totally ignored by HO.
    - "Increase-the-advertising-budget" was the usual and routine HO solution to drop in local or national sales.
- While local staff liked the salaries and working conditions, there were various kinds of local-global *emotional gaps*. Periodic staff engagement and competency surveys were conducted by management consultancy organisations under the supervision of HO. The findings were seldom discussed with the international branches.

Rishi discussed his views with his HR and marketing heads. He was convinced that for long-term sustainability, *global-local* approach had to give way to *local-global* approach of management. *Local* contextual creative energies had to be nurtured to meet *local* creative challenges. *Localness* had to become an integral part of global operations.

However, as his own management strategy, Rishi was not interested in announcing his views till he had evidence to support his views. Without bringing about any major changes in the prevailing working operations, with the full cooperation of HR and marketing heads, he wanted to introduce some *creative* management elements in the local operations. His approach included:

- He proactively started a *self-education* programme about the country, its history, economics, cultures, festivals, customs, language, food, etc.
- He wanted to interact with as many customers as he could. He believed that customers and employees were the most effective brand managers.

- While interacting with his corporate team, he would often enquire and express curiosity to understand the why, when, where and how of events and activities.
- He became an active listener. In his own way, he wanted to make his organisation an aware, curious, *context-conscious* and *customer-focused* organisation.
- He introduced an open-door policy.
- Along with the HR head, he took active part in local festivals and the events of personal interest to employees like birthdays, anniversaries, etc.
- With full cooperation of the marketing head, he introduced *self-determination* of sales targets for the marketing teams.
  - Once the teams had decided their own targets, along with marketing head, he would meet each team and try to find out the reasons and methods behind arriving at their targets. He also promised his support in achieving the targets.
  - With full support of the team and marketing head, invariably Rishi managed to enhance targets.
- Rishi was aiming to exceed all past performance levels in revenue as well as profits *without asking for any changes* in international management procedures or new investments from HO.

With a confirmed track-record of high performance to support his suggestions, he wanted to propose more creative and appropriate *local-global* approach in global-local management to HO. However, as he was implementing his plans, he often wondered:

- Were his concerns about the importance of local-context in global management justified?
- Was he on the right track with the right approach?
- What were his other strategic options to achieve his objectives?

What is your critical evaluation of Rishi's approach?
- Suggestions for making his approach more effective?
- Please suggest two alternate approaches to achieve the objectives.

*****

Context and Change

Change changes everything. Whether to proactively remain aware of its implications or ignore it and be trapped in the "boiling-frog syndrome" is the choice for managers to make.

In a globalised, interdependent world, business innovations and new business players create new challenges for established business players. In an uncertain, complex, multi-faceted, fast changing business environment, it is hard to predict which innovation will shake up which industry — when, how and with how much intensity.

Change changes context as well as creativity options. Each industry, as well as each business unit, is unique and operates in a defined context. Commercial value adding activities do not happen in a vacuum. For each commercial activity, there is a context and reason, as well as a cost-and-benefit perspective. A business process is a chain of contextual creativity and interdependent activities. In a fast changing business environment, creativity needs of business units keep changing, because context changes with change.

Different industries and business units operate at different speeds. Each has its own unique context. Also, each commercial activity has a specific purpose, a defined goal and a time-frame. There is a beginning and an end. Each product has a life-span. Most services are perishable. There is an objective, imagination and an implementation effort associated with each activity.

In the business arena, each product and service has a demarcated market zone and a specific customer context. Considerations of costs, price, customers and revenues are an integral part of the commercial creativity process. Also, each innovative idea and creative activity has a unique context, focus and purpose. Some have well specified time-frames.

There are a variety of creative actors, acts and activities in the commercial arenas. Context defines their roles and options. We can take the analogy of a football game, where some team players are positioned to create creative ways to score goals, while others are positioned to be creative in protecting their goal-post. However, unlike a limited time football match, dynamic creative thinking in business is a continuous, open-ended activity.

Discussing his views on context and creativity in business organisations, a senior business consultant said:

> In the world of commerce, each business unit is unique, has a distinctive context, has a situation specific system of cost, revenue streams and customers, as well as a management philosophy. Personally, I feel creativity and design-thinking cannot be transplanted. Creativity has to be seeded and design-thinking nurtured in a contextually appropriate way.

Caselet 6.2

Contextualising and Individualising Creativity

Soon after joining as the Dean of a well-known business school, while examining the historical data, Flocy realised that the performance of the school had not been satisfactory. Student applications as well as placement of students had been on a decline.

Before formulating any action to introduce change, Flocy wanted to proactively learn and understand the realities of the situation and gain an insightful understanding of the *context*. As a part of her learning mission, she was keen to understand the views of various stakeholders. She interacted with current as well as former teachers, students and employers of former students, as well as entrepreneurs.

She arranged meetings with business executives, human resource managers and business leaders in the area. As she was keen to get an understanding of the general reputation of the business school also, she interacted with general public as well as parents of the former students in the area.

With a reasonable and realistic understanding of the context of her school, along with the class teachers, she arranged to interact with the students. Her personal curiosity was to understand *why* they had opted for the school, *what* they expected to gain from their association with school, and *how* they wanted to use their learning from the school.

With a fairly good understanding of the situation, Flocy arranged an informal weekend *brainstorming* session with her faculty. The one line agenda stated:

- To assess our present situation and explore future options.

Along with the three industry representatives in the region, she also invited three former students of her business school and three start-up entrepreneurs. Before proceeding with the brainstorming session, which she wanted to use as a platform to seed culture of *critical, creative* and *constructive* thinking at the school, she wanted to visualise and explore the options before her. Some the issues which she was considering included:

- What were the options for her and her faculty to make students proactive in their own career planning?

- She recalled the words of her school swimming instructor — there are two ways to learn swimming, you can sit before your TV set, listen, take notes and memorise all the instructions by the best swimming coaches in the world, or just jump in the water and discover your own swimming talents. She wondered:
    - How should she introduce her students to the world of commerce?
    - Should they be asked to take up a live business project on the very first day of classes? Why? Why not?
    - How else could she make them get a feel of the ground realities? Or context of their future careers?

- ○ Besides being self-reliant, she wanted her students to develop proactive learning, creative and constructive attitude.
- She was also keen to introduce the concept of "life-long learning"
- She wanted to explore ways how the business school could be associated or support their life-long learning efforts.

What would be your approach — As Flocy? As a teacher? As a student?

*****

Context, Creativity and Strategy Dynamics

A context is a given situation. Change changes situations. Change creates uncertainties, complexities as well as opportunities. Creativity is creative problem solving. Strategy is a roadmap to the future. Thus context-creativity-strategy are intertwined. Context may be seen as the take-off platform for creative strategy.

To formulate growth plans, corporations create a vision statement — vision to see, create and navigate their own future and move from the present context to the future context. Vision helps in visualisation and defining of future context. In a fast changing business environment, context changes with each move. Complexity and diversity in business operations makes design-thinking approach a necessity.

Corporations have to reinvent themselves over and over again in response to ever changing demands of their customers, challenges from competitors and needs of local markets. Change and uncertainty are the only constants in the market place. Customers, as well as expectations of customers, keep changing. Customers need to be served, in new ways. New contexts evolve continuously.

Discussing creativity in the business context, a senior business consultant said:

> In the world of commerce, creativity is not consumed. Each successful effort takes us to a higher plane and platform of

creativity. Each creative effort, successful or not, gives us a new context for new creative and innovative efforts.

Like any other aspect of life, success and failures are an integral part of business. Over the years, entrepreneurs have been searching for answers to the same questions—how can I add value to the existing products, services and business processes to optimise profits? They are continuously searching for new, creative solutions for their basic business aspirations.

Caselet 6.3

Infusing a Contextual Creative Soul

As part of a team research project to interview a business executive, Uma asked her friend to meet her at the gate of The Art Gallery (TAG), located in the city shopping area. On reaching TAG, she discovered that she was much earlier than the appointed time. Her colleague was unlucky with her bus connections. To make use of the time, she decided to go around TAG.

This seemed to be her lucky day. The gallery was full of paintings, but without visitors. During her school days, she had been a keen student of art, painting and music.

While interacting with the gallery's curator-manager, she discovered that TAG was not a successful business venture. As a student of business, she was curious to know why a well-known art gallery, located at a strategic location, with a large parking lot, should be a business failure. Why was a home of creativity in need of commercial creativity?

In her efforts to collect business data and facts, she discovered that TAG had a tradition of exhibiting well-known artists. Most visitors were art enthusiasts and art collectors who came to TAG to buy or trade their collections. Its main revenue sources were exhibitions and commissions. In the past it had been profitable.

Uma thought that in an art gallery, creativity should flow throughout the organisation. Yet, the curator-manager hardly talked of any creative activity. It seemed to her just like another "trading house". Was this art gallery in need of creative management, she wondered? She discussed her observations and feelings with her friend when she met her.

Uma and her friend decided to take up TAG as their class study project. Because of its current business activities, they profiled TAG as *a paintings exhibition and trading centre*. There were hardly any elements of curiosity, questioning or creativity at TAG; just coloured canvases with price tags.

They felt that TAG had the potential to be the creative heart of the city. Appropriate creative energies had to be encouraged and contextualised. Being in step with change was essential.

Since they planned to present their views and strategies on how to introduce creativity, design-thinking and creative management at TAG, they named their project as "Contextualising Creativity: infusing an art gallery with a contemporary and contextual creative soul".

They developed a "flexible, multi-activity business model" around their vision of TAG. Their value proposition was to provide multi-faceted life enrichment experience through learning and art appreciation. *Creativity* was to be the attraction for visitors to TAG.

As a business model, every activity did not have to generate profit. Some activities would subsidise others, but TAG was to be an overall profitable venture.

With an aim to re-create and contextualise creative culture, they did some research to identify creativity requirements in the area. They met people from all walks of life and sought their views. Taking account of the operational parameters, they prepared their suggestions.

- To promote understanding of the relevance of creativity and art in the contemporary life-style, they suggested:
    - Art and Creativity Appreciation (ACA) seminars at TAG.

- Each seminar was to be creatively planned for different segments of society such as children, young adults, working persons and senior citizens.
- International art and creativity seminars were to be conducted for different art and creative activities.
- TAG would organise creativity events, functions and celebrations in different areas of art—paintings, dance, drama, music, etc.
- TAG, as a social platform for the city, would organise lectures and conversations on value and uses of creative thinking by prominent people. To make them participative, more than one person would be invited to lecture and interact with participants on different subjects in:
  - Different forms of creativity.
  - Technology, Creativity and Culture.
- TAG would hold creativity enhancement classes for different segments of society in areas such as painting, poetry, acting, singing, story-telling, writing, music, dance, cross-cultural events, sports and management.
  - To make TAG an inclusive thought sharing platform, individuals from different organisations would be invited to design creativity learning programmes.
- With help of students, TAG would create an interactive digital platform for national and international participation.
- They also proposed to invite students, faculty and experts in digital technologies and share their views and experiences of creativity in the digital world, for example, how robots can create art and music.
- A critical and creative element in the business model suggested by them was that instead of fixed fee or price, participants and consumers of services at TAG would be requested to make appropriate contribution for the cause of creativity.

They concluded their class presentation with these questions:

- Were their suggestions and actions meaningful and workable?
- Can each activity be revenue generating?
- How can an art gallery make creative use of digital technologies?
- How can TAG become the creative soul of the city?
- Would each-week-a-new-creativity-week be a workable proposition?

*****

In a multi-faceted, dynamic, fast changing business environment context, creativity and strategy get interweaved. One can visualise context and creativity from many perspectives. Creativity is energy. It may also be seen as an event, activity or a process. In a given context, creativity usually has a short life-cycle. But it re-creates itself in different forms or *avatars* in a new context for a new purpose. Contexts also changes with change. A business process is a continuous process. Business managers creatively manage a dynamic mix of past, present and future.

A Narration

Work-Style of an Artist Manager

Creativity may be proactive as well as reactive. It is a mind game. It may be an idea in the mind of a manager or an act of ideation or transformation on the canvas. There seem to be many similarities between the work-styles of managers and artists.

Explaining his work-style, an artist said:

> Usually, I like to work on several paintings at the same time. I spend a lot of time wandering between the easels; adding new lines of colours or shades on different canvasses; experimenting at each step with new techniques and tools

to highlight themes, contexts, continuity or contrasts. Each time I lift the brush, a new context appears. There is lots of experimentation. There is new focus as well as new discipline in emotions and colours. Creativity also incorporates the art of navigating through fuzzy ideas.

Once, I visited a motorcycle assembly line with the assembly line manager. As you know, assembly lines have well defined interdependent activities. You may visualise an assembly line as a value chain. Each activity is a new step in value addition in a defined unique context. In many ways, each stroke of my brush moves similarly towards the canvas. Each brush stroke of colour has a new, unique defined context. Also, each colour creates a new context for the next.

For me, each canvas speaks a different visual language, whispers a soliloquy with different tune, a new *raga*. Also, there is a unique contextual obsessive intensity in each canvas. I usually like to work alone in complete silence. However, at times I have loud music on. There is a connectivity in creative energies. At times I instinctively put some colours on a canvas and let the theme, lyric and the symphony of colours evolve. My work is a collection of ideas and emotions expressed with colours on canvasses.

Sometimes a fuzzy idea comes in my mind. I can hear the humming. I get a craving for putting it on canvas, a strong intuitive desire to paint. The idea develops. Ideas also have a speed dimension. I arrange my colours and canvas. I start painting. I pause. I look. I analyse. I paint again. I pause. I delete. I change colours. I re-paint. At times I find myself competing against time. Then I finish the painting, with few finishing touches. I look at it the final time. I close. End of creativity and innovation cycle in creating the painting. This may take few hours, a few days or even a few months. Some ideas remain unfinished. Perhaps like a software designer or designer of a digital app. Can you please tell me where and when I was being creative and where I was not? There is another very different creative and innovative process of selling the paintings and earning my living — my revenue stream.

I am also a businessman. My business jargon may be somewhat different from yours. I have my unique cost equation that includes ideas, observations, thinking, time, incubation and innovative creativity in producing my product. Also, my own unique revenue equation with a roughly defined customer profile. I have my own unique creative business strategy. Like another businessmen, I also have to know the emotional profile of my customers. Also, like any other business unit, creativity and innovation are an integral part of my overall business process. I live creativity and innovation every day. They are integral part of my being. I do not talk about them. I use them. I make my living from them. I feel this must be true for other professionals in their own unique contexts. I think, I am living the life of a creative manager.

*****

To be strategic one has to be creative. Also to be creative one has to be strategic and target focused. In a fast changing business environment, it becomes essential for business managers to re-evaluate their assumptions and contextual parameters for each new step.

Digital technologies have created internal as well as external disruptions for business organisations. Constant awareness is essential. Along with target focus, managers need to have a good understanding of the business environment. The last link, where product or service interact with their customers, is the most critical. There is always an element of luck or chance. Risk management is an integral part of creative strategic thinking.

As will be discussed in detail in the next chapter, experimenting and learning must become integral part of strategy design and implementation. Designing and integrating resilience as well as preparing for mishaps is an integral part of strategic thinking. The creative DNA of an organisation can evolve and improve through experimenting, systematically observing, listening, appreciating, respecting and re-thinking about customers. Organisations also need a canvas, perhaps many different canvases, to reflect their ideas and focus on them. For optimal results, context, creativity, focus and mission must be appropriately aligned.

Context, Creativity and Global Business Dynamics

With the prevailing VUCA business environment in the global commercial arenas, each business activity needs to be contextually and creatively managed for optimal performance. The interdependent, global business network keeps changing. Each creative effort, while contextually focused, must also be viewed from the overall purpose of business, a micro-macro mixed perspective and a simple approach of knowing where one is and where one is going.

Business units simultaneously operate in global cyberspace and local physical space. Each has distinct culture. Given the multi-faceted and multi-cultural challenges, customer focused creative design-thinking has to be incorporated in each corporate activity. The critical factor is to appreciate the need for understanding, defining and clearly demarcating context before initiating creative thinking. Also, it is important to distinguish between incremental creative efforts and disruptive innovations. Each requires different contextual and creative design-thinking approach.

Whatever the approach—incremental or disruptive innovation—enhancement of profit, net earnings or surplus is the main objective of business organisations. Profit, however defined, is essential for survival and self-sustaining growth of business operations. Managing costs and revenue streams becomes very challenging in the competitive VUCA business environment. From the current contextual creative thinking perspective, at any one time, the context and concern of corporate managers may be cost reduction or enhancement of revenue streams or profit maximisation. Or, a mix of cost reduction as well as revenue enhancement.

Discussing his perception of business option dynamics, a senior bank executive said:

To understand international business complexities and associated risks, we need to simplify them. I feel it is very useful to study business operations from local contexts. Focus on simple variables—costs or revenue streams—one at a time. No doubt, the devil is in the details. But to appreciate the significance of details, one has to have an insightful understanding of the context and local operations. For optimal results, banks, like any other business units, adopt and adapt to local business exigencies. Individual local units around the world add up to make global giants.

Local or global, each activity in business is a mix of cost and revenue generating components. Each activity has its unique context, role and operational constraints. Insightful creative inputs are required to map activity, understand its role and define its significance. Creativity is also required to find ways to simplify activity, make it more effective, at a reduced cost or to increase its productivity.

In a dynamic, cross-cultural environment, understanding of cultural sensitivities is essential. Even in local operations, while the basic cost-revenue equations for business models may look simple, each variable is jam-packed with dynamic complexities. Both cost and revenue have their individual as well as interrelated, intricate, interdependent relationships. Thus, the context has to be clearly defined and demarcated for both.

In the present era of global interactive connectivity and numerous start-ups, every day we read and hear about some novel business models with new, creative and innovative designs, products and services. Making creative use of the digital technology options, the new business operation may be a simple or an integrated complex mix of real brick-and-mortar and virtual products, services and business processes. As in the case of large diversified shopping malls, customers may use different options. They may make traditional visit to the mall or procure multiple products on-the-move, with home delivery options.

In the global context, the new ventures may be by a single individual with a global reach or global, crowd-funded and multinational partnerships, with a very-very narrow demarcated customer profile(s) and market(s) in remote part(s) of the world. The venture may just be an addition of a few new variables in conventional business processes or very new creative ideas to take new evolving technologies like 3D printing or robots to next levels of successful commercial operations. The new competitive challenges may emerge in many forms and from any part of the world. For optimal response, insightful understanding of context, competition, customer behaviour and environmental characteristics are critical.

A Narration

Understanding Context: A Critical Business Success Factor

Sharing his experiences in the global business operations, a senior business consultant said:

> Before I answer your question, please let me elaborate and narrate my perception of context in multinational operations. For me, understanding the nature and nuances of *local* context from *local* perspective defines the differences between success and failure of business. My experience tells me that internet and global social media have accentuated local and national sentiments around the world. Understanding of context is critically important.
>
> For any complex situation or challenge, context should be carefully defined and demarcated, more so in a multi-cultural and physical-virtual mix environment. Business process is a chain of value-adding creative activities. These business activities are often conducted in different situations, in different countries and at different times. To appropriately evaluate efficiency and efficacy of a creative activity, we need to understand its context. Also, we must be aware of the risks and unknowns associated with our assumptions.

Let me illustrate my statements with a few examples. In my spare time I paint and also compose music. If you were to evaluate my painting or song, you can do it as a painting or song as a whole. Or, analyse the moods and expressions of each colour in the painting, analyse each line or note in the song. It depends on your knowledge and insightful understanding of the activities. Some international marketing people think of India, European Union (EU), even Africa, Asia and Latin America, as a single marketing unit. Others spend years to understanding just a state in India or a country in EU. One can analyse the auto industry, or an auto, or an individual part in an auto or just the business process associated with one part of an auto. An automobile is sum total of its parts.

Contexts, perceptions and insights change at each step. As it is said, the devil is in details. I see new challenges and opportunities in understanding the details of contexts. Each context provides a distinct growth platform.

Let me give you another set of examples. For meaningful and insightful understanding of Mahabharata or Ramayana, one has to understand the *unique context* of each act. Each act is a case-study in ethics, values and philosophy of life. It is for a manager to decide what he or she is looking for. Just the big picture from distance or insightful details. It all depends on his or her ability and aspiration to understand the problem and associated challenges.

It is my personal feeling that the success of organisations such as Microsoft, Google, Apple, Amazon, Facebook, Alibaba and other such business units is the result of insightful understanding of the techno-business context by their founders.

Now to answer your question, if I had one hour to solve a problem, I would roughly spend 15 minutes in understanding the context and causes, 10 minutes to analyse and understand the problem, 10 minutes to evaluate at least two or three solution options, 10 minutes to visualise the overall business process with the selected option, 5 minutes to meditatively visualise it all from customer perspective, 5 minutes to make an overall final review and 5 minutes to present my solution to my team for their consideration. As you can see, I give extra importance to understanding of the context. In international business, it is critical to visualise individual activities and policies from local perspectives in the local context.

*****

Brands, customers, as well as markets have cultural-references, emotional-associations, locations and nationalities. Products and services may also be seen as packaged emotions. Many products and services cross continents and oceans to meet their customers. Products and services, as well as customers, travel to meet one another in a social, economic and emotional framework, as well as in a cultural context.

Success in multi-cultural business arenas require talents of observing and active listening, contextual defining of problems and finding contextual, creative, value-adding solutions. To sharpen their creative management edge, corporations would have to initiate and assimilate contextual, cross-cultural creativeness in their corporate DNA and creatively manage it.

Caselet 6.4

Context: A Business Strategy Perspective

While doing research for his various class projects, Neville often experienced lack of contextualisation. He felt search engines were more speed focused and less context focused. Search engines indicated their performance in terms of speed and number of files searched. To him both seemed out of context. He had to do his own search for his specific needs.

Even where business organisations had made extensive use of data analytics, learning machines and artificial intelligence, the emphasis, he felt, was on speed rather than context. As he saw it, there was an obsession with speed.

He visualised extensive wastage as well as customer frustration. He had a feeling that the digital technology entrepreneurs were technology focused and not customer focused. It was more dominated by "technopreneur" rather than entrepreneur thinking. He had a feeling that the technopreneur survived on the basis of their monopolistic positions rather than competitive offerings.

For his Creative Management class project, where the faculty had given them freedom to choose any topic as long as it was related to business, he decided to present the topic: contextualisation of information as a business opportunity.

Neville's business approach was to contextualise and simplify information for his customers. He wanted to adopt an evolutionary, learning led growth, approach.

He wanted his venture to be a First-Call Help Centre—a centre that provided simple, contextual and reliable information. Through his class presentation, he wanted to test the validity and commercial feasibility of his business analysis.

He wanted to start his venture with classification of his customers. To start with, he identified following set of customers:

- Students—Senior school and university
  - Educational matters—proactive and creative approach
  - Career options—guidance and mentoring
- Senior citizens
  - Healthcare
    - Various options in assisted care
    - Friendship and mutual healthcare providing group formations
  - New innings in life
    - Re-employment and career options
    - New, creative hobbies and learning
  - Entertainment

- Working women and housewives
  - Childcare
  - Work-from-home, flexitime options

He was considering a flexible, business growth model with a number of revenue streams, such as:

- News and information letter which would accept advertisements
- Possibilities of membership with very nominal fees
- Facility for members to advertise, form cooperative groups, etc.
- Providing mutual help — with some earning for help partners

He wanted to start his venture in partnership with his friend. As he made his presentation in class, he wondered about the commercial viability of his project and:

- How to start his venture.
  - With minimal initial cost
  - Revenue generation options
  - He had already initiated discussions on alternate designs for his website

What are your views on his thinking and approach?

*****

As in other activities, proactive contextual planning, strategic thinking, coordination of various resources and experimentation are an integral part of business operations. As will be discussed in the next chapter, strategy starts with knowing where we are and why, before we decide where we want to go and how.

The global business units walk on their local legs. Multinational organisations may also be visualised as a banyan tree drawing its nourishments or business benefits from various local roots. Local markets and local customers are the critical determinants of the local business context. However, it is essential to remember that local business operates in a global environment. Business managers have to have a clear understanding of the local-global as well as global-local dynamics. Strategy to craft the future starts with knowing where one is, that is, the context.

Be it in multinational business or in cloud operations, the real challenge is in effective localisation and contextualisation of products and services vis-à-vis customers. The commercial playground (market) is local and the goal (customer) is local. The context is local. Incorporating local thinking, local touch, local smiles as well as local sentiments is essential for global-local as well as local-global success. Thus, business managers need to be aware of global happenings while being locally focused.

As stated earlier, the life-line of any business is the local customer— they are the revenue source. The critical importance and implications of this observation for creativity and innovations will be discussed from different strategic perspectives in the next chapter.

*****

Creative Management: *A Role Play*

1. Assume the role of the CEO of any MNC of your choice. Suggest strategies to improve its local operations just by improving "contextualisation" of its products and services.
2. As a CEO of a local company aspiring to go global, formulate strategies to "contextualise" your products and services for different international markets.

*****

7

The essence of strategy lies in creating tomorrow's competitive advantages faster than competitors can mimic the ones you possess today.

C. K. Prahalad & Gary Hamel

Designing Integrated Creative Strategy

Strategy is a plan of action designed to achieve a goal. The traditional parameters of strategic thinking and planning in business as well as in war are defined by the two questions — *where* do you want to go, and *how* do you plan to get there? Appropriateness of strategy is determined by the *success* in achieving the *predetermined* goal.

Overall goals in business may be to enhance profit, by reducing cost or increasing revenue. Strategy helps in identifying and defining priorities for managers. It helps in allocating resources and making decisions. Every activity in a business process has elements of costs, revenue and strategy. An activity without defined objective and strategy would be of little value in business.

The *real* management challenges are in managing the details. As the world of business has moved on from the agriculture-era to the industrial-era and now to the digital-era, there is a need to re-think concepts of strategy as well as management. New situations require new thinking. The nature and pace of change has changed. The business environment is disruptive as well as volatile, uncertain, complex and ambiguous (VUCA). The continuity of business process and impact of high-velocity, multi-faceted change must be visualised in new contexts. As will be discussed later in the book, for *sustainable success in business*, a creative management approach is essential.

Strategy: Experimental Process for Discovering and Creating Future

Business is a continuous process. Faced with unexpected, disruptive, fast changing competitive business environment,

Designing Integrated Creative Strategy

managers need to find reliable ways to know where they are. Only after knowing their context in the new dynamic digital landscape would it be possible for them to decide their future course of action. To design integrated creative strategy to discover and create the future for the business organisation, the first phase of strategy for creative business managers would have to be to know where-they-are.

As discussed in earlier chapters, a business process is a complex chain of diverse activities. Each activity in the process has a unique context, purpose and goal. Contextual strategic thinking is essential. Business process may also be seen as a network of diverse strategies that require creative as well as integrative design-thinking.

Strategy may be viewed as a process for discovering and creating future. The front end of the process, a small team of aware and informed executives, may be seen as the antennae, eyes and ears of the business organisation — a future focused business intelligence team, a team with skills to sense opportunities, challenges and risks, a team with capabilities to *initiate* the process of designing integrated creative strategy to develop future focused products, services and business models. An experimental future exploring approach.

In a fast changing, uncertain, complex and ambiguous business environment, targets and pathways become fuzzy. Strategy moves slowly — step-by-step. Strengths, weaknesses, opportunities and threats (SWOT) equation of business changes with each step. Each stride creates *new* challenges, risks and growth opportunities. Each step requires review of context, options and strategy. Business process may also be seen as a chain of diverse, dynamic and inter-dependent strategy cycles. Strategy supporting systems and structure need to be flexible and adaptive.

Every business has a context, a purpose and a process. A continuous, customer focused action plan, with specified objectives, should be an integral part of every business operation. Starting with the context, strategy is an integrated action plan that incorporates predetermined business purpose. Besides coordinating overall business process, strategy is also designed to navigate business as well as its products and services in dissimilar market places to meet expectations of diverse set of customers. All this within the framework of overall business objectives — profits, cash-flows and satisfaction of stakeholders.

Strategy also includes developing insightful understanding of the expectations of customers, who are the life-line of business, knowledge of their shopping behaviour, as well as their decision making process for selection and purchase of products and services. A business strategy may be considered successful when the products and services offered by the business managers are bought by customers. Business is a continuous adaptive process. In a high speed, disruptive, VUCA environment, strategy has a short life-cycle.

For products and services, strategy design is the optimal mix of perception and performance. In a multi-cultural business environment, contextualisation and customisation of products and services is essential. Business units try to enhance accessibility of their products and services. Strategy designers have to understand the why, what, when, where, who and how (5W+H) of the use of products and services. In disruptive, fast changing, VUCA business environment, 5W+H questions need to be asked more often.

As discussed in earlier chapters, business units operate in two distinct yet intermixed environments — *virtual* cyberspace and *real* physical space. Increasingly, customers connect with organisations through various mobile digital technologies or smart phones. Understanding of why, when, which, where, what-for and how (5W+H) technology is used by customers has also becomes an integral part of strategy design process. To know, how customers acquire and use information is an integral part of strategic analysis and planning. Customers are the essence of business purpose as well as of strategic intent.

Business organisations operate in dynamic, turbulent and fast changing VUCA business environments. Along with change, digital technologies are disrupting every business activity. Digital disruptions are creating new risks, opportunities and challenges. Transforming unexpected opportunities into competitive advantages is also part of strategic thinking. New problems need new creative solutions. Thus the business strategy design has to be creative, comprehensive and contextual. Managers have to be aware as well as adaptive to cope with VUCA elements prevailing in the business environment.

Strategy-Tactics Dynamics

Notwithstanding the differences in scope, time-frame, size or levels of operations, the words "strategy" and "tactics" are often used interchangeably. As will be discussed later in the chapter, accelerated pace of change, VUCA, globalisation and digital technologies have made strategy and tactics more interdependent and intertwined. A new dynamic strategy-tactics mix approach is essential. For effective communication within the organisation, it is essential to define the terms clearly and contextually.

In some situations, tactics are designed so as not to indicate strategic intent. Just as each move of a competitor in a game of football or chess may have different objectives, the actions of competitors, too, can have different objectives in business arenas. Tactics are used to test and understand the thinking of competitors as well as customers. As a strategy within strategy, to stealthily achieve business objectives, tactics are often used to camouflage real intent.

In a fast changing and disruptive environment, effective coordination of diverse activities is critical. As in a fast moving football match, each move has to be analysed from different perspectives, such as scoring a goal as well as defending one's position. It includes attack, defend or confuse, and create a situation to rethink strategy. In a dynamic, interconnected, global business environment, insightful, contextual understanding of – why, what, when, where, who and how of business and strategic use of tactics may have transformational impact on overall strategy. Innovations and innovative new business models from any part of the world can change the nature of the business game and rules of competition. Black-swans can come from any direction from any part of the world. Strategy implementers must be aware, adaptive and creative.

Business units often adopt different tactics to develop their business intelligence. In diverse, complex, fast changing, uncertain, multi-cultural environment, business managers may often have to progress, one step at a time, stop, think, evaluate and move (STEM) approach in implementing their strategies. Every step forward requires revalidation of strategy and a new contextual and creative approach.

A Thought Provoking Interaction

Strategy or *Shraddha*

In my efforts to gain an understanding of the use of different strategies which Sri Krishna had designed in the Mahabharata war, I interacted with a *Swami ji* (a title of respect for religious teachers) who was also a visiting professor in a business school. As he was explaining nuances of Sri Krishna's war strategy with the example of the encounter between Arjun and his *guru*, Dronacharya, I asked him, "*Swami ji*, how can these strategies be adapted in hyper-competitive business arenas?"

Swami ji thought over my question silently. Then, with a smile, he said:

> Professor, I thought you wanted to discuss the issues *strategy* and *war* ethics in the Mahabharata war. I know strategy, tactics and war-games are popular topics in business schools. Strategy in Hindi means *rananeeti*. *Rana* means war; *neeti* is policy. It implies the *right* path or rules of war.
>
> Professor, is business a war game? Or is it a socio-economic venture? Are people working in business organisations the same as soldiers in the armed forces? Should they have same values, thinking and mindset? Is "command-and-control" and "do-as-told" way of governance appropriate for social organisations? Are "war" and "competition" synonyms?
>
> Professor, you mentioned creativity and context before we talked about strategy. Is it fair, meaningful or even desirable

to talk of *war* and *competition* in the same context? Or use same terminology? Are continuous social activities for long-term social welfare and progress the same as short-term wars? Should we have the *same* mindset in competitive markets and destructive war-zones? Personally for me, war is a very undesirable situation. On the other hand, cooperation and competition in games, sports, tournaments and business leads to growth and development.

What is the difference between a mother watching her son in a football match, and watching or imagining him as a soldier in war? Should we talk about a competitive football match, business or branding activities and war in the same context? I have heard business teachers talk of business wars and brand wars—brands being used as bullets and bayonets to conquer markets.

In the present era of global connectivity, interdependence and context of *vasudheva kutumbhakam*, we face situations that require collaborative problem solving approach for promoting international business. Should we talk about corporate CEOs as army commanders in war, in the same context? Do they or should they have the *same* mindset? Expressions? Values? Ethics? Rules? Success criteria? Whom do we want to *kill* in commerce? Why? When? What do we want to win? Why? For whom? I think we need to ask many questions, as we did when we were discussing situations in Mahabharata.

I feel entrepreneurs design business for *mutual* benefit, for *continuous* win-win situations. Think of a farmer in his farm, or a shopkeeper in his shop. Business is a continuous social activity that promotes social welfare. It is based on mutual trust and goodwill. *Shraddha* (reverence) and *sadbhavana* (goodwill). It is based on the philosophy of *vasudheva kutumbhakam*—the world is a family. On the other hand, war is an anti-social activity. As I see it, competition and war are two separate and distinct activities. The World Olympics or World Cup football and cricket tournaments are different from World Wars. Contexts, mindset and objectives are different. Businesses create, wars destroy.

Professor, I think you want to talk about creativity and competition in business. Business is a game of relationships, mutual trust and respect. Think of a painter holding his brush, a designer creating a product, a chef preparing a dish or a football player in a match. Who is their source of inspiration? What are they trying to achieve? How do they evaluate their success? Can you feel or visualise *shraddha, saadhan* and self-actualisation in their efforts? Or do you see war?

Professor, as a *sadhu* and a seeker of knowledge, I have a right to be wrong in my assumptions and learn from my mistakes. I feel we need to take 'destructive war-elements' out of 'creative-competition' in business. Think of our students in the class. I like them to compete, learn and develop with mutual trust, goodwill and smiles. We all learn together. We should try to create creative, collaborative as well as competitive learning experience for them, not with 'war-like strategies'. Let them walk together as colleagues, competing, cooperating and co-creating new products, services, business models and start-ups.

Professor, every time I visit a business school, I feel there is a need to re-contextualise business thinking. Business leaders and business teachers need to do some zero-based thinking. Commerce is an integral part of society, with a unique purpose. Within a competitive framework, we often face collaborative problem solving situations. We need to rediscover and re-define business and management and question traditional assumptions, thinking and theories. We all need a more creative, contextual, compassionate, competitive and co-creating world of business. Can we create a business model with *shraddha* in place of strategy to win trust and goodwill of customers in business?

I had many more questions to ask and discuss. But *Swami ji* had to leave for the airport to catch a flight. I wondered, how to take "war-like thinking" out of creative business competitiveness? Is it possible? Why not?

*****

Designing Integrated Creative Strategy

High velocity change impacts strategy-tactics dynamics. Change is multi-dimensional. While strategy-tactics designers may factor-in expected changes, managers executing strategy may encounter unexpected changes. Managers may need to design and experiment with new tactics. Strategies are designed on various present-future assumptions. Unexpected moves of competitors or changes in environment may warrant re-evaluation of strategic options.

Change and digital technology are omnipresent. Digital technologies have the potential to impact every activity in the business process. In an interdependent system, change impacts every business activity differently. Analysis and taking corrective action as well as learning, unlearning and relearning have to be an integral part of on-the-move creative strategy process. Improvisations and *jugads* may also be seen as contextual tactics to navigate strategy through VUCA situations. Each move forward may have to be creatively redesigned.

Discussing this point, the senior partner of an international business consultancy organisation said:

> In the prevailing international business environment, every assumption and concept needs to be continuously and contextually revalidated. Be it the well-known 4Ps (Product, Price, Promotion and Place) marketing of Philip Kotler, McKinsey's 7S (Strategy, Structure, Systems, Shared-values, Skills, Style and staff) framework, Michael Porter's Five forces (Bargaining power of suppliers and buyers, Threats of new entrants and substitutes and industry rivalry) model or Jagdish Seth and Rajendra Sisodia's 4As (Awareness, Acceptability, Affordability and Accessibility) marketing model, all need to be contextually validated. Business arenas are faced with high-speed, multi-directional and multi-source disruptive forces.

In the present context, where all business activities such as procurement, operations, finance, marketing and human resource management are simultaneously experiencing fast-paced changes, strategy becomes a multi-faceted, multi-speed, creative business journey.

In an uncertain, globalised, multi-cultural and disruptive business environment, strategy has to create its own pathway as it moves in the direction of its destination. Business targets — the customers — have acquired their own dynamics. Strategic passage is a creative journey over turbulent waters and not on a static pathway on a map. Strategy journey becomes a pattern created by successive improvised tactical acts and a sum total of tactics.

Expressing his views on this topic, the CEO of a multinational organisation said:

> At times, tactics can go contrary to strategic thinking. Even if you analyse the strategic journeys of the three great Indian strategists — Krishna, Shakuni and Kautilya — you will realise that while being target focused, they often adopted *contextual tactics* which were not in line with the overall strategic objectives. In war, chess and other games, as well as in business, tactical withdrawals are often done before launching an offence.

Strategy is designed as well as implemented in uncertain fast changing business environments, that is, in dynamic contexts and shifting targets. To navigate strategy through unexpected turbulences, creative strategy designing skills must also be assimilated in the strategy implementation process. Strategising the strategy is essential.

Designing and Implementing a Creative Business Strategy

In a fast changing business environment, creative business strategy may be seen as a continuous process. Business is a continuous, creative process. Strategy designing, implementing and review may be viewed as an integral part of the business process — a creative business-strategy process.

Business ventures are created by the people and for the people. Products and services are developed by entrepreneurs to transform purchasing power of their target customers into business revenue streams. People ideate products, services and business models, and transform innovative ideas into viable commercial propositions. A business strategy would be as good as the knowledge, empathy and creative thinking of the people designing it, their understanding of target customers, business environment and market landscape. A business strategy starts with people and is people (customer) focused.

Strategy is also designed to create competitive advantages. Competitive advantages move with customers. Customers define and change future opportunities and strategic options. Creative strategy is proactive, flexible and customer focused. Continuous experimentation, learning and unlearning are an integral part of creative strategy.

For effective implementation of strategies, appropriate organisation structures and support systems are essential. To design appropriate strategy-structure mix, coordination and alignment of different business activities would have to be done on a continuous basis. Depending on the location, nature, scope and objectives of the business, each activity of business faces different kinds of disruptions and challenges. Each activity has a different role and requires different skill-sets. To remain relevant and useful, creative energies need to be recharged and contextualised, at least at the speed of change.

A Narration

Integrated Creative Strategy: A Continuous Process

Sharing his perceptions and experience of designing strategy, the CEO of a multi-product company said:

> Integrated creative strategy for us is our core competency. For us, it is a continuous process of designing, implementing and reviewing. It is an amalgam of our purpose, priorities and business processes. Our creative dynamics start with customers. Our purpose is to serve ever changing priorities of our customers. Our business teams such as procurement, operations, finance and marketing, have

insightful understanding of the products we produce and the segment of customers we serve.

All employees participate in designing our strategy. We regularly monitor our performance and review our strategic process. Periodically, we also make an overall assessment of the impact of change on our value-chain and business strategy. This is done in three different steps:

1. Review of the changes in markets and business as observed by regular monitoring reports and structured information and observations from our front line marketing personnel.
2. Periodic zero-based assessment of our business position and new options. This is initiated by our in-house team of industry data analysts. It includes data of potential products and service substitutes.
3. Comparison and contextual amalgam of the above two findings.

The unique feature of the above exercise, which involves a series of meetings, is that it is inclusive and participative. Creativity, zero-based and design-thinking are an integral part of our organisational culture. A small group whose members are appointed on rotation basis from different departments serves as a starting or focal point. All employees are requested to share their observations with this group.

Initial meetings are informal where a few former employees, distributors, retailers, customers and start-up entrepreneurs connected with industry are also invited. Sometimes, management consultants are also invited to take part in the process. Customers are our main focus. Adopting a design-thinking approach, some alternate future scenarios are developed and the strategy process is reviewed and re-evolved.

As we operate in very competitive business arenas, both in cyberspace and physical, for us business and strategy are combined open-ended, value-adding, continuous processes. With inbuilt review and mid-course correction options, we constantly try to align and harmonise our different activities such as procurement, processing, finance and marketing.

When required, we introduce new technologies, with the aim to improve our services to customers. This summarises our story of designing, renewing and realigning strategy and business process.

I would like to know from you and your students, how can we make our integrated strategy designing process more effective?

*****

Strategy is also about being aware and managing the uncertain future, navigating and managing business operations in multicultural VUCA business arenas, designing integrated creative strategy processes and creatively managing new technologies. New ideas, new business models, new ways of working and creating, as well as selling new products and services in diverse markets are some of the new challenges. Customers as well as political, economic, social and technological (PEST) environmental factors keep changing. High-velocity multi-faceted change is a critical strategic challenge for creative managers.

Change impacts strategy. Change does not work itself out. Managing internal and external change, as well as internal and external continuity are integral part of creative strategic management. Change also makes repositioning of business a continuous process. Creativity, as stated earlier, is the art and process of using imagination to solve problems or transform innovative ideas into commercial reality. Change, risks and challenges, as well as opportunities, move together.

Caselet 7.1

Strategic Transformation of a Bookshop

As a child, Mehru often visited her family bookstore located in the city commercial centre. She went there to play, read, do her homework, as well as help in little tasks. She enjoyed being with books. She also liked the smell of new books.

Now, as a student of business administration, she became more curious and questioning about the commercial aspects of its operations. She realised that books were one of the most popular items for e-commerce operators. She wondered about the strategic options available for small, traditional bookshops.

Could the same digital technologies that are used by global operators be creatively used or adapted by traditional bookstores to create a niche for themselves? She was searching for a contextual, creative niche with its own business model for her family bookshop. She also wanted to explore options of becoming a publisher.

Making use of digital technology options, she was keen to transform the family bookstore into a proactive information and knowledge centre. She wanted to adopt the try, evaluate, add-value and move-on (TEAM) strategic approach, creating team and operational network as she moved on and be an active player in the future "sharing economy".

To test the operational possibilities and commercial value of her ideas, she presented her thoughts as a class project in her class.

- Her objective was to create a commercially viable niche for her family bookshop.
- She wanted to start her venture by compiling list of regular customers.
  - She would also try to collect a list of customers who were no longer using services of the store — dissatisfied or otherwise.

- She would try to find new customer friendly ways to collect as much information about the customers as she could.
- She wanted to make appropriate use of digital technology to create an informal information and learning oriented relationship with current and potential customers with a family-like interactive bonding.
- For appropriate, relevant and timely information to customers, she wanted to:
  - Segment her customers by
    - Topics of interest
    - Age and profession
    - Frequency of business interactions

  to invite customers on appropriate occasions like new books launches, etc.
- Moving on with the TEAM strategy approach, her other plans included:
  - Celebration of national events by giving information and knowledge perspective
  - Create a real-virtual mobile anytime-anywhere platform for:
    - Intellectual conversation and exchange of views
    - Poetry reading, book reviews, meet the authors' events, etc.
    - Reflect and share life experiences and stories
  - Knowledge theme events like history, space, stories, authors, etc.
  - Student, business, career development, senior citizen events, etc.
  - Book launch events and hold seminars with authors
- Hold events with other information related organisations such as travel, sports, entertainment, media, etc.

- Promote creative writing among customers and public.
- Arrange creation of creatively designed bookshelves for homes.
- Create strategic alliances, for example, occasionally rent out a part of the shop space for cooperative promotion with other similar organisations. Also, to request space from others for a limited time-span.
- Occasionally arrange mobile bookshop at schools or functions.
- She wanted to discover and experience the cutting edge of book and publishing industry and invite ideas from every one.

As she completed her presentation she sought:

- Feedback for her start-up or digital transformation venture approach.
- She requested opinions on how to prioritise her activities
- She was also keen to know, how she should design her strategic plan to:
  - Initiate and develop business niche development process (BNDP)
  - Structure strategy support system and identify growth route
    - Synergise activities, especially mutually supporting activities
  - Develop inventory of skill and talent needs to create, develop and fortify her business niche

*****

Strategy, Technology and Competitiveness

Information and Communication Technologies (ICT) are an integral part of strategy planning and business competitiveness. Digital technologies have inextricably fused personal and professional lives, as well as organisational operations. Smartphones are increasingly being used by customers to connect with business organisations. Big data and high speed analytics are being used by strategy planners. Automation and artificial intelligence are becoming integral part of organisational systems. The world of commerce is in a state of flux. Innovations and speed of creativity are emerging as critical success factors (CSF) in the business arenas.

Technology must become an integral part of strategic thinking, designing and implementation. Simultaneously, operating in virtual-cyberspace and real-physical space, organisations have become a complex mix of human-machine networks. Systems supported by artificial intelligence and predictive analytics are becoming integral part of operations as well as management support systems. Elements of complexity theory — classification of problems according to inherent difficulties — are being redefined. Creative use of artificial intelligence, robotics, automated data collection and high speed analytics systems can provide instant feedback. Digital technologies are creating disruptions as well as providing support for flexible, creative strategic approach. The creative business organisation design must synergistically balance and accommodate a dynamic mix of commercial, technical and human priorities.

Some of the other dynamic factors, both internal and external, that managers need to consider while initiating strategic design-thinking in a business organisation include:

Customer dynamics: Mobile connectivity and the large variety of digital apps available have empowered customers. Customers are better informed with more options. This has created new uncertainties, complexities and ambiguities for strategy designers.

Competition dynamics: In a connected world, competition and disruptions may originate from any part of the world. New business models are redefining rules of competition. Strategies need to be change-sensitive and flexible.

Competition against time: Business transactions are taking place with the click of a mobile phone button and at the speed-of-thought. Ideas, time and speed of creativity are the new defining factors of competitiveness in many industries.

New bonding dynamics between the business organisation and customers: In most industries, traditional personal contacts with customers are being fast replaced by interactive digital technologies. Business organisations need to re-evaluate the effectiveness of their traditional trust-bonds with their customers.

Power of one: Making use of social media, one dissatisfied employee in the organisation or one dissatisfied customer outside the organisation can create global ripples. Cyber security and theft have also become critical issues.

Digital technology dynamics: Digital technologies are dynamic and disruptive. Almost all aspects of business are intertwined with digital technologies. For effective strategy design and management, strategy managers need to develop at least two early warning systems:

Quick environment scanning techniques: Depending on the nature of the industry, this would include continuous scanning of political, economic, social and technical (PEST) changes.

Quick enterprise scanning techniques: Again, depending on the nature of the industry, it would include continuous scanning of procurement, operations, finance and marketing (POFM) processes, or overall changes in cost and revenue streams. Also, it is important for strategy designers to remember that different departments in a business organisation operate at different speeds.

Comprehensive Creative Strategic Approach: Digital technologies have created interconnected and interdependent systems. Neglect of any activity or function may prove to be detrimental to the organisation. Strategy designers must take an inclusive and comprehensive view of business operations. Creative and integrative design-thinking approach is essential.

Countering complexity: Complexity has to be countered by classification of problems and simplification of problems and processes for employees and customers. Simplification should be an integral part of business strategy. Digital technologies are user friendly.

Designing Integrated Creative Strategy 171

Speed and Change: In a globally connected, digital technology mixed, business environment, cross-cultural trans-national business transactions happen at the speed-of-thought. Thus, competitive realities may shift unexpectedly. Awareness should be an integral part of organisational culture.

Change, Strategy and SWOT balance: Change would impact strengths, weaknesses, opportunities and threats (SWOT) of an organisation. Strategy designers must constantly re-evaluate impact of change on corporate SWOT position vis-à-vis competitors.

Coordination and alignment on-the-move: To remain relevant and useful, strategy must change with change. As change changes the internal and external environment of the organisation, strategy managers have to creatively coordinate and re-align activities and processes on-the-go to remain customer focused.

Business navigation strategy: To navigate business operations through a turbulent, multi-cultural, VUCA business environment, strategy must be designed with a constant review of context and course correction options. Creative managers would need to adapt, using stop, think, evaluate and move-on (STEM) approach.

Globalised interdependent world: Cyberspace, social media and globalisation have introduced many new unknowns in the business environment. In a globalised interdependent world, unexpected competition can erupt from any part of the world. Being aware of global geo-political and geo-economic developments is essential for business strategy designers.

Artificial intelligence, data and analytics embedded systems: In designing as well as implementing strategy, managers have the option to make creative and innovative use of digital technology options. Digital technology apps can be creatively used as strategy support systems.

Cyberspace opportunities and risks: Cyberspace offers many new opportunities for business organisations. It also exposes organisations to global risks. This requires new creative management and strategic thinking. Cyberspace is the new global business arena for creative cooperation as well as creative and innovative conflict.

Multi-cultural and multi-technology business arenas: Business arenas are becoming multi-cultural and providing multi-technology options for customers. Business managers need to be aware, insightful and comprehensive in their strategy designs. Business operations are interdependent networks. Each activity has to be analysed and synergistically synthesised in the system. Being technology as well as business savvy is essential for business managers.

Social media and corporate communication strategies: In a multi-cultural interdependent world, comprehensive local-global integrated corporate communication policy must be an integral part of the overall business strategy.

New situations require new thinking. Old data, old information, old assumptions, even with the most sophisticated analytical tools, will provide irrelevant guidance.

Caselet 7.2

Leading Customers Creatively: *A Strategy Perspective*

Travelling across Europe with his family, Vikram realised the uneventfulness of the tour. His parents had taken leave from their respective jobs and taken him on a holiday to experience Europe and its diversity. Their tour was arranged by one of the leading travel and tour operators in the world.

Instead of diversity, what he experienced was similarity. He had already seen most of the places on television or on computer. All hotels and transport facilities were similar. Even the tour guides spoke with similar accents, expressions and mannerisms.

This was supposed to be a good educational experience for him as well as an opportunity for family to experience quality

Designing Integrated Creative Strategy

time. Their interactions were mainly with other tourists. The conversations involved exchange of list of visited places and the usual small talk. From his perspective, the tour had failed to achieve its objectives.

As a dissatisfied customer and a student of business administration, he visualised a business opportunity. He was keen to explore possibilities of designing a customer-focused business model for tourist and travel industry. He wanted to make his offerings a truly international learning and global-bonding experience.

His informal discussions with a few people who had experienced being tourists and used travel agencies confirmed his own experience. He also interacted with some travel agencies to find out the why, what, when, where, who and how of their trade.

Over the years, the industry had been structured around a well-defined business model. Travel agencies promoted similar pre-designed itineraries and destination packages. He wondered how to break into a global, structured industry. To start with, all he had was his belief of an unsatisfied demand for cross-cultural learning and his limited skills in digital technology. He decided to present and discuss his commercial start-up options in class.

- He wanted to start with an interactive website to connect with potential customers.
- His first target was students from schools, colleges and universities.
- His first offer was cross-cultural experiences and learning:
  - Learnings that would help students in their future careers
  - Help them gain an understanding of the evolving global-village
  - Help them develop cross-cultural sensitivities
  - Help them become better informed global citizens
  - Inculcate curiosity and proactive learning about global cultural diversity

- His plan was to create travel adventure and cultural learning experiences. He decided:
    - To limit each group size to 20–25
    - Travel with first few groups to gain personal experience
    - Try to identify one or two member from each group to lead future groups.
- His plan included student tours during academic holidays. He arranged with some well-known schools in destination cities for renting their hostel facilities. He had done some of his homework and selected few destinations with:
    - Well-known educational institutes
    - Interesting cultural diversity
- He was keen that the travel learning adventures be designed interactively with students. He wanted students to get a feel of the "ownership" of the travel and activity agenda.
- He was keen that students get a chance to interact with local students and families. With the help of the local student body and an NGO, he was able to create a shortlist of families who would like to host students.
- With appropriate strategic alliances with some other students in other countries, he wanted to promote his business concept and model on a reciprocal basis. He would grow and expand the business as he learned the nitty-gritty of tourism.

As he prepared his presentation for class, he wondered:

- Had he missed out on any major link in his operational framework?
- How could he make his purpose more purposeful for his customers?
- What alternate business models can he develop?
- How can he identify new growth options?

*****

New Risks: Data Security and Social Media

The digital era is also associated with new forms of risks, some known and some unknown. As business organisations navigate through a turbulent and disruptive multi-cultural business environment, risk management must become an integral part of the comprehensive strategy design. Some risks may originate from:

Competitors: With the availability of various hacking options, competitors may use hacking as a tool of competition.

Data theft: Digital data is easy to store, retrieve and use. Business data, information and intellectual property can be hacked and stolen by hackers located in distant places.

Speed of theft: Data can be stolen as well as transferred at high speed to the desired destination. Also, hackers can use sophisticated ways to hide their identity.

Data fraud: Use of digital technology in business processes exposes organisations to various kinds of frauds. Digital technology savvy customers, employees and business partners can create fake data and information deceptions.

Unsatisfied customers: Social media with global reach can be used by customers to express their dissatisfaction which may do significant harm to business reputation.

Cyber-attacks: Cyber-attacks may originate from known and unknown sources from around the world.

Ease of destroying data and information: Just a click of a button can destroy enormous amount of valuable data. This may be done by mistake or deliberately.

Data security must be an integral part of all strategic planning and design.

Business Diplomacy: A Strategy Design Imperative

Diplomacy is the creative art of human relationship management. The business process is a relationship based network. Business operates in diverse, dynamic, multi-cultural, multinational and multi-media business arenas. Business arenas are also a dynamic mix of virtual-cyberspace and real-physical space with distinct social and work cultures, mindsets as well as speed of operations. Notwithstanding the extensive use of automation and artificial intelligence empowered learning machines by business organisations, business is still a game of human relations. Creative business diplomacy is an imperative.

Business management is also a creative art and science of human-to-human (H2H), human-to-machine (H2M) and machine-to-machine (M2M) relationship management.

In business, diplomacy is a continuous process of observing, listening and learning as well as discovering and evaluating cross-cultural and trans-national relationships. It is the art and science of negotiating strategic alliances as well as facilitating business operations in sensitive VUCA business arenas.

We may think and perceive of the world as a global village or a global arena, flat or uneven multi-cultural jungle with many fault lines. Business organisations, in general, suffer from a social trust-deficit. Also, global markets are getting more dynamic, segmented, multi-cultured, multi-layered and complex. Managing human relations is becoming more complex.

As will be discussed in the next chapter, besides products and services based competition, business is also a cross-cultural operation of negotiations, strategic-alliances, joint-ventures and co-operative research. Strategic commercial relationships are integral parts of business ventures.

Cross-cultural emotional intelligence is essential for commercial organisations. To navigate and position business activities, products and services in sensitive multi-cultural, volatile, uncertain, complex and ambiguous business arenas, business leaders have to learn the art of creative business diplomacy. Business diplomacy helps create value and provide sustainability for business organisations in turbulent, multi-cultural business environment. For harmonious and optimal growth, business organisations should integrate creative business diplomacy in their national as well as global business operations management thinking.

Creative business diplomacy may be seen as a constant search for improving real and virtual technology based bonding with all stakeholders. In the global business arena, managers have to often negotiate culturally as well as politically sensitive strategic alliances, acquisitions, mergers, partnerships, join-ventures, franchise or licencing agreements. For successful win-win multi-cultural negotiations, creative business strategy managers have to be culture as well as diplomacy savvy.

The same words, expressions and body language can have different meanings in different countries and cultures. Communication is integral part of management. To successfully operate in a multi-cultural world, global business players must acquire knowledge of cross-cultural work-methods, time-perceptions and communication methods as well as body-language and dress-code sensitivities.

A Narration

Business Diplomacy in Multi-cultural Business Arenas

While on an assignment in one of the middle-east countries, during an informal interaction with two senior, lady, business executives, I asked, "In your view, what would be the unique distinguishing elements of 'Arab style' of management from those of American or European style of management?" I knew that the lady executives were MBA degree holders from well-known international business schools.

After a short discussion between themselves in Arabic, one lady said, "Sorry we are confused. Can you please rephrase your question?" I thought for few moments and then said, "OK, let me try. If my company had responded to one of your business tenders, and you had to tell me that we were unsuccessful, how you would do it?"

They were still confused. I elaborated further, "I think an American would be direct, frank and blunt in telling me that our company did not make it. A British would be diplomatic. A German would like to use technology and say, 'We would let you know by e-mail'. A Japanese would be silent and hesitate in giving the bad news. Different cultures, different ways, different expressions. How would you say it?"

There were mixed expressions of surprise on their faces. Again, they got into a lively discussion. After a while one of them said, "Dr. Saumya, we would *never* say *no* to you."

Surprised by their response, I asked, "Then how would you *say* no to me?"

Almost in unison, both of them said, "We would say *Insha Allah*."

There was a pin drop silence between us. They had big smiles on their faces and I was totally surprised and confused. Then one of them said, "Please do not be confused. This is the way it happens in our family also. When our children ask us for something and we want to deny their request. We say *Insha Allah*." I was more surprised.

I asked, "I am sorry. I am lost. It is my turn to ask for elaboration. Please, can you explain?"

Again, there was a short interaction between them. Then one of them said, "We use the expression *Insha Allah* on different occasions to communicate different feelings. To comprehend the intent or meaning, you have to actively listen to the *tone* and carefully observe *expressions* on the face."

As she finished her statement, we all burst into laughter with joy — the delight of mutual learning, the confusions, charms and challenges of cross-culture interactions.

*****

Diversity in its various forms, is an integral part of business organisations. More so in international business. Diversity in different forms such as race, religion, culture, history, gender, nations, professional expertise, values, education and age can create various forms of conflicts and frictions in organisations. As discussed earlier, in a turbulent, fast changing disruptive environment, for survival, business organisations have to be self-adaptive.

While operating in a multi-cultural environment, it is important to remember that globalisation has given rise to need for local identities. Understanding the sensitivity of local sentiments is essential. Diversity management—internal to organisations or for modulating external multi-cultural environment—requires business diplomacy skills.

Each nation and culture has its own set of etiquettes, social interactions and work habits, as well as perception of good and bad, right and wrong, fair and unfair. Business organisations have to develop working relations with international business partners. Creative business diplomacy is essential for creating win-win commercial relationships.

Emerging Challenges in Strategy Designing

Digital technologies and globalisation have created many disruptions, several new challenges and a variety of new opportunities. Almost every business activity has been impacted by new applications of information and communication technologies. The nature and landscape of markets has been transformed. Fast changing VUCA business environment has created many new challenges for strategy designers.

Trust creates sustainable bonds between customers and business units. As in most other social relations, digital technologies are the medium that connect customers and business units. Unlike industrial-era mediums, smartphones have embedded artificial intelligence. Strategy designers cannot ignore the role of digital technologies in business operations. Strategies need to be designed to manage disruptions and transform opportunities into competitive advantages. The challenges and opportunities for strategy designers include *winning and sustaining the trust of customers*. Strategy designers need to gain insightful understanding of the role of digital technologies in the purchase process of customers and marketing process of business units. Making appropriate use of their knowledge they can design strategies to:

Personalise and customise products and services: By creative use of digital technologies, business units can enhance the quality of experience of their customers. As discussed earlier in this book, in multi-cultural environments, contextualisation of products and services is of critical importance.

Co-creating partnerships: Products and services are designed for customers. Continuous connectivity provides opportunities for business organisations to be connected with customers and seek their inputs while designing their products and services for them.

Strengthen bonds of trust: By appropriate use of information and communication technologies and well integrated communication policies, business units can enhance relationship bonds with all their stakeholders.

Proactive strategic moves: By being proactively aware and sensing directions of change, strategy designers can formulate proactive strategic moves to gain competitive advantage.

Digital technologies can provide many strategic advantages for strategy designers. Such as means to sense change by high-speed data-analysis and take proactive corrective action. By designing effective real-time feedback systems and being aware of changing perceptions customers and other stakeholders, business organisations can develop sustainable competitive advantages.

A Narration

Seed Curiosity, Harvest Creative Strategy

While sharing her views on creativity and strategy, a lady fashion designer said:

> For me creativity is the synonym for strategy. Seed curiosity. Ask questions. Define problems. Outline or ideate possible targets. And then, just watch various kinds of creative strategies evolve in your team. What we call *target* or the end product, may also be seen as a value adding innovation.

Creativity for us is a continuous as well as reiterative process. Visualising, creating, erasing, re-drawing and re-creating are integral parts of our creative process. As we erase, we look for new options, new thinking, new ideas. The creative mind, like the mind of a proactive strategist, looks for new options and opportunities. Creative minds do not wait for opportunity. They tests ideas. A strategic mind uses tactics and prototypes as experiments. While moving towards an innovative solution, ideas and tactics get amalgamated. The creative strategy process also positions the product for customers.

There are many similarities in the two activities of creativity and strategy. The differences, as I see, are in approach, attitude and time-frame. In our business, there is more openness, zero-based analysis, contextual proactive and intuitive thinking in the innovation-creativity (IC) approach. IC is creativity trying to transform innovative idea into a commercially viable product. There is always a target and time-frame associated with the IC process. With us, the creative process operates under many constrains such as cost, time, context and customer preferences. I feel, our IC approach is more broad-based, zero-based, as well as evolutionary in nature. Conventional strategy operations are usually top-down instructions and implementation commands oriented.

With our scale of operations, for us, it is a two phased process. First, creative strategy is used to transform innovative ideas into a desirable and affordable final products for customers. In the next phase, it helps us in selling the products. Here, I would like to emphasise that creative strategy is a proactive dynamic mix of contextual skills and knowledge. With change in context and purpose, it changes its composition.

Each organisation is unique in designing strategy, creating support structure and systems.

*****

Creativity is a multi-faceted energy that flows throughout the organisation. For desired results, the creative energy of each activity must be synergistically connected with other activities in the business value chain. Creativity and strategy may be seen as synonyms in some business situations such as marketing operations.

The nature of business, its purpose, strategy and the structure of the organisation are interdependent. For optimal results, it is essential to match strategy and the structure of the organisation. The form and function, structure and strategy must be in harmony. Also, in a fast changing disruptive VUCA business environment, both strategy and structure must be flexible and adaptive. The dynamic, reciprocal, interdependent relationship between strategy and structure should be creatively synergised by creative managers.

Caselet 7.3

Designing Take-Over Strategies

Rishi had read few *Panchtrantra* stories. He had read how a *strategic thinking* rabbit was able to lead an arrogant lion to his death. He had also read about *strategic thinker and planner* Chanakya, who had created the largest empire of his time by using only his brain power. Chanakya did not touch a single weapon himself.

As a student of business studies, Rishi wondered why small *aware and fast-thinking* start-ups cannot takeover bigger *lazy, slow-thinking* corporations. With medium size corporations as his target, he wanted to develop a framework of appropriate strategy and structure a team.

To share his thoughts with his class, Rishi developed a short presentation to initiate discussion on the topic. Starting with the end in mind:

- He started with the statement of his assumptions
    - Internet provided him global possibilities in
        - Sourcing knowledge and identifying talent
        - Developing appropriate target focused professional network

Designing Integrated Creative Strategy

- After selecting his *target* — a medium size corporation — he would be able to
  - Create an appropriate real-virtual global *team of experts* to
    - Do due-diligence: the business evaluation of the target corporation
    - Do SWOT and PEST analysis
- If needed, create another *credible* team of experts to
  - Create alternate strategic plans for business turn-around
  - Prepare appropriate action plan for business development
- On the bases of his *credible* management team
  - Approach financial institutions with his team for financial support to
    - Take-over of *management* operations of the *target* organisation
    - As collateral, *ownership* can remain with the financial institution

The overall strategy being:
1. Based on general information, identify one or more take-over *target* companies
2. Create appropriate and *credible* team or *structure* to
   a. Study and work-out alternate ways to *improve* performance of the target company *to give higher returns to stakeholders*
   b. The real-virtual team would be appropriate mix of:
      i. Well-known experts, working or retired from around the world.
      ii. Credible proven knowledge base would be created.
      iii. To digitise operations of the selected target, some start-up entrepreneurs associated with the industry may also be associated.

    c. Positioning of new creative management team would be the target.
3. Management change-over bid will be made through financial institutions with a *credible plan to give them higher financial returns* on their investments.

He felt confident that, with his own initial studies, he would be able to select the target and with future profit sharing options, he would be able to create a credible team to implement his strategies. He presented his plans to the class for evaluation and discussions. He curiously awaited the reactions from of his class.

*****

Strategy designing has become complex and dynamic as cyberspace has added many new forms of diversity as well as new dimensions to traditional diversity elements in the business arenas. In the diverse, dynamic and disruptive VUCA business environment, strategy implementation requires continuous contextual analysis and synthesis. Critical evaluation, unlearning and relearning with future focus, become essential with each move.

Every step would require a new coordination and re-alignment of organisational operations. The challenges faced by managers to remain customer focused in the turbulent environment will be discussed in the next chapter.

Discussing her views on the subject, a senior business executive in the consumer durables industry said:

> Customer behaviour is changing so fast in so many ways that the front line marketing executives are asked to share their observations as often as possible. Increasingly, we are empowering them to take decisions on the spot. I feel our targets are always tentative. Data is always incomplete. Our executives have to imaginatively and creatively visualise and analyse the situation and make decisions.
>
> In the present fast changing environment, one can never be sure of the situation or the context. Changes in customer behaviour, strategic thinking of competitors and digital technology options are moving in all directions. It is hard to plan and set meaningful or firm targets.

Designing Integrated Creative Strategy 185

Flexibility has to be built into strategy design as strategy requires re-designing with each step. Various changes in strategy design have to be incorporated during strategy implementation due to shifts in customer behaviour, market landscape and policies of competitors. As will be discussed in the next chapter, each strategic journey creates its own patterns and pathways.

*****

Creative Management: *A Role Play*

You have been appointed the Officer on Special Duty (OSD) in the office of the CEO. You have been given the responsibility to initiate the process of designing integrated creative strategy for your organisation. Your firm is a multi-product company. It has sales offices in ten countries. The CEO has told you that you are free to decide your approach and create your team.

To initiate the process and make it inclusive, the CEO has already sent an email to all employees requesting them to participate in the exercise and give their suggestions. Many employees and department heads have sent in their suggestions. The main suggestions include:

- Department heads of procurement, warehouse, shipping and distribution have suggested that they would like to focus on improving efficiencies of their operations by making use of digital technology options.
  - They would like the CEO office to decide the strategic priorities.
  - They want to be intimated what is expected of them.
- Department heads of finance and human resource have just indicated that they would be happy to take part in the meeting to formulate strategy.
- Marketing and international business departments have sought time and permission to engage services of some marketing research companies to gain understanding of:
  - Market dynamics in different countries

- Re-evaluate the nature of competition in each market
- Develop action plan for each market
- Evaluate communication and sales promotion strategies.

- As a new manager on the job, how do you perceive your role?
    - Would you like to take charge and "direct" the process? How?
    - Would you let the process "evolve" but prod participation from all? How?
- Would you like all departments to be on the same page? Or,
- Would you let marketing and international business departments lead and other departments play a "supporting" role?
- How would you "structure" your managerial venture to develop and design an integrated creative strategy for the organisation?
    - To help you in coordination, would you like to create a "team" of team leaders or department heads? Or,
    - You would like to have a direct, one-to-one communication with each department head?
    - How would you go about structuring your strategy and also to make your organisation:
        - Multi-context, multi-market and multi-customer focused?
        - Collaborative and synergise inter-department learning?
        - Operating in a complex and dynamic environment, how would you incorporate experimental iterative flexibility while designing integrated creative strategy?

Please state your assumptions and present your approach in designing your strategy.

*****

8

That's been one of my mantras — focus and simplicity. Simple can be harder than complex; you have to work hard to get your thinking clean to make it simple. But it's worth it in the end because once you get there, you can move mountains.

Steve Jobs

Customers, Competition and Creativity

We are all customers for some products or services at different times, in different contexts. However, who, why, when, where, what and how (5W&1H) of customers is a perpetual mystery for marketing managers. Also, each product-service mix is a distinctive synthesis of ideas, knowledge, technology, inspirations and initiatives. It is an outcome of creative design-thinking.

Business is a competitive, multi-faceted and multi-skill game. At any given time, business units create and sell an enormous variety of products and services to a great variety of customers in dissimilar markets. Digital technologies and globalisation have introduced many multi-faceted new diversities in the business arenas. Competition has become complex, uncertain and fuzzy. To remain competitive, managers require more awareness, analytical abilities and creative design-thinking capabilities. Creativity is an integral part of product and service designing, manufacturing, as well as designing of strategy, marketing and selling.

Discussing the point of product-service mix, a senior marketing executive said:

> For a marketing person, I think, there is no such a thing as a "product". In the market we only sell services. Products are just "packaged" services. In the market, customers are looking for services, be it diamonds or designer shirts, cars or coffee, TV sets or holiday travel. In the market, customers buy services or packaged services as products.

Business arenas have been transformed by globalisation and digital technologies. Business players need to re-evaluate relationships between their creative product-service mix and their customers. Brands communicate in many different ways. Mobile phones and digital technologies have introduced many new mediums between products and consumers. New languages and new messages need to be created for effective communication between business organisations and their customers.

Understanding New Digital-Customers

Purchasing is based on trust as well as perception of value-for-money. How to create and nurture bonds of trust with customers is a critical challenge for business organisations. To understand the nature of customers and their purchase behaviour, it is essential to know who they are; why, when, where and how they buy; and what they buy. Also, to understand how they are changing with change. The (5W+1H) need to be periodically evaluated.

As stated earlier in another context, be it an individual purchasing products and services for self-consumption (B2C) or an industrial customer purchasing supplies for industrial use (B2B), customers form the life-line or *jeevan-dhara* for business organisations. To keep pace with the change, new perspective and understanding is essential. Organisations and customers interact in virtual-cyberspace as well as real-physical space in numerous complex, dynamic ways. This creates new creative and competitive challenges for business managers. It is essential to creatively harmonise the dynamic real-virtual mix of customers and business.

Customers and their smartphones have unique interdependent relationships. Smartphones are a complex mix of technology and emotions. Customers are creatively using their mobile phones as computers, personal information support systems, and for instantaneous checking of e-mails, messages and maps. Smartphones are used as entertainment systems, time planers, newspapers, as well as mobile working platforms. With their ability to do any-time and any-where tasks, smartphones have become *trusted assistants* of their users. Even wearable technologies have to get associated with smartphones to enhance their utility and acceptability. Artificial intelligence empowered smartphones may be the *real* customers of the future. Perhaps smartphones may merge with wearable applications. All this is changing the nature, context and speed of challenges, opportunities and competition.

For effective and meaningful understanding of their digital customers, marketing managers have to have an insightful understanding of the role of smartphones in the shopping process of their customers. Depending on the appropriateness of knowledge, smartphones may be bridges or barriers between marketing managers and their customers. Digital technologies have become more and more user friendly and addictive. Many business organisations and creative managers are trying to design new innovative ways to *lock-in* their customers. Speed is a critical success factor. Competition against time seems to be a norm for most organisations.

Information technologies have become omnipresent and are inextricably intertwined in the life-styles of customers as well as work-style of business units. With chip embedded products, a new relationship has evolved between product designers and their products. Products are becoming the source of information about their own consumption cycles. New artificial intelligence supported, data-driven creative digital-marketing and advertising has evolved. Besides intertwining with physical landscape of business, Internet-of-Things (IoT) is creating a different and distinct cyber world of commerce. New strategic and creative management thinking is essential.

With various kinds of business models as well as apps in the smartphones, each marketing variable has become more complex and dynamic. New situations require new thinking. New business dynamics, new forms of business-customer-product relationships and new forms of competition are creating new creative design-thinking challenges for business managers.

In a competitive, fast changing, disruptive, business environment, the question — how do customers relate with their products and services — often remains unanswered. Information and data have a limited useful life-span. With continuous flow of new data and information, the mood, options, attitude and shopping behaviour of customers, as well as the context of market research keeps changing. Data-analysis and observations from social media constantly provide various new customer behaviour insights. Tracking the shopping process of their customers and adding new, appropriate, value at each touch point are the new creative challenges for business strategy designers.

An important challenge for the digital marketing teams is to gain an insightful understanding of the role of digital technologies in the shopping process of their customers. Artificial intelligence (AI) has empowered smartphones. Smartphones have empowered customers. Real time data-analytic systems can provide instant information to marketing managers. It is important for business managers to understand the decision making dynamics—relationship and dynamics between customers making use of their own judgement, and the AI based options recommended by their smartphones. It is important to keep in mind that AI becomes *more intelligent* with each interaction. AI updates its learning. Creative use of AI is adding new complexities, challenges and opportunities for business managers.

Customer empathy—emotionally being in the shoes of customers, or wearing hats of customers to understand their perspective—can be a critical source of competitive advantage. Digital technologies can be designed to provide individual customer level digital data. Marketing managers need to map the shopping journeys of their customers. With appropriate embedded sensors, products can be made *smart* to communicate their locations as well as consumption pattern. Making products generate data about their purchase and consumption pattern can be of critical importance for marketing teams. For this, marketing managers would have to decide—What should they know? Why? When? How?

Caselet 8.1

Creating Smart Products and Business Organisations

Rishi wanted to get reaction from his classmates about his idea to develop and design smart products and smart processes to create smart products. He was aware of the fact that in the world of business, ideas have to pass the market test to be considered creative or innovative.

As a student of business administration, he was mindful that the 'smart products' would have to add value for customers as well as business organisation. Like the smart cars, he wondered whether it was possible to create smart business organisations. Design products that enhance customer experience and also provide useful data to marketing managers. In his own way, he wanted to explore and experiment with Internet-of-Things (IoT) as well as data based designing of smart products options.

- Impressed with the information about self-driven cars, he wondered, why can't products be designed to do their own promotion as well as suggest future product development options? Self-designing and self-selling products.

- Why digital technology and artificial intelligence cannot be used to develop self-sustaining bonds between products and their consumers?

- He was keen to explore possibilities of using product packaging to create bonds and be more 'interactive and communicative' for products, business units and customers. Use packaging as a marketing tool.

He wanted to explore possibilities of developing platform for some devices and sensors that would enhance utility of products for customers and also provide data on consumption pattern of customers to product designers. Initiate the virtuous cycle of product improvement and brand creation. He was aware that business is also a game of relationships. Customers had to be integral part of the product development.

Customers, Competition and Creativity

With the above objectives in mind, he developed a short presentation to provoke questions on the why, what, how, when and where of sensors in products to make them more useful and smart for customers and business organisations.

- He wanted simple low-cost "links" or "sensors" to be non-intrusive,
  - Mobile phone compatible
  - Enhance utility of products for customers and
  - Generate required personal consumption experience data of consumers for business organisations.
  - Create a unique selling proposition for each product.
  - The product package would be used as guide with:
    ◊ Comprehensive information and illustrations
    ◊ Promise of full refund or replacement
- Initially the products he had in mind were books, precooked food, health-care and games and sports – Chess, golf, tennis etc.
- His ideas for books included:
  ◊ Devices that would enhance book use experiences
  ◊ Instant education guidance while reading book
  ◊ Instant audio-video reference to concepts discussed in books
  * Self-learning and teaching books
- For games and sports his ideas included
  - Chess boards that would help players become better strategic thinkers
  - Golf irons that provide guidance to improve performance of players
- For precooked food and health care items his ideas included
  - Age, gender, work and life style specific expert guidance

These were his tentative ideas. He was keen to get a critical and creative feedback from his class, and also know whether he was moving in the right direction? Which product to start with?

*****

Business-Product-Customer Digital Bonding Dynamics

Whether digital technologies act as bonding agents or barriers between products and customers depends on the creative management abilities of business managers. Digital technologies are ubiquitous as well as intertwined with the work-processes of business and shopping journeys of customers. With massive data being originated from smart phones and electronic transactions more and more business organisations are adopting co-creation of products. Integrative design-thinking in business operations includes customers as well as business partners.

New product development or bringing about incremental changes in products are complex multi-faceted processes. Depending on the nature of business, the new product or service development cycle may consist of — market research; customer need analysis; solution idea generation; screening of ideas; concept development; feature specifications; testing of the new concepts; technicalities and development of prototypes; checking legal and market standards; developing distribution networks; assessment of market size; product designs; price; packaging; assessment of alternate break-even points; developing product launch strategy; cash-flow assessment; communication plan; developing marketing process and structure; use of critical path method; post launch evaluation etc. Each activity is unique as well as interdependent. Each activity - individually as well as a part of complex-interdependent-mix, in the overall process of new product and service development effort requires extensive inputs of insightful critical, creative design-thinking. Each activity has its own input-output reliability and limitations of contextual relevance issues.

Appropriate market research tools must be used to get an overall understanding of the various fault-lines as well as trends in the markets. Managers must be judicious about the limitations of research tools and data. Managers need to make extensive use of critical thinking and curiosity. Appropriate and contextual use of imagination is critical to understanding dynamics of customer mind-set. Some customers evaluate product value with head and others with heart; some with logic others with emotions. The mixing and matching of logic, emotions and commercial priorities are often in conflict between business units and their customers as well as consumers.

Business process, as discussed earlier is a chain of unique creative interdependent activities. All products and services conceptualised, created and sold by business units incorporate imagination, innovative idea and creativity. Creativity is needed not just to conceptualise and create products and services but also to generate matching value perceptions in the minds of the potential customers. In the market place, it is important to remember that, value has value only when the person valuing the value appreciates the value of the offered value proposition. Imagination, design-thinking and creative management play critical role in creating products as well as communicating their value to the potential customers.

Caselet 8.2

Creating Customer-Product Creative Dynamics

Faced with a declining market share, the well-known ParkShore Medical Equipment Manufacturing Company, popularly known as PMC, had head-hunted Rishi to head the product development division. At the management consultancy organisation, where he was previously employed, Rishi had been an important team player in some of the business turn-around teams.

PMC's medical equipments were extensively used by hospitals and medical labs. However, during the last few years, PMC had lost its market share and profitability. To gain an understanding of the product-customer relationships and the nature of competition, Rishi adopted observe, question and listen (OQL) strategy and an informal "W" questioning approach.

With the help of local company representatives, he tried to visit as many sites as he could that used the medical equipments made by PMC as well as those of competitors. He visited hospitals, met doctors, medical staff and technicians who had been using these equipments.

After a few days of his own personal learning, he called a meeting of the front-line sales staff to assess the situation from their perspective. He also wanted to validate his own observations.

He was able to get an insightful understanding of the market situation. Simply stated, PMC products had not kept pace with the change. There was an urgent need to upgrade the products and product-service mix.

In his assessment, PMC had to be transformed into an aware, customer focused, learning, creative and innovation focused organisation. Personally, he was keen to introduce the concepts of *operational simplicity* in the product designs and *customer focus* in business operations. He wanted a customer friendly, design-thinking approach.

He wanted customers to be a part of the product designing process. He was keen to transform "us and them" kind of relationship with customers into an integrated "design-team". He was also keen to use digital technology and global connectivity to create an integrated "real-virtual" global design team.

Rishi wanted to move PMC to the cutting edge of medical equipment technology in the areas of its operations. He also wanted to introduce some new, innovative medical equipments in the product range.

- He wondered how to move from
    - Past to present? Or,

- Present to future? Or,
- Leapfrog from past to future?
- How to introduce awareness about:
  - Need for change, and
  - Risks associated with change, also,
  - Risks associated with *ignoring* change, or,
  - Avoid the "boiling-frog syndrome".

As he was planning to call meeting of department heads to discuss his observations, he wondered, as a matter of management diplomacy, should he interact with:

- Department heads one by one with his OQL strategy? Or,
- Call a *brainstorming* meeting with all department heads?
- He was also keen to do a zero-based analysis to identify the gap:
  - Where we are? And
  - Where we could be, with available technology options?
  - He wanted to have a personalised as well as generalised approach.

He wondered how he should introduce or initiate:

- Culture of critical and creative design-thinking
- Practice of customer focus
  - Think of customers as an integral part of business process
- He was keen to create customer-product development synergy
- He desired to ideate innovative products in the organisation with customers.

He wanted change to evolve from within the organisation. He was keen to explore possibilities of seeding customer and competition focused curiosity and creativity in the organisation. What would be your approach?

*****

Business is an open-ended continuous process. Future focus is essential for business leaders. Creativity, by its very nature, is future focused. Given the fast changing business environment, business organisations have to manage their today with tomorrow in mind. The future will be very different from the past and the present. Many unexpected, disruptive changes will happen in the business arenas. As will be discussed in the next chapter, with ever increasing VUCA in the business environment, imagination, ideation and creative thinking would become an integral part of creative management process.

Discussing the importance of future focus and creative thinking, in a fast changing business environment, a senior marketing executive said:

> It is amazing how often our team members talk of their past experiences in our product development and marketing process evaluation or future planning meetings. The habit of excessively looking at the rear-view mirror is obvious. It is a very dangerous habit in a fast changing, turbulent environment.

Past, present and future are a never ending chain and require continuous learning, unlearning and relearning. What and how fast to learn, unlearn and relearn depends on the dynamics of the context and competitive forces.

Caselet 8.3

Business, Customers, Consumers and the Empathy-Gap

While waiting at the bus-stop, Rishi observed a small girl struggling with her sweet. She could not unwrap it. She asked her mother for help. It reminded him of his own childhood and his various experiences with his toys, sweets and food items.

As a student of business, in class, he heard his teachers repeatedly talk of change. Yet nothing seems to have changed in the world of sweets, toys and childhood.

He wondered why? Was it because business organisations were *only* concerned about *customers* and their *sales* and cash-flow? Was there a *blind-spot* between business organisations and actual users of their products? Was it because of the gap between business organisations, their customers and the final users? How many business organisations are really concerned or want to know how their products are *consumed* — By whom? When? Where? How?

In his class also, he had often heard about the shopping behaviour of *customers*, but not *consumption* pattern of products and services. With digital cyber connectivity, could there be a consumer back-lash against products and services that lacked contextual consumer-empathy? Was it another aspect of global-local contextual gaps?

He was keen to understand the world of business, customers and consumers — conflicts of self-interest and commercial constraints and gain an understanding of empathy-gaps. He also wanted to understand the impact of e-commerce on business-customer-consumer gaps. How does "virtual-economy" impact design of products and services?

As a student of business, he also deliberated whether there was a "hidden" digital business opportunity? Can he empower consumers? How could he design a business model for services based on his observations?

To gain a wider perspective on his ideas, he requested permission to discuss them in class. His presentation in class included an outline of his business plan.

- His focus would be *consumers* rather than *customers*.
- Gain an understanding of customer-consumer relationships and gaps if any.
- Contextual Empathy of Consumers (CEC): Keeping in view the cultural diversity of markets, he wanted to study — while designing products and services, how concerned are product and service designers about CEC?
- He wanted to develop two indices:
    ○ Ease-of-Use (EoU) index for products and services

- ○ Contextual empathy of consumers (CEC) index incorporating cultural factors
- To develop his *information base*, he would collect information on the *inconveniences* suffered by *consumers* of products and services.
- Interacting with consumers, he would also develop a *design* or *profile* of *user-friendly* products and services.
- Make use of digital technology options to interact with consumers.
- His initial plan was to start with consumer items such as:
  - ○ Products and services used by children and senior citizens.
  - ○ Fast moving consumer goods and general house hold items
  - ○ He would focus on issues such as design, size, packaging, etc.
  - ○ He would focus on convenience-of-use, re-use and disposal, etc.

His aim was to create:

- A data and information base about the *negative experiences* experienced by consumers while using products and services.
- To develop an *ease-of-use* index for products and services.
- To develop a *contextual empathy* index for products and services.
- Identify solutions with the help of product or service users.

He wondered whether, with above information, could he enter the business world and design a sustainable business model? Could he create a management consultancy organisation with an understanding of customers, commerce, culture, competition, context, compliance, change and empathy, that is, 7C+Empathy? In other words, (7C+E) consultancy? He requested his class colleagues for their feedback.

*****

When a global product is introduced in a local market, to be accepted by local customers it should be made local culture-fit as well as life-style fit. For optimal results, the value offered by product must "speak" in the local language — perhaps, a global-local mix with some factor-X that is added for differentiation.

Even the most popular global brands require creative local adaptations. The global-local gap in value offerings of a global product and local expectations may sometimes only be due to minor interpretations of language or colour connotations on the package. Small misrepresentations make big differences in cross-cultural operations. It would be advantageous for global corporations to use local language and expressions and also create a local "face" and roots. Globalisation has enhanced local aspirations.

National as well as global business organisations need to acquire multi-cultural sensitivities. Each nation is the sum total of many diverse communities. Even in the age of global connectivity, popular internet symbols and jargon, each community is evolving its own code of conduct and communication. Product and package designs as well as communication and colours used on packages need to reflect positive sensitivities of potential customers. Merchandising and product presentations should also be cross-culture as well as diversity sensitive.

Caselet 8.3

Competing and Exploring on the Edge

In her high school, Mehru had done a class project on newspaper reading habits. She had studied how different segments of readers read newspapers differently. Later, she found dissimilar patterns in the reading styles of magazines. She was aware that news and views are *manufactured* items.

As a student of business, she was keen to know how digital technologies have impacted traditional newspapers and magazines. She was keen to visualise possibilities of digitisation of print publications. To test her understanding, she decided to examine business perceptions and opportunities for a business publication. She took permission to use this as a class project.

When she visited office of a business publication and told them about her desire to use their publication as a class project, they were surprised. Welcoming her, the assistant editor said, "While we have been in business for a few decades, as far as I can remember, no one from a business school had ever visited us. We are just a small, specialised business publication or trade journal. Why would our business be of interest to business school students?"

Newspapers and magazines, like other media, depend on two revenue sources—subscriptions from readers and advertisements from advertisers. In effect, the purchasing power of readers is sold to advertisers.

In the commercial world of newspapers and magazines, editors and publishers show their priorities by allocating prime space to readers or advertisers. Advertisers are attracted by the quality and quantity of readers. The reader-advertiser equation constitutes the core of media revenue dynamics and business.

From the business purpose perspective, Mehru wanted to define a business publication as a provider of reliable and relevant business information to its readers.

Her digitisation objective was that with the minimum possible disturbance to existing operations of the publication, Mehru wanted to use paper publication as a base and explore the frontiers of information business. Her overall learning approach included the usual "W" questions.

- Understanding customers—overall customer profile:
  - Who are they?
  - Where are they?
  - How do they get information?
  - Why do they need information?
  - When do they need information?

Customers, Competition and Creativity 203

- Understanding information need of customers:
  - Their ways of sourcing, using and storing information.
  - How do they share information?
- While continuing to be an information provider through the magazine, she was keen to expand the information provided — news and views operations.
- Starting with magazine readers as the base, she wanted to explore possibilities of creating an interactive platform with the objective to:
  - Synergise present and the planned future digital venture.
  - Make the platform customer focused, simple and user friendly.
  - Provide real time information to customers without hurting the business interests of the magazine.
  - Create a knowledge base and explore possibilities of becoming a cutting edge information and knowledge provider in the selected business areas.

As she tried to visualise the processes in her venture, she wondered:

- How to define the value proposition and purpose, and create purposeful information products and services?
- How to use the existing readership base as "consultants" or "idea generators" for her future venture? How to:
  - Understand their information needs?
    ◊ Format and contents desired by them?
  - Gain from their experience to enhance the use of magazine?
  - Enhance purposefulness of the magazine with their inputs?
- How should she initiate the process of creating network of relevant and reliable information providers?

- How to transform magazine *readers* into co-creators, partners or stakeholders in the cyber venture?
- How to transform *advertisers* in magazine into co-creators, partners or stakeholders in the cyber venture?
- What marketing strategies to adopt to expand her information community and for attracting new advertisers?

With this, she invited ideas from her class.

*****

Complexity: New Creative Challenges

Complexity and creativity are integral part of business operations. A situation or a problem is said to be complex when we require extra or more critical and creative thinking to simplify it. Digital technologies, cyberspace and social media have added various forms of new complexities in the business arenas.

Complexity is an integral part of change in the business arenas. Change changes business reality, context and customer behaviour. Change enhances complexity. New situations require new critical and creative thinking. To manage transformation, complexity or change, the business processes need to remain simple, flexible and adaptive (SFA). Being creative and customer focused is imperative for managers to maintain relevance of their business organisations.

Complexity is complex because it consists of many different parts or diverse inter-related activities. Each complexity in each business process is unique. It would require contextual and complexity-specific approach to define it, demarcate it and simplify it. To manage complexity we need to creatively classify its components and divide them into related groups. Then each segment must be creatively understood in its operational context, eliminating whatever is identified as unnecessary or can be eliminated and then assemble back the simplified version. This also helps in contextualising business.

Complexity in business originates from many sources. Change changes contexts. Competitors change competitive positions. No actions or wrong actions also create complexities. Source and context of complexity must be critically analysed.

Multi-faceted change changes contexts and competitive positions in business arenas. Complexity is also created when irrelevant activities are not eliminated from business processes. Corporations may, at times, also create problems and complexities for themselves by their own proactive out-of-context acts.

As the nature of complexity differs, so also must be the approach to it. Creative thinking may initiate changes in products, services, business models or business processes. Depending on the nature and scope of their business, business organisations need to develop a systematic approach to anticipate, understand and simplify complexity. To simplify, business organisations may have to pass through following stages:

Defining complexity: Complexity needs to be defined and demarcated. From business perspective, complexity may be seen as a new and unexpected *friction causing factor* in the business process.

Defining the context: Business complexities occur and their solutions have to be found in their specific contexts. Complexity may be defined in terms of its area and activities where it is causing friction:

Cost equation: Complexity may be adversely impacting the cost equation of the company.

Revenue equation: Complexity may be causing obstructions in the revenue streams.

Operations and manufacturing: Complexity may cause frictions in the overall operations. This may impact both cost and revenue streams.

Mapping complexity: Keeping in view the interdependent nature of business processes, it would be advantageous to map the impact zone of complexity.

Analysing complexity: Besides overall evaluation, before proceeding with the solution, it would be appropriate to analyse and understand the 5W+H of complexity. Divide complexity into simpler parts to analyse it.

In inter-disciplinary, multi-department and multi-cultural activities, it may be advantageous to define or visualise complexity from different perspectives. This will help in bringing all participants on the same page. Analysis will need to be integrated by participative and creative design-thinking. Business managers have to make use of their business diplomacy skills to develop unanimity.

Caselet 8.4

Creating a Cutting-Edge Venture with Ancient Wisdom in Healthcare

Vedant's uncle had been suffering from a chronic disease for a long time. The family had consulted a few doctors and followed their advice. They had also consulted medical experts in some well-known hospitals. However, there was no discernible improvement in his condition.

His health improved and the disease retreated after his recent consultation and treatment from an Ayurvedic *hakim*. Ayurvedic treatment is a traditional healthcare treatment — low cost and said to be with practically no side effects. Besides giving some low cost herbal medicines, the hakim had suggested some changes in diet.

The family and friends were full of praise for the hakim. Vedant knew that his uncle and family had consulted the hakim almost as the last option.

As a business student, he saw a business opportunity. He wanted to be a catalyst for the Ayurvedic system of healthcare, which involves a holistic mind-body-soul perspective. He was keen to share his vision with his classmates and get their feedback. As a class project he prepared a short presentation.

- He wanted to create a platform for sharing traditional healthcare knowledge.
- He wanted to create an interactive, global, any-time anywhere consultancy website.
- He was keen to revive the traditional healthcare ways by:
  - Credible information
  - Confidence building
  - Promoting global collaborations in research and development
- He wanted to develop a comprehensive global knowledge base for healthcare

As he progressed with his project, he began to wonder:

- How should he start his venture?
- He wanted his venture to evolve and be self-supporting as early as possible
- He wanted to develop and progress organically.

He sought alternate approaches or solutions and feedback from his class.

*****

Being Competitive

To be competitive is an imperative. Competitive markets and competitors are unforgiving. In the world of business, being competitive implies being "better" connected with customers, being more trusted by customers and providing more authentic value, that is, products and services, to customers.

Besides the unique industry requirements, in the present connected, globalised, knowledge-era, to be competitive, business units would need to be:

Customer focused: Today, customers have almost global options and competitors are just a click away. Being customer focused is an imperative.

Context awareness: Notwithstanding globalisation, business managers need to be context aware. This would include political, economic, social and technological (PEST) elements in the business arena and an understanding of the nature of competition.

Connectivity or bonding: An insightful understanding of the "glue" or value propositions that bond customer and the products or services.

Commerce physiognomies: Emergence of new business-models with new innovative features is a norm in most business arenas. Proactive awareness is essential.

Creativity capabilities and competencies: Creativity is a critical competency requirement for survival in the knowledge-era business arenas. Creative business managers must be able harness and utilise organisational creativity to counter competitive challenges.

Technology savvy: Digital technologies are omnipresent. Appropriate, competitive and creative mixing and matching of technology in the business processes is essential for business units to remain competitive. Artificial intelligence must be creatively used for and effective decision support system.

Any shifts in customer expectations, business context, customer-product bonding, commercial process, creativity competency and technology effectiveness (5C&T) can disrupt the competitive position of a business unit. Defining problems, ideating, designing and optimising solutions in a dynamic ecosystem is a continuous, creative management process. In a turbulent VUCA business environment, problems have to be continuously re-framed and re-contextualised. Analysing and contextual synthesising are an integral part of creative management.

From a business perspective, change implies need for re-creation—new learning, unlearning and relearning. The business journey is a continuous journey of creative construction as well as creative destruction. To keep pace with change, critical and creative thinking must be an integral part of organisation culture. As will be discussed in the next chapter, creativity has its own economic parameters.

Sustaining Competitiveness: A Creative-Excellence Paradigm

Given the uncertain uncertainties, it would be advantageous for corporations to develop an appropriate contextual, long-term competitiveness, that is, a creative-excellence paradigm for their business operations. With ongoing change and uncharted future, business units have to discover and create their own future on a continuous basis, making each move forward a learning, unlearning and relearning process.

With many unknowns in the local-global market places, every business organisation should question its traditional taken-for-granted assumptions. It is possible that someone somewhere may be developing a product, service or business model that may present itself as a direct competitor. A black-swan may appear. A VUCA situation may develop.

Change changes everything. Before business units try to understand their competitors, it is important that the organisations know themselves. It would be advantageous for business units to do self-evaluation vis-à-vis their objectives. What do the business units want to be? What is their purpose, value-proposition or solution-offer and for which socio-economic problem? What is their unique value proposition for their identified segments of customers?

By asking such questions and evaluating their own responses, business units can do their own strength, weakness, opportunity and threat (SWOT) analysis vis-à-vis their objectives. In a fast changing political, economic, social and technical (PEST) environment, this should be done periodically. In a fast changing environment, customer-product bonding needs frequent realignment.

Sustainability implies a long-term thinking mindset. Business units need to think in terms of perpetual existence. The life-line or the bond between the product and its customer needs to be nurtured. The focus of creative thinking must change with changes in customers and context.

If we think of the commercial organisation as a social-solution, for its growth and sustainability it would need a reasonable amount of revenue and profit generating capabilities.

It would need to be an appropriate commercial solution for the society in which it operates. It would also need to be culturally relevant, a good corporate citizen, as well as be competitive.

In any competitive business situation, one has the option to *just* focus on competitors and *just* try to beat the competitors; or aspire to excel — be the best, not just to beat competitors, but be as well as one can be — one's best. There is a discernible difference in focus, perception and thinking, as well as the mindset between the two. There is a difference in being *just* focused on the performance of competitors and being focused on *being the best*. In a competitive market place, the competitors' level of performance may also be seen as the minimum acceptable performance level.

While being fully aware of and managing the competitive business challenges, managers can also aspire to be the best in their areas of operations. Being best is not just comparing cost items and revenue streams with competitors, but building overall optimal commercial, creative capabilities in their organisation. This requires creating a customer focused, self-actualisation culture — doing one's best for the customers and society in which one operates. By asking, "Is this our best? Can we do better?" maybe a thought process in line with the self-actualisation options.

Discussing this topic, the CEO of a large organisation said:

> When one is just competitor or market focused, one tends to think of options such as acquiring and eliminating competition. There is an element of hate. We start playing close to the legal lines, make secret deals with competitors. We tend to use money and power to minimise competition. This gives us immediate results. Developing internal corporate creativity talents is a long-term activity. Usually, we tend to think short-term and want immediate results.
>
> I myself have a short-term tenure. Should I be thinking long-term? Why?

Ideally, for competition in business, as in sports, to be beneficial to society, each aspirant and each participant should have a fair chance to compete and win. Whatever the stated rules, business units have to compete in real situations, for example, in arenas of patents and intellectual property rights. Some may visualise the market place as an arena of commercial wars and justify their practices with the dictum—all is fair in love and war. Business-political nexus takes on many forms. All these factors are an integral part of the dynamics of a globalised commercial world.

When strategising for competition, the focus is outside the corporation. Competition takes place in the market place. Acts of competitors provide the initial impetus for strategic thinking, strategic planning, actions, setting time-frames and targets. In a way, it may not be wrong to say that it is a reactive-thinking process. In competition, players often play reactively. To excel, one has to be more proactive.

Competition implies more than one player. Competition is competition when there is more than one player. Competitors compete to do better than others. Policies of competitors determine the benchmarks, performance measures and targets.

When aiming for excellence, the main focus is inwards—the corporation in search of itself, to be best for its customers. Aspirations for excellence originate from within the corporations. Customers, as the prime movers, become an integral part of the organisation.

The desire to be one's best comes from within the organisation. It is a proactive thinking process.

A Storyline

Competition versus Excellence

The difference between learning for excellence and learning to compete may be observed from historical events. This is well-illustrated in the mythological story of Arjun and Eaklavya, in Mahabharata.

Prince Arjun was getting training at the royal ashram of Guru Dronacharya with other princes in a competitive environment. He was adjudged as the best among them in archery.

At the same time Eaklavya, who was refused training by Guru Dronacharya, proactively taught himself with just a statue of Guru Dronacharya in front of him.

Arjun learnt his art in a competitive environment and he was the best in his group. But self-taught Eaklavya, who wanted to do *his* best, excelled. Eaklavya proved to be far better than Arjun. The rest, as they say, is history.

*****

In the world of business, one can creatively mix and match the philosophy of excellence with competitiveness. Creative strategic actions need to be contextualised. Pursuance of excellence, with awareness of challenges from competitors, would enhance sustainability of business organisations. It can be synergistic. In a diverse multi-cultural environment, pursuit of excellence must be multi-focused.

As customers are becoming more and more technology savvy and information empowered, every customer's touch-point is becoming critical. An insightful understanding of customers' decision journey has become essential. To excel, managers have to be technology savvy as well as customer focused. With various knowns and unknowns, as well as unknown unknowns in the business arena, it would be advantageous for corporations to develop an appropriate, contextual, competitiveness-excellence, creativity paradigm for their business operations.

As challenges and opportunities originate from many sources at an increasingly fast pace, it is essential for organisations to consolidate their operations and also prepare for new competitive challenges on a continuous bases. Managers have to become multi-focal. To refresh their global-local information and knowledge base, they have to wear many hats. While keeping a watch on competitors and matching their challenges, business units also need to endlessly ask themselves, "Is this the best we can do for our customers?" Thus we can match competition, yet aspire for excellence. As will be discussed in the next chapter, creativity must be customised and contextualised to match the perceived needs of corporations.

*****

Creative Management: *A Role Play*

As an officer on special duty in the CEO's office, you have been given the responsibility to institutionalise creativity in the organisation. Taking a long-term view, management is keen for this so that their multi-product and multinational organisation can retain its competitive position on a sustainable basis.

You are free to select the organisation — real or imaginary. You have to prepare and present your action plan.

*****

9

Capital isn't so important in business. Experience isn't so important. You can get both these things. What is important is ideas. If you have ideas, you have the main asset you need, and there isn't any limit to what you can do with your business and your life.

Harvey Firestone

Economics of Creativity in Commerce

Economics is a branch of knowledge concerned with study of how individuals, organisations and governments make choices regarding allocation of scarce resources. Economics is also concerned with production, consumption and transfer of wealth. During early stages of the industrial-era, generally accepted inputs for industrial production processes were land, labour and capital. Later, entrepreneurship was added in the list of inputs of production process. In the current digital-era, innovative ideas and creativity are considered critical economic resources.

The world of commerce is created and designed by entrepreneurs. They are individuals with creative ideas. Many kinds, modes, forms, colours and shades of creativity are used by them in their business operations. They conceptualise, design and produce new products and services desired by customers and society. In commerce, creativity includes creative design-thinking. Entrepreneurship may be visualised as creativity in action. It is the proactive, creative, entrepreneurial spirit that initiates business ventures.

Entrepreneurs initiate change and create a future for themselves as well as for the society. Entrepreneurs work for themselves. They serve their self-interest by creating value for the society.

Economics: Some Perceptions

Generally, economic observations are divided into macroeconomics and microeconomics. Macroeconomics is the performance of the *aggregate* economic system and microeconomics is behaviour of *individual* business units or consumers. In a globalised, interdependent world, economics has social, commercial and political, as well as geo-economic and geo-political implications. Along with mathematical economics and philosophy of economics, there is an economic perspective for almost every social activity, such as, political economics, consumer economics, behavioural economics, energy economic, Islamic economics, Marxian economics, feminist economics, experimental economics, and many more.

Economics means different things to different people at different times in different situations. Economics is associated with money, employment, education, happiness, healthcare, housing, travel, hope, opportunity, quality of life-style, freedom, fashion, security and much more. In different contexts, it is also seen as inflation rate, trade-flow, stock-market movements, price levels, variety of products, quality of products and services, brands and availability of products and services. It is also associated with quality of media, news, entertainment, training, sports, games and much more.

Economic perceptions of young parents investing in the education of their children are different from those of senior citizens investing their savings for retirement. The state of economics is different for a house wife managing the household on a fixed income and a lady executive travelling on a corporate account or a young unemployed person or an old person in need of healthcare. Also, economic rules and expectations are different for different segments of society, at different times. The socio-economic perceptions towards people commissioned in the armed forces are different from those people training themselves to be corporate executives or other professionals.

Perceptions of economic resources also differ. Money is perceived and valued differently by people who save for a rainy day and bankers who use money to make money by lending it—encouraging investments or consumption. Economics is also reflected in low interest to an individual money saver and high returns for bankers, corporations or stock market speculators.

Economics is also a game of raw numbers and data. Money also talks. People with more money are perceived differently than people with less money, be it in a casino, market place or social gatherings. Some people study economics as a branch of knowledge concerned with production and consumption goods and services. Others study it as a science of wealth creation. Economics is also viewed as a social science concerned with the general welfare of people.

Discussing his perceptions of economics as a social science, an entrepreneur said:

> Frankly, I do not see much difference between workers trying to maximise their salaries, my efforts to maximise my profits, or national governments trying to optimise their tax collections. All want to maximise their revenue, growth options and purchasing power. Nations encourage exports so that they can import more. Economics is the art and science of increasing wealth, purchasing power or capacity to consume or enhance welfare.

On another occasion, explaining perceptions of economics, a business consultant said:

> I think of entrepreneurs as social artists. They create commercial tapestry on a social canvas. Each product and service associated with commerce is creative. Each is a mix of creativity and design-thinking. Each has its own unique socio-economic space in society.
>
> Every business organisation has a social and economic purpose. Business and management are creative arts. Business organisations need to rediscover economic value of creativity.

Caselet 9.1

Activating Creativity in Maslow's Pyramid

Rishi joined marketing division of an International Organisation (IO). He was given overall charge of a country marketing operation and reported directly to the VP. The organisation owned some well-known global brands.

Soon after joining IO, he realised that while the company had been able to maintain its profit levels by increasing the price of its reputed brands, the sales volumes had slipped. He was also aware that the next price increase may have a very detrimental impact on the sales volume.

The country where he was working had one of the highest per-capita incomes in the world. The organisation was known for its high employee benefits. However, when interacting with employees and colleagues, he found the frequent discussion topics were cost of housing, living, education, healthcare, entertainment and luxury cars.

At business school, he had read about Abraham Maslow (AM), the Need Hierarchy theory and the pyramid. He wondered about the position of his colleagues in the socio-economic pyramid. Why did he never hear words like self-esteem, self-actualisation, confidence, respect for others, commitment, ideas, and desire to be creative or innovative on the job? He wondered whether creativity or being creative and desire for self-actualisation were just a state-of-mind.

He wondered, whether he could transform culture of his organisation and translate it into enhancing the competitiveness of his organisation, higher productivity, lower costs and higher sales and profits?

Without discussing his thoughts and ideas with anyone, he was keen to experiment. It was to be his *no extra real cost venture*. Quietly, he just wanted to "seed curiosity" and introduce elements of critical and creative thinking in the "sluggish, sleepy and comfort trapped" socio-economic AM pyramid of his organisation. While interacting with his team and colleagues:

- Informally and judiciously he started introducing "curiosity and desire for awareness" by asking simple and general questions about business environment and competitors.
- Casually but carefully he started "planting seeds of curiosity, questioning and creativity" by casually asking contextual questions relating to the purpose of business and their own aspirations.

Economics of Creativity in Commerce

- In his own informal way, he had been able to make his team members aware of the common link between their own "actualisation" and "the purpose" of their organisation.
- He realised that as he *seeded* curiosity and creativity he also created *social-capital* as a by-product in his organisation. Design-thinking evolved.
  - He himself felt more motivated and involved in his work.
  - He also began to notice enhanced commitment, team-spirit, involvement, motivation, sense of ownership and a proactive learning attitude in his colleagues, individually as well as in teams.
  - The organisation reported higher performance levels.

Without changing any system or any new investment, he had been able to make his teams creative as well as more productive. He wondered how should he:

- Measure or calibrate his success?
- Celebrate his success?
- Discuss "Economics of Creativity" with his colleagues?
- Calculate return on investment (ROI) of his creativity initiative? (ROI is gain minus cost, divided by cost.)
- Tell his boss or company about his experiment?
- Go about institutionalising creativity and innovation in the organisation?
  - Should the company human resource department (HRD) adopt this as a "formal" policy? Or
  - Should each division and department be encouraged to evolve their own creativity initiation ways and programmes?
  - Should HRD develop contextual or divisional *creativity-coaching* programmes?
  - How could digital technology be used to institutionalise creativity?

- Where there any trade-offs in his seeding of curiosity and creativity?
    - How should he do a "cost-benefit" analysis?
    He is keen to know your thoughts.

*****

Creativity: Estimating Return on Investment (ROI)

In business, Return-on-Investment (ROI) is a critical key performance indicator (KPI). It is used to compare cost and corresponding performance or the overall contribution made by a resource, investment or an activity.

In a competitive, uncertain and fast changing digital business environment, creativity is a critical success factor (CSF). To estimate the cost of creativity in an organisation, we would have to evaluate the cost of activating, instigating or nudging dormant *creativity resource* in the mind of employees of the company.

Depending on the nature of the business, usually while recruiting employees, business units match experience, skills and talent of candidates with that of their defined job profile. Many organisations outsource the recruitment process or use artificial intelligence embedded systems to shortlist candidates. Usually, the final interviews by company executives are used to evaluate emotional and culture-fit of the candidates with the work-culture prevailing in the organisation.

While discussing this topic, a senior human resource manager said:

> We expect a new recruit to fit in with the existing job-profile and work-culture. For smooth and harmonious working, we like to ensure existing job-slot fit. We have well defined job profiles and key performance indicators for each job. Training is an integral part of our divisional activities.
>
> Creativity is a very abstract term. It is not a part of the job description. For transparency in recruitment, we need well defined *measurable* parameters.

Benefits of curiosity, questioning and creative culture get reflected through changes in the organisational revenue and customer relations. To calculate ROI from creative thinking by employees and the overall creative culture, we would need to have cost estimates for "creating" a creative thinking environment and creative management. What are the main cost items for creating a creative thinking environment in a business organisation? Depending on the nature and scope of the business, the process of *seeding, nurturing* and *harvesting* of creativity in commercial or other organisations may include:

Initiating awareness: Creativity quotient of an organisation depends on the curiosity quotient of its employees. Depending on the nature and size of the business, seeding of curiosity, questioning and creative design-thinking may be informally done by senior managers or team leaders. Business units are networks of teams. Synergistically coordinating teams is an integral part of creative management.

Contextualisation of the enquiry or curiosity: A business process is a chain of diverse, interlinked and interdependent activities. To translate overall curiosity into creative value adding challenge, curiosity has to be contextualised and given a focus. Purpose focused, contextual and value adding ideas have to be generated. As stated earlier, this may be done either in a formal or an informal manner.

Depending on the size, spread and complexity of the activity or department, further division of context may be essential. This would be applicable to transnational divisions such as procurement, marketing, finance and operations. Further subdivisions would be essential for complex products. Analysis, synthesis and integrative design-thinking are an integral part of creative management.

To nurture creativity in complex technology or multi-cultural activity areas, some creative division heads may also like to introduce concepts of:

Coaching: Coaching requires positive, individualised attention to people. Depending on the situation, managers may create self-managed teams and act as coaches rather than managers.

Mentoring: Mentoring is for overall guidance and coordination of different specialised activity areas. Mentors may also need to supervise experiments by some individuals or teams from departmental or overall business perspective.

Overall coordination of selected creative ideas: As stated earlier, creative ideas are value adding ideas. As business organisations are a group of varied specialisations, and business processes are dynamic, interdependent chains of diverse activities, overall coordination by senior staff is essential.

All these activities may be seen as an integral part of creative design-thinking culture and creative management. Depending on the nature of business and the work style of managers, initiation of creative design-thinking would be a low cost activity. Some managers think of creativity as a *free* resource with zero-cost or *minimal additional cost*. Creativity requires a continuous awareness and commitment to purpose. Digital technology with almost zero marginal-cost operations offers many low cost, interactive, communication options for creative managers.

Generally speaking, seeding contextual curiosity and creativity, as well as nurturing of creativity in an organisation, is a low cost activity. Besides enhancement of competitive position and revenue, other direct and indirect benefits from creative thinking culture include an involved and motivated work-force, higher customer satisfaction and more purpose focused work-culture.

Caselet 9.2

Performance: With and Without Creativity

Rishu saw a young postman, apparently in pain, stretching himself in front of the letter box of his condominium. He went to enquire about his health and offer any help he could. While interacting with him, he came to learn about the job-description of a postman. He also realised that architects of the condominium had paid little attention to size, shapes and location of letter boxes. Little consideration was given to the convenience of postmen.

On doing some more research, he came to know how, over the years, by mutual learning and adapting best-practices, most post-offices around the world had standardised their operational activities. It is like a global network. Post office services around the world have been active in cooperating, coordinating and improving their operational services — picking up, sorting and distributing letters, magazines and small packages.

Around the world, post-offices provide the most economical local, national and global delivery services. He was aware that global connectivity and interactive social media had reduced the importance of conventional letters, but distribution of products is a critical success factor in e-commerce.

In many countries, post-offices are the oldest and most experienced organisation in distribution. Then why is there a mismatch between e-commerce and post-office? He wondered why, in general perception, post-office services were becoming relatively irrelevant in most parts of the world? Was it just a public-sector verses private-sector mindset? Was it lack of creative management?

As a student of business administration, Rishu was keen to present his questions as a class project. Assuming that all students were aware of post office operations, for his presentation he adopted a format of questions. He questioned:

- Had post-office services become disconnected from their customers?
    - Who are the current and potential customers for post-office services?
        - Individuals?
        - Commercial organisations?
    - What other logistics services can post-offices undertake?
        - For individuals?
        - For commercial organisations?

- Were post-office services in need of a creative evolution?
  - To be digitally-fit for the digital-era?
- Taking into account the new realities of digital technologies and e-commerce
  - Do post-offices have to redefine their value propositions?
    - For individual citizens – young and old
    - For commercial organisations – small and big
  - How and what post-office should do to fit in with new e-commerce growth areas?
    - Local logistics
    - National logistics
    - Global logistics
- How should curiosity, creative and participative design-thinking be implanted and nurtured in post offices?
  - How to *knowledgise* or make traditional industrial-era post office operations knowledge-era fit?

He invited ideas from his class.

*****

New Economic Realities and Creativity

Industrial-era industrialised agriculture. Digital-era is digitising industrial-era operations. Besides various other factors, speed of operations is a distinguishing characteristic of the digital-age. Digital technologies have connected and empowered individuals. The interactive social media has transformed global life-styles, social, economic and political power structures. With more and more creative use of bits and bytes, the digital economy, with its own set of rules and currency, is growing at a fast pace. The new era, with new complexities, requires new multi-cultural thinking and new creative solutions.

The business economics of land, labour, capital and entrepreneurship has transformed into economics of talent, ideas and creative management. Algorithms and automated operations have restructured commercial operations. Cyberspace has created its own commercial arenas with their own currency. All this has impacted commercial structures, business processes, job profiles and talent requirements. Creativity and innovations are the most important source of wealth in the digital economy.

Innovative ideas remain a figment of imagination until creative inputs transform them into viable commercial options. Creativity, creative design-thinking and creative management are the underlying critical success factors in the new evolving economic order. To appreciate the economic significance of creativity, we need to have a clear understanding of its role in different industries as well as in the overall economic system.

Commerce, Creativity and Design-Thinking Kaleidoscope

Commerce is the creative process of using economic resources to produce and make available economic goods desired by people. Given the freedom of choice, it gives people the opportunity to improve their material life-style and happiness. Creativity, as discussed earlier in a different context, is the ability to use imagination to develop new products and services. Creativity helps in enhancing human happiness.

Discussing the topic of creativity, design-thinking and economics, an artist-entrepreneur said:

> The term business economics should be perceived as economics of creativity and innovation in commerce. Every product or service is a creative work—a distilled, compact and packaged work of art. Creative inputs come from many sources. There is no greater art than the art of commerce, more so in the current hyper-competitive ever changing environment. Curiosity and creativity help in activating dormant, perishable economic resources. In the current fast moving economic system, we need to think of economics of creativity, as creative design-thinking and innovation on-the-go.
>
> Having worked in industry, I would like to caution you, please do not underestimate the agony, hardships and failures that go into creating new, successful products. To be creative means

getting out of one's comfort zone and learning to operate in a complex, uncomfortable and uncertain situations. In business, creative ideas have to pass through many techno-economic filters. It can be a very frustrating and iterative process. Navigating and managing creativity through various structured as well as dynamic business disciplines is itself a very creative management exercise.

Along with various internal and external changes, the business platforms and paradigms are changing at an increasing speed. The life-styles of consumers are changing. The markets have become multi-cultural. The consumption patterns of products-services mix are changing. The traditional brand-bonding with customers are changing fast. Life cycle of business models, products, services and business strategies is becoming shorter. Managers have to think-creatively, act-creatively and present creative products in a creative way to technology savvy customers on-the-go.

As will be discussed in the next chapter, in the current unforgiving business environment, creative management, in fact, on-the-go creative management, is an imperative for business survival and growth.

Creativity: The New Invisible Economic Resource

Creativity is an invisible economic resource. Creativity transforms innovative ideas into socially useful and commercially viable products and services. It is, thus, a prime mover of social change, economic development and future aspirations.

Entrepreneurs may also be seen as creative economists. Making use of economic resources, artists create art on canvas. Sculptors create sculptures. Entrepreneurs create socially useful products and wealth. Artists, musicians and sculptors have the option of working under undisturbed conditions at their own pace and with their own rules. Business entrepreneurs work in noisy, complex, multi-cultural and competitive markets and disruptive environments, within the confines of prescribed rules and regulations.

Discussing the relationship between creativity and commerce, a senior art critic said:

> Commerce and the so-called creative arts have very close relationships. The super-rich invest their wealth in creative items such as paintings, sculptures, jewellery and other items from museums and galleries. Creative designer-products have high market value. Commerce provides value to art. Even artists do not know how their art is evaluated or how it is priced. The invisible hand of economics has an invisible role in pricing the invisible creative thinking and activities like art objects.

From a market perspective, there are also many similarities between the products of creative arts and those of commerce. Both make use of experience, imagination and instincts. Cost and creativity are integral part of both. Creative and innovative thinking are an integral part of designing contextual business processes, products and services, as well as art items. The challenge for both is in using their creative talents in contextual and creative ways to survive and grow in a given market. Customers are the life-line for both.

Caselet 9.3

A Creative Adventure: Traditional to Modern

During festive shopping, Uma was surprised by the price difference between some of the very labour intensive traditional cultural items and those mass produced by machines. She wondered why the labour intensive traditional cultural items should be so low priced. On enquiry, she came to know that, besides some other reasons, the limited market and limited traditional designs were critical constraints.

She wondered about overcoming the traditional limitations and expanding the business in a simple way, incurring minimal costs. The artisans were located in rural areas, away from commercial cities. The commercial traders often used the distant and isolated locations of producers to suppress prices of traditional goods.

She wondered whether she could help the traditional artisans enter the competitive global business arenas. She wanted to explore creative use of digital technologies. Adopting it as a class project, she presented her views in class:

- She wanted to create a website where individual artisans could display their products. Her plan included:
    - The website would be like an artisan department store.
    - Artisans would be able to display their past, current and future product designs.
    - The site would be interactive.
    - The prices would not be displayed. Potential buyers would have to bid for the products.
    - A fixed percentage of sales would accrue to website entrepreneur.
- Branches of Cooperative Grameen Bank would facilitate:
    - Finance for business operations of artisans.
    - Local, national and international financial transactions.
- Since some artisans were located in remote areas, for delivery of products to customers, artisans would make use of the postal department.
    - Appropriate arrangements would be made with postal department.
    - Products would be insured.
    - Delivery would be assured within a time-frame.
- She also wanted to explore possibilities of introducing information about this pre-industrial age community and creative experiences to knowledge-era consumers.

She was keen to create a platform for artisans and a simple, customer focused business model. She was curious to know from the class whether she was on the right track. She was also keen to know about other options that may be available.

*****

Disruptions in business arenas become critical when they impact relationships between business organisations and their customers. Increasingly, that critical link is through the mobile phone screens. Business organisations have to find creative, credible and interesting ways to create space for their products and services in the new mobile life-style of their customers. Creative strategies have to be designed to attract and retain the interest of customers. Real-time understanding of the shopping journey and decision cycle of customers is essential.

Creativity, by nature, is future focused. In the prevailing, fast changing, socio-economic environment, there is a critical need for imaginative and creative management thinking. Curiosity, questioning, intuitive thinking and the quest for imaginative solutions are integral parts of individual and corporate creativity enhancement. Business is becoming more and more of a risk infested competitive game.

Discussing the need for creativity and innovations in the world of commerce, a senior business consultant said:

> I feel creativity and innovations happen everywhere in business. How can a business unit survive unless it keeps pace with change? Change is a natural process. No one can stop it. With change, customers change, and the expectations of customers change. Change and creativity go hand-in-hand. To cope with accelerated, multi-faced changes, we need accelerated, multi-faceted inputs of creativity.

Creativity is a mind game. Creativity, in multi-cultural fast changing business arenas, is a process of contextual observations, awareness, listening, curiosity and questioning, as well as of instincts and intuitions. Creativity is a sensitive, emotional and highly perishable economic resource. Creative talent and creative processes need to be managed creatively.

Caselet 9.4

Creating a Learning Story: *Acting the Roles*

During informal interactions with a few executives of an international bank, Rishu came to know that due to a *variety* of reasons a number of banks were faced with "bad-debt problems", that is, non-performing loans or debts which cannot be recovered. These are usually associated with business failures.

Rishu recalled a quotation of Bill Gates, "It's fine to celebrate success, but it is more important to heed the lessons of failure." As a student of business administration, he foresaw a good learning opportunity in non-performing loans.

He wanted to share his views in class:

- How students could use "bad-debt" cases as learning opportunities.

- He was sure that at least in some cases, students may be able to come up with some alternate solutions to revive non-performing loans.

- After discussing with some of his classmates, he felt confident that business schools and banks could collaborate in the study and revival of some non-performing loan cases.
  - It would provide very useful, real-life learning opportunity for students.
  - Banks would benefit from new ideas and the creative energy of students.

- To test their creative abilities, along with some of his classmates, Rishu and his team were keen to study and adopt a "bad-debt" case for revival.

- The team identified a non-performing loan case with the bank.
  - It was a private construction company that had taken loan from the bank to construct a small shopping complex, but was in difficult times due to

◊ Litigation with some clients.
◊ Slowdown of business, in general
○ By interacting with the different individuals involved, they felt that they would be able to resolve the issue by:
◊ Re-engineering the loan
◊ Transform the shopping complex into a co-operative venture.
- They presented their case study to the class and also requested the business school Dean to explore possibilities of creating more such learning opportunities for students by:
○ Strategic learning alliances with some banks
○ Create a student-faculty learning group of bad-debt cases
○ Explore appropriate acquisition and merger (A&M) possibilities for non-performing business units.
○ Create a "Faculty, student & alumni business consultancy group".

Rishu and his team invited feedback from the class.

*****

Creativity and the Business Score-Card

Can or should creativity be an item on the score-card of business units? A score-card is used to evaluate performance vis-à-vis a specified goal. To be purposeful, the score-card must be contextual as well as activity specific. While indicating the past performance it must also provide guidance for future actions also. Creativity is the core competency in the knowledge-era. Since creativity is a Critical Success Factor (CSF), its needs and availability status must also be reflected on the corporate score-cards.

Each business is unique. Each business has its own set of 5W+H considerations. Business units must plan according to their own circumstances. Each business must contextualise its strategic design-thinking and performance norms as well as its score-card. Score-card has to evaluate and reflect business performance from the perspective of the dynamics of context as well as business objectives.

Each score-card must also provide inputs to analyse and create an opportunity to pause, think and reflect. Besides informing stakeholders, business score-cards must also guide business managers in re-crafting the future of their business. For on-the-go customers, on-the-move value-creation and value-proposition enhancement has to be planned and executed by creative managers.

Financial results sum up the operational health of business organisations. Business is an open-ended process. Financial results reflect the past. Creativity is futuristic. In a fast changing business environment, future focus, contextual innovation and creative capabilities are of critical importance.

As we move from industrial-era to digital-era, depending on the nature and scope of business, a comprehensive business score-card should indicate:

Financial performance: Different financial ratios are used to analyse and gain insightful understanding of financial performance.

Customer bonding: Because of the multi-faceted changes in customers' shopping behaviour and their expectations, the life-line of most business organisations is under stress. Customer loyalty shifts may happen unexpectedly and impact the commercial health of the organisation. Continuous health monitoring is essential.

Evaluating customer digital links: Business organisations operate in a dynamic, fuzzy and foggy environments. Along with the data of sales, business organisations need to evaluate *trust-bonding* with their customers. The situation is complicated by use of diverse digital apps by customers and organisations.

Real-time monitoring: Appropriate use of digital technologies can provide real-time inflow of customer data. Understanding significance of each touch point of customer in their shopping journey is essential. This is true for business-to-business (B2B) as well as for business-to-customer (B2C) marketing operations.

Real-time evaluation: With options of speed of data collection, analytical and predictive tools, it is possible to monitor and evaluate decision making pattern of customers.

Front-line critical and creative thinking: The competitive advantages of a business organisation originates on the front-lines. Critical observation and appropriate creative response to challenges at the front-line would provide sustainability to business operations. Digital technologies provide options for real-time monitoring and evaluating options.

Future thinking: This involves developing alternate future scenarios. While consolidating today's advantages, business organisations must prepare for tomorrow. While *following* customers, business units must also experiment with creatively *leading* customers, thus exploring their own future. This must be evaluated and recorded. This also provides sources for organisational learning and creative future planning.

Customer and core-process focus: For appropriate and speedy response to various changes in the shopping behaviour of their customers, the core-processes of business organisations need to be in dynamic sync with the life-styles of their customers. Monitoring, evaluation and continuous optimisation of synergy between customer relationship management (CRM) processes and enterprise resource planning (ERP) systems is essential.

Evaluating awareness, agility and creativity: In a fast changing business environment, a continuous corporate learning strategy to be aware, agile and creative would ensure appropriate business health. Depending on the nature of business operations, it may be evaluated on the basis of:

Awareness: Providing early warning or indicters of changes in consumer behaviour as well as external environment.

Agility: Keeping different divisions informed of the need for improving and aligning productivity, processes and systems.

Creativity: Analyse and indicate areas where new values may be added for customers. Periodic evaluation of corporate creativity abilities, capacities and competencies is essential.

Creative communication strategy: Communication strategy is usually designed to reinforce corporate-customer bonding. Globalisation and social media have created various new creative challenges in designing comprehensive, multi-cultural communication strategies.

Resilient and responsive core-processes and organisation architecture: The score-card must indicate the systemic and structural health of the organisation. Along with learning culture, organisations need resilient and responsive systems to remain competitive. This can also be an evidence based evaluation. Efficiencies can be measured and evaluated.

Moving as an integrated unit: To be in tune with the changing shopping behaviour and expectations of customers, it is critical that organisations move as an integrated system.

A continuous creative journey: Business is a journey of continuous creativity. For sustainable competitiveness, business organisations need to constantly evaluate their creative capabilities.

Moving up the creativity spiral: To remain on the cutting edge of technology, business organisations have to constantly move up the creativity spiral.

Customer fatigue: Life-cycles of products, services and interest-spans of customers are reducing. Customers are constantly exploring for enhanced value products and services.

Corporate systems fatigue: Working in a competitive environment, corporate systems also come under stress. Managers need to be aware of corporate systems stress levels.

Besides the above factors, based on the continuous assessment of political, economic, social and technological (PEST) environment and being aware of the dynamics of one's strengths, weaknesses, opportunities and threats (SWOT), business managers need to use score-cards as a guide to move up the value-chain for their customers.

In a disruptive, fast changing, business environment, the *irrelevance-gap* between the past and the future increases unexpectedly. Constant *relevance* monitoring of data, information and knowledge is essential. This would also apply to business score-cards. Unlike other sports and games, business is a continuous, perpetually changing, long-lasting, socio-economic process. It needs continuous creative renewal.

While reading business score-cards, to get a more comprehensive understanding of performance, we need to take account of the current as well as the long-term, futuristic and sustainable perspective of the organisation.

Organisations are living, creative organisms. To judge them only by limited financial score-card score may often give misleading information. How the creative energies of an organisation are nurtured and optimised is the challenge for creative managers. This will be discussed in detail in the next chapter. The challenge is also how to measure them in the score-card.

Creativity a Low-Cost High-Value Adding Renewable Resource

It is often said that there is no such a thing as a "free-lunch" in economics. However, there are some very valuable human talents and capabilities which cannot flourish in *system-strong* organisations. What if those talents can be cultivated with minimal *spare-time* efforts? Or, just as experimental managerial challenges? From a business perspective would we be justified to think of *creativity* as an *almost free* and renewable resource?

In business context, creative thinking may be viewed as a mindset — a creative solution seeking mindset. Just a change in attitude, just being curious and asking appropriate questions, one can be creative with whatever one has and whatever one may be doing. To be creative, organisations do not require anything other than what they already have — people. All that the organisation requires is *seeding* of curiosity, nurturing of questions and creative management.

Some managers assume "know-all" postures and try to control every aspect of the business process. Others nurture creativity at all levels of the organisation. It is for the management to decide whether to adopt a "do-as-told" or "think-and-share" policy and adopt a learn-together manage-together policy. The potential of creativity is present in every organisation. To use it or not is the management's decision. In that sense, it may not be wrong to view creativity as a *free resource* for management.

Human beings are creative by nature. Business organisations are organised and managed by people and for people. Even when working in a strict "do-as-told" system, human beings observe and know the weaknesses of the system they operate in. To improve or to make the system more efficient, managements have the option to get an outside expert advice on payment or activate the dormant *inactive* creative energy in the organisation. To activate the internal creativity process, managements just have to *seed* curiosity and adopt a creative management approach.

People working in commercial units assimilate a variety of information pertaining to their defined and demarcated scope of work, as well as about the overall business operations. In many situations, all that managements may have to do is to encourage creative talent of the corporate team members to become customer focused.

By initiating, nurturing and harnessing dormant corporate creative talent, corporate managements will have more options for developing competitive advantages and aiming for excellence in their areas of operations. Creativity creates opportunities and designs strategies. It does not wait for opportunity — it creates its own path.

A Flashback

Spiritual Creativity in an Organisation

During my quest to understand the role of creativity in business organisations, I had good fortune to interact with a *Swami ji* (spiritual guru). He was also a visiting faculty at some business schools. To my very first query he said with a smile, "Creativity is the essence of life. Business organisations are living organisms. Creativity and life go together."

Economics of Creativity in Commerce 237

I was curious to know more. I asked, "If business organisations are living organisms, can *business* organisations be spiritual?" Again he smiled and said, "I think, all living being are spiritual. But we all differ in our perceptions and degree of spirituality."

I was more curious and more confused. I asked him again, "*Swami ji*, can we visualise, feel or assess spirituality?" He asked me to elaborate my question. I said, "Is there a way to experience spirituality or measure it? *Swami ji*, I am sorry to be so crude in my choice of words, but is there a way to know, calculate and say that one *business* organisation is *more spiritual* than the other?"

He answered:

> Professor, you have asked me a difficult question. I do not know whether I will be able to answer it fully. Spirituality is very subjective, personal and has many facets. Each living being is unique. In our present context, I think I can only try to provide some indications. I will try to create some dots. You will have to connect the dots in your own context and create your own spiritual pattern. Also, you have to develop your own definition and scale to measure levels of spirituality. Try it as an experiment. It may be a good learning experience.
>
> In our present context, let us take a simple approach to spirituality. Organisations are living beings. All living beings have at least four characteristics—*physical* structure, *intelligence* or mind, various kinds of *emotions* and creative *energies*. Business organisations exist in a context, community and political, social, economic and technological environment. As for individuals, so also for organisations, *vasudheva kutumbhakam* (world is a family) would be a valid perception.
>
> Spirituality may also be seen as an attitude—being aware, appreciative, empathetic, but unattached. A spiritual person is a mindful seeker, a seeker of truth, seeking to be aware and to know who we are, seeking to be in harmony with surroundings, seeking to be connected with context and beyond. Business organisations also need to be aware, in harmony and be connected with their customers as well as other stakeholders. They have to be in search of ways

to enhance purposefulness of their business purpose and happiness of their customers and mankind in sustainable ways.

Each living being is unique. I think, a student of management should be able to develop an appropriate, contextual, measuring unit or matrix for corporate awareness, mindfulness, harmony and connectedness for an organisation, besides developing measuring units for a business organisation's physical assets and systems, human-human and human-machine relations. In addition, it should be possible to measure mindfulness or attitude of the corporate team towards the purpose of the business organisation, emotional involvement of corporate personnel towards corporate goals, how corporate creative energy is nurtured, as well as used to make business purpose more purposeful for customers and society.

Please keep in mind, business is a continuous dynamic process. It is conducted in an ever changing, multi-cultural, dynamic physical and cyber environments. So, as in our own life, spirituality in business organisations may also be seen as a continuous, dynamic, balancing process between internal and external systems and operations. Business organisations need to be continuously *mindful* of their business purpose and customers, as well as *connected* with their business associates, stakeholders and surroundings. The corporate team celebrates joys of their life through commitment to business purpose and happiness of their customers.

You may recall some of the dialogues in Gita between Arjun and Krishna. These are question-answer sessions between a human and an *avatar* and are initiated by Arjun's search for duty, purpose and *dharma*. I think, business units must also stay in similar questioning mode with the society in which they operate. As living, social organisms, business units need to think of themselves as an integral part of society in which they operate. They need to question themselves and define their own social purpose and *dharma* for themselves and the society in which they operate.

Have I confused you? Or have I been of some help in understanding the dynamic nature of corporate spiritual dots? Try to link the dots of corporate spirituality to create a meaningful and purposeful pattern or an image of a "corporate soul"? Please try to visualise and experience it. Think, discuss with others and try to identify the dots and create different patterns. Keep trying from different perspectives.

I hope I have been able to present the essence of Swami ji's thoughts.

Perhaps, to gain an understanding of the above stated concepts, some students may like to develop a "spiritual matrix" for an organisation of their choice and discuss it in the class. I would also like to explore further and develop the above concepts.

*****

Social-Capital: A Synergistic By-Product

Social-capital or camaraderie is a very valuable by-product of creative and design-thinking culture and creative management initiatives. Social-capital is mutual trust, appreciation and understanding between corporate team players. Informal individual bonds, small informal initiatives and proactive contextual improvisations often transform organisations. All these are living and dynamic components of social-capital.

Social-capital may also be seen as a customer and business focused *social-network* within organisations or a social-bonding that facilitates business operations. It is an informal social-network based on mutual trust, reciprocity, shared interests, shared-learning, information and knowledge. It is the result of the shift from "I" to "we" perception. It is a glue that bonds a team or the mortar that holds corporate bricks together.

Creative problem solving and design-thinking encompass exploring alternate options, sharing of diverse views and perspectives, which often result in *creative-conflict* situations. It creates awareness and mindful understanding between different activity experts as they experience the value of others. They learn to value the value of others. This creates *value-bonding* between the organisation's team players and enhances quality of social-capital.

Unknowns, surprises, complexity and ambiguity are basic features of cooperative multi-disciplinary search for creative value-adding solutions. As will be discussed in the next chapter, blending diverse creative ideas and options into appropriate contextual value-adding solutions is an integral part of creative management. Each creative conflict resolution generates shared-learning and forms the building block of organisational social-capital. Finding commercially viable solutions in a dynamic, multi-cultural world requires participative design-thinking. Creativity and design-thinking develop corporate-stories where every corporate team member has a role.

In the present context, social-capital may also be viewed as value-adding contextual information and knowledge-sharing teams in search of common creative solutions. At micro level, it may be a team of a department such as procurement, operations, finance or marketing. At the macro corporate level, it may be teams sharing their vantage point perceptions with other teams for overall business solutions. Corporate social-capital results in coordinated departmental teams. Corporations operate as a team-of-teams, all with a common objective to enhance the purposefulness of business purpose.

Creativity and social-capital are interdependent as well as synergistic. The co-operative creative problem solving process creates social-capital, and search for creative value-adding solutions becomes more effective with appropriate social-capital. In the globalised multi-cultural environment, social-capital is a critical constituent of organisational culture, as well as in the evolutionary process of the corporate-soul.

While use of dormant, creativity talents of employees provides direct benefits in rationalisation of costs and timely re-enforcement of customer bonds, there are also some indirect benefits. The benefits include:

> *Participative management*: The policy to invite creative ideas from employees gives rise to idea sharing and a participative culture in the organisation. This policy creates more committed and harmonious corporate environment.

Reputation management: Aware, committed and customer focused employees help in creating a favourable reputation of organisation.

Motivated employees: As employees get involved in the organisation operations and realise that their observations and ideas matter, they would be more motivated. This will result in better overall performance from employees as well as of the organisation.

Aware employees: Idea and thought sharing opportunities would make employees more aware of their role and will be reflected in their interactions with customers, colleagues, business partners, as well as general public. Aware employees would also act as business intelligence bases as well as early warning systems as they encounter dissatisfaction within the organisation or with customers.

Change agents: Committed employees would become change agents and see change and growth of their organisations as an opportunity for themselves.

Loyal employees: As employees feel more engaged, involved and responsible, their attachment with job and organisation will increase.

Improved corporate health: With more aware and involved employees, corporate-customer bonding will improve, which would result in better business performance and a healthier corporation.

Cost fitness: With market, competition and performance aware employees, the organisation will become cost aware and remain cost-fit as well as cost competitive.

Appropriate business model and technology options: Competition and competitors aware employees will proactively suggest and promote appropriate restructuring of business operations and use of appropriate technology options.

Proactive cost-benefit analysis: Aware corporate team members would proactively be concerned about the cost-benefit balance of activities.

Navigating the Organisation: To navigate the corporation, products and services in a turbulent, multi-cultural, fast changing business environment, it would be advantageous for the management to have cooperation of creative corporate team.

Excellence competition focus: Operating in proactive and creative business culture, employees would desire a more holistic, long-term healthy organisation. This would also make them proactive in continuously learning and career development; developing the organisation as they develop themselves.

From the economic perspective, the question to-be or not-to-be a creative manager seems irrelevant. Whether one thinks of traditional industries or digital-technology industries, business-as-usual or management-as-usual is no longer an option. For their survival and growth, business organisations need to activate their organisational creativity. As will be discussed in the next chapter, in the prevailing disruptive VUCA environment, creative management is a strategic imperative for business organisations.

*****

Creative Management: *A Role Play*

Select any company from any industry. As its new CEO, you are keen to create a sustainable, creative ecosystem in your organisation.

- Please give a business and organisational profile of your selected organisation.
- Please discuss economics of your approach.
- Please give business and commercial reasons for selection of your approach and strategy.
- Would you focus on competitiveness or excellence? Why?
- Identify some critical success factors.
- Identify and analyse factors which may tend to disrupt sustainability of your approach.

- Also, please suggest ways how artificial intelligence or digital technology systems may be used to enhance sustainability of creative ecosystem.
- How would you measure or evaluate your economic success?

*****

10

It's not the strongest of species who survive, nor the most intelligent, but the ones most responsive to change.

Charles Darwin

Creative Management

Success is celebrated. It creates heroes. It has many visible and invisible designers, diverse causes and many contributors. Each success has unique context, reasons and creative design-thinking mix. However, at times, success is a "back-swan", an unexpected event, even for the winners.

Success is result of past acts. Does success have a relevant message for the volatile, uncertain, complex and ambiguous (VUCA) future? Is it end of an innovation-creativity cycle?

How does one define success in business? A new revenue generating product or service? A new cost effective business model? A well negotiated deal? What is the life-span of success in business? What do business organisations celebrate when they celebrate success?

Each success has a complex chain of decisions associated with it. Also, different elements of mystery are associated with each decision.

Success in business is designed by creative efforts of the past. It is often assisted by learnings from on-the-way failures. It is an evolutionary development—a contextual, creative and customer-focused process.

Creative Management Imperatives

To create future success stories, organisations need to unlearn and relearn, face moments of chaos, re-contextualise, and re-start with zero-based thinking. New success needs new ideas, new creative and innovative thinking and a new contextual and creative management approach.

Business is a dynamic, complex, creative, continuous and ever changing process. It is also a chain of experiments. To be in tune with change, as living organisms, business organisations need to inhale-in future and exhale-out the past. As discussed in earlier chapters, unless appropriately managed, present success in business may mark the beginning of future failure.

Many known and unknown factors are associated with decisions that create success in business. Business processes may also be visualised as dynamic success-failure mix operations. Success introduces managers to the market, failures give them an opportunity for insightful understanding of themselves. Managers need to analyse, learn and move-on.

Making decisions is an integral part of management. However, we do not yet have a generally agreed upon criteria to *evaluate* decisions. How does one evaluate decisions when they are made? We normally judge decisions by results. A winner is *assumed* to have made the right decisions. Winners are almost always right. *Sabal ko nahi dosh gusai* (Strong have no faults).

In a fast changing business environment, each business decision has elements of probability, possibility and chance. Luck — the unknown x-factor — often plays a very critical role in success. Success, however defined or measured, has a limited life-span. In the open-ended, creative and dynamic business process, it is just an event — an on-the-way happening or a milestone or a situation to pause and reconsider future options. Whatever the causes, success is the result of *past* decisions. Creative decisions are futuristic. Creative management is future focused and is an imperative for sustainability of success.

In the uncertain and unforgiving business environment, effective use of imagination and creative abilities by corporate team members is a critical success factor. Creativity is a mind game. However well designed the rules and policies of an organisation may be, their final implementation rests with the individual team members. Managerial ability to initiate and nurture innovative as well as creative capabilities of employees is a critical competitive advantage. Dynamic and synergistic alignment of creative-right-brains and logical-left-brains of corporate team members is an integral part of creative management.

Business leaders are perpetually searching for answer to the question—How to design a proactively learning, creative and continuously innovative organisation? How to create sustainable, creative and dynamic customer-focused business processes? Creative management process includes contextual synthesis of creative and analytical thinking.

The globalised interdependent world is flat. For some industries, geography and locations have become less important. Competitiveness does not depend on where you are but how good you are. The bits and bytes of digital technology can effectively bite from any part of the world. The new business models are very disruptive. Faced with the business disruptions from different known and unknown competitors, business managers are critically re-evaluating their options, some from zero-based perspectives. Various constructs of creative management are becoming integral parts of corporate thinking. New multi-faceted cross-cultural challenges call for new contextual creative management thinking. Various forms of creative management paradigms are evolving.

To navigate business operations through diverse, uncertain, globalised, multi-cultural and information empowered environment, managers not only need to be aware of their current situations but also the consequences of their decisions. For some organisations, every act may have a global reaction. Real-time feedback, proactive resilience and agility are essential. Managers need creative ability, agility and creative resources to restructure their value propositions and bounce back faster than their competitors.

The new combinations of ideas, internet and digital technologies, are challenging conventional business operations in many different ways. New threats and opportunities are arising from digitisation of business activities. There is need to rethink about traditional business processes as well as management theories and philosophies. Industrial-era management or business-as-usual is no longer an option. In a fast changing VUCA business environment, zero-based critical and creative thinking is essential. New, contextual and appropriate creative management paradigm is an imperative.

For most business organisations, the opportunities and options, risks and rewards, as well as swiftness and dynamics in the markets have increased many folds. Start-ups can bite even before they become visible. Many new unknowns have emerged in the business arenas. Markets have become very uncertain and unforgiving. To ride the disruptive waves, harness new technologies and re-design traditional business models, creative design-thinking and creative management approaches are essential.

While VUCA, diversity, pace and risks have increased manifold, the business objectives are the same—enhancing purposefulness of purpose for customers and enlarging business growth options. The digital technologies and global connectivity are creating new challenges. The same technologies and globalisation also offer many new options and innovative solutions, thus the enhanced need for creative management. The premise of creative management is the belief that every team member in the organisation and associated with the business process, counts. Also, that customers are an integral part of corporate creative-design-thinking and creative management operations.

Creative management is also about *seeding* curiosity. It is a process of nurturing and harvesting creativity in every facet of business operations, being aware and encouraging proactive questioning and learning by employees and contextual shared learning. As discussed in earlier chapters, a design-thinking approach helps in integration of diverse perspectives as well as in developing synergistic, value enhancing bonds between different departments. All this is done while remaining purpose and customer focused.

To create a sustainable base for corporate creativity, creative aspirations of individual employees need to be creatively aligned with corporate purpose. This means creating a business purpose focused, creative challenge for creative managers.

Caselet 10.1

Sowing Seeds of Creativity and Synergising Network

During high school days, Rishi had done some social work in rural areas. While a student of business administration, he wondered whether a rural village or a set of closely located villages, could be visualised as a potential business unit. Would seeding of curiosity and creative thinking bring about transformation in economically under performing, sleepy villages? Could he initiate a mix of business and social objectives in the venture?

To get an understanding of the potential developmental opportunities, he had discussions with local banks, microfinance companies and some NGOs engaged in socio-economic development work. He was looking for ways to motivate villagers to facilitate acceptance of the change he was planning to introduce. He was keen to "seed" curiosity and creativity in the minds of residents. He wanted to make residents proactive in their development efforts. He wanted to explore possibilities of *seeding* curiosity, initiating and *evolving* an economic development process.

To sow seeds of curiosity and provoke desire for *change-and-gain*, he thought of some simple developmental changes like:

- Along with traditional agricultural practices, farmers could also explore possibilities of planting medicinal plants or flowers. He had created marketing systems for both items.

- He thought about the possibilities of using simple ways to add value to the traditional products produced by the farmers and artisans.

- He had visualised plans to sow seeds of curiosity in specific traditional livelihood and agricultural areas and then link them in a synergistic way to evolve cooperative business models.

- To start with, he thought about developing poultry, animal husbandry and handicrafts.
- As there was significant distance between the villages and nearest town, he thought about upgrading of educational and technical training facilities.
- As set of villages he had selected had a picturesque location, he also thought about the possibilities of developing a simple:
  - Mind-body-soul retreat for busy urban dwellers.
  - A simple low-cost back-to-nature mind-body-soul retreat:
    - To disconnect from technology addictions — a digital detox.
    - Yoga and meditation facilities.
    - Simple nutritive organic food.

As he prepared to present his project in class, which he wanted to use as his learning platform, he wondered:

- How should he "seed" curiosity and creativity in the villagers?
  - Who should be the first target group?
  - Which stories or methods should he use to create curiosity?
  - How and where should he arrange informal meetings?
  - How could he make use of a design-thinking approach?
- Should he:
  - Form a single team? Or,
  - Create a network of local people for different activities?
- Starting from class, should he also think of the project and prepare for it as:
  - An after university career venture? Or
  - Just as a class project?

Creative Management 251

- What are the opportunities for him to make economic use of digital technologies to achieve his goals?
- He was aware that this was not a traditional business development project, but a socio-economic development project.
- Can it be visualised as a "start-up" business venture?
  - A hybrid social-business enterprise?
  - Is there a business model for him in this venture?

He was keen to get feedback from his class on his overall thinking.

*****

Creativity and Business-Discipline Dynamics

Creativity is generally associated with limitless freedom. Business is a controlled and disciplined activity. It is a competitive game of products and services, as well as costs and revenues. In a turbulent, fast changing, business environment, managers need more effective control mechanisms. In such a disruptive situation, is there a need and place for new, creative, management thinking? Are there any possibilities, at all, of adding value by contextual creative thinking?

Change is accelerating. Managers need to be aware, closely listen to the sounds of the markets, comprehend fast analysis of relevant data, and sharpen intuitions and gut instincts. Before acting, managers need a clear understanding of the nature of change and competition. To be meaningful, the creative business decisions must match the speed of on-the-go customers clicking their mobile phone buttons. Can creative management mitigate the risks involved?

Navigating business operations through digital disruptions is an integral part of creative management. As discussed earlier in the book, with the full cooperation of their corporate teams, creative managers know how to enhance sharpness of their business focus, design appropriate controls to enhance the value of creativity and also synergise the creativity-discipline mix. Like the continuous business process, to be effective, creativity in business must be a continuous process, too. There is a need to instil questioning and creative design-thinking into the DNA of the corporate culture. To move up to more insightful competitive levels, creativity must create its own continuity.

Seeding curiosity, creating and managing clash of ideas, high-speed analysis and synthesis, as well as executing ideas efficiently are essential parts of creative management. In a fast changing, uncertain, business environment, where competitors are relentlessly prowling for new markets, besides protecting their business turfs, corporations need to proactively spot new opportunities and transform opportunities into reality by generating and testing new ideas, products and services, to give enhanced value to their customers. There is a need for a new, creative business culture, with new skill sets and mindsets. To be commercially effective, corporate creativity must be customer focused, disciplined and operate within defined business parameters.

In business operations, customer focus is essential. At times, managers may have to be very narrowly focused on a business issue or an activity, without losing the overall business perception. There is an increasing need for a holistic, mindful, creative management, where creativity contributes in creating new value propositions for business.

Traditional Management Wisdom and New Realities

The industrial-era rules of business have changed and are further changing at an accelerated pace. Digital technologies are transforming industrial-era organisations. Life-styles and work-styles are changing. Information empowerment of customers, e-commerce options and on-the-move mobile phone connectivity are transforming business-customer relations. In many cases, technology is defining customers' shopping options. Business at the speed-of-thought is becoming the norm. There is a need to reinvent management.

Artificial intelligence enriched self-learning machines and remote controlled robots are taking over skilled jobs in many industries. High speed data gathering and computing power enriched predictive analytics are becoming effective decision support systems for business managers. Life cycle of products, services and even business success is reducing fast. Creative ability to transform ideas into commercially successful products and services is the new competitive advantage.

Digital technologies are impacting every phase of business as well as management processes. Cyberspace, internet and social media have introduced many new unknowns in the business arenas. Even one unsatisfied customer in a remote part of the world can create a global impact. Business managers have to learn the new cyber business language, nature of risks, as well as new ways of doing business. A new creative mindset is needed to design and manage the dynamic mix of cyberspace business operations with traditional physical space business processes.

To cope with multi-faceted changes, there is an urgent need for industrial-era organisations to reinvent themselves and *knowledgise* their operations. Commercial units need to become learning, creative and innovative organisations. Along with new wealth-creating creative strategies, there is a need for new, appropriately designed, contextual, flexible, learning, organisational architecture. To stay relevant and profitable, there is a need for new creative management thinking.

Along with the need for new attitude, skills and knowledge, we also need to reconsider role of strategy in business operations. When entrepreneurs start their ventures, strategy is an integral part of their business process planning. Every enterprise was once a "start-up". As business units expand and different functions take on specialised roles, strategy planning and implementation also emerges as a specialisation. With the advent of digital-era and globalisation, the nature and rules of business are changing. We need to rethink the role of management as well as strategy in the prevailing dynamic, fast changing context.

Even if managements were to go by the traditional industrial-era approach, in the prevailing fast changing and disruptive business environment, to answer the old strategy question—*Where do you want to go*—managements would need to know *where they are*. They need to keep in mind the costs, risks and anticipated gains, before deciding *where they would like to be* and *when*. Business managers must know *where they are* and *how* will they get there? The future is fuzzy. Business would have to navigate through disruptive VUCA environment. Strategy designers need to rethink their traditional roles.

In the present context, where digital technology innovations can impact every activity in the business network, traditional strategy planners would have to ask many more questions before they can initiate the strategy formulation process—questions such as: How can the current competitive position be evaluated? How can the current *overall* business position vis-à-vis competitors be known? How can we decide where to go? Time frame? Cost? Risks? With fuzzy targets and uncertain strategic roadmaps, creative management becomes an imperative.

A Short Story

What Do We Do after Success?

Sitting in a university lawn, some business students were considering options of what to do with their spare time. They had a spare day but no activity plans. The university was located in the outskirts of city. They were faced with the traditional strategy questions—*Where to go? How to get there?*

Someone suggested they should go to the city. He also named the target place. All happily agreed. Almost immediately, an animated debate started on *how to get there*. Many ideas and counter ideas were presented. There were some strong disagreements. Some ego issues also cropped up.

One student convincingly presented his somewhat complex proposition. It involved taking a few interconnected bus routes rather than simpler ways presented by others. As he concluded his presentation to the group, he confidently said, "If you follow my plan you will save 15 minutes."

A student, who had been quiet throughout the discussions, shouted, "Eureka!" Then, he politely asked him and the group, "But, what will we do with the 15 minutes which we will save?"

For few moments, there was a total silence. They looked at one another and then everyone burst out laughing. Many business organisations face this dilemma. What to do after success? This is the usual 5W+H question.

*****

Success and Creative Management

From the creative management perspective, success and failure may be visualised as two sides of the same coin. For their next step, both require re-validation of their context, un-learning and re-learning attitude, zero-based evaluation of new options, and a new creative design-thinking approach.

In an open-ended, continuous, creative, business process, how should *success* be evaluated? By calculating return-on-investments made to create success? How can life-span of success be estimated? How does success impact the future of business? Global business arenas are graveyards of *once successful* corporations. Does success in business create barriers for future success? Who creates them? How? Why? When? Where?

Keeping corporate creativity alive, ignited and focused is an integral part of creative management. Creativity is future focused. Creative management takes a continuous long-term view of the business process. With each passing event, *what-next* is the obvious question. Re-assessing context, options, environment and moving on with appropriate creative strategy is constantly required.

As in other situations, so also in business, success or failure are never final. Success or failure may be perceived as outcomes of short-term creativity cycles, in a long-term continuous business process. Football teams win some games. They lose some. They win tournaments. They lose tournaments. *The game continues*. The teams continue to play. Success and failure are an integral parts of the continuous process. Win or lose, each *next* game is *new*. Each *new* game incorporates *new* contextual, creative, design-thinking. *New* analysis. *New* learnings. *New* strategies.

Why *once* innovative business organisations stop being innovative? Does the answer lie in their attitudes towards success? Do they have a short-term view in a long-term continuous process? What are the alternate ways of celebrating success? Depending on the nature of business and area of success, the alternate ways of perception may include:

End of a creative cycle: Be it innovation of a new product, service or business model, success would indicate just an *end* of a *creative* cycle—and the start of a new one.

Reaching destination: Success may be seen as having reached the *end* of the *journey*. This will merely be an illusion in a long-term operation.

Success in scoring *a goal* does not mark end of a match or a football tournament. Similarly, innovating a new product, service or a business-model does not mark the end of the business journey. Success in scoring a goal just creates a transitory win-lose situation in an open-ended, long-term tournament. It is an unlearning-learning situation for *both* sides.

The results of next round would depend on their attitude—Who learns and unlearns faster and how winners celebrate success and for how long. How losers bounce back is important in the ongoing process. This point, along with other perceptions, is well illustrated in the popular *Panchtrantra's* Hare and the Tortoise story.

Why do people who have failed elsewhere often succeed in business? Why are *once* successful but later failed companies almost a norm in business? Why does present success often gets in the way of future success? Perhaps, business managers often forget that each success is unique—it happened in a specific context, under specific circumstances, and in a given time-frame. Each success is an *end* of a successful creative cycle. New success requires new zero-based creative design-thinking. An approach to continuous success process may include:

Corporate need for continuous customer-focused creative excellence: In a fast changing business environment, business managers need to continuously align their business value propositions with those of the changing expectations and shopping behaviour of their customers. As discussed in earlier chapters, managers need to be fully aware of the competitive challenges as well as opportunities, while being excellence focused.

Learning from success and failures: As a learning organisation, each success and failure in the business should be critically analysed. Each new experience involves learning, unlearning and relearning to be in step with change.

Need to move on: Being over-obsessed with grand success can be fatal. Success tends to create an emotional intoxication. It tends to create blind-spots towards the need for new long-term thinking. Continuing with the same strategy in a changing environment can be very harmful. Often, corporations develop fat, managers create comfort zones and new innovative and creative thinking gets neglected.

Understanding nature of change: Change impacts *every* business activity. Zero-based design-thinking is essential. Success should be seen as an end of a creative cycle. The need to renew creative thinking in the new changed context should be recognised.

Appropriate attitude towards success is important. Managers need to celebrate success, learn and move on. Learnings from the present success should be creatively used for more effective bonding with customers in the future. Continuous, proactive, innovative and creative design-thinking are integral parts of creative management. Creative strategic management has to ensure appropriate corrective actions as well as on-the-move value creation. Strategy must create its own strategy to be continuously flexible, creative and remain customer focused.

Discussing this point, a senior partner of an international management consultancy firm said:

As we know, success has a thousand fathers while failure is an orphan. On the other hand, failure has a thousand lessons while success is often a blank page—a page on which every employee wants to write his or her name.

Success is very difficult to define. In business, what is success—product, service, business-model or the brand value? Brands are often created and sustained by very complex creative processes, with inputs from many experts. Success in the marketplace is dynamic and ever-changing. It has to be creatively nurtured. In competitive markets, targets are fuzzy and dynamic.

As business leaders and organisations get obsessed with celebrations of their success story, they often tend to overlook some critical success factors such as context and creative origins of the success. Like everything else, success has a lifespan. Markets are very unforgiving. By the time organisations realise that their success has lost or is losing its market relevance, their original creative organisational network has withered away due to negligence. In business, creativity is very contextual and very perishable.

In the fast changing VUCA business environment, business managers have to be proactive, creative, as well as multi-focused. Even a short pause may have serious consequences.

Creative managers need to be careful not to get "trapped-in" by history or success. The overall nature and pace of business is changing. Industrial-era is being transformed into information and digital-era. New high-speed knowledge-era thinking is essential. Organisations have to become learning organisations. Creative managers have to make appropriate use of digital technologies. It is time to create a creative and contextual amalgam of creativity, strategy and management functions.

Looking in the rear-view mirror would be of little use, perhaps dangerous, in a fast changing business environment. Business managers need to critically examine and be continuously aware of the creative and disruptive powers of digital technologies and the power of their competitors. Even new "invisible" start-ups in distant parts of the word may prove to be disruptive. Managers have to creatively manage change, unexpected disruptions, as well as continuity. New contextual learning, critical and creative thinking are essential for managers. With the fast shifting scenarios, zero-based thinking becomes essential.

Caselet 10.2

Self-Managed Business Organisations

Having read about self-driven cars, smart roads, smart cities and Internet-of-things (IoT), Rishi, a business student, wondered — why not self-managed business organisations (SMBOs)? He had also read about artificial intelligence (AI), predictive analytics and Enterprise Resource Planning (ERP) software solutions.

He wondered if computers can outsmart the best Chess and Go players in the world and manage interplanetary space ventures, then why "they" cannot be effective business managers? AI systems have high-speed self-learning abilities and almost unlimited memory. AI systems are more *logical* and more *systemic* than human intelligence (HI). Then why can't AI embedded systems manage *simple* cost and revenue streams of business organisations? What and where are the *real* gaps between HI and AI, he wondered?

Why can't AI empowered business organisations create sustainable and creative "commercial partnership" with mobile phone dependent customers? Chess and Go are considered to be very complex and creative games requiring analysis, synthesis and integrative thinking. Business CEOs usually play much simpler games. Then why can't Chess or Go winning computers manage business organisations?

Supplied with appropriate data, can AI systems be designed to:

- Do political, economic, social and technological (PEST) analysis? Why not?

- Do strengths, weakness, opportunities and threats (SWOT) analysis? Why not?
- Keep business organisation customer focused? Why not?
- Generate and analyse customer intelligence, shopping behaviour data, etc.?
- Evaluate customer or brand relationships? Why not?
- If AI systems can suggest "appropriate and corrective" Chess or Go moves, can AI systems suggest "appropriate and corrective" managerial actions? Why not?
- Can AI systems act as creative managers and design-thinkers?
    - If computers can mix and match priorities of king, queen, rooks, bishops, knights and pawns in chess, then why not of procurement, operations, marketing and finance for optimal business results?

Thinking of business realities, he thought of driverless cars. Unlike car drivers on the busy roads, with many new unknowns during rush hours, business managers have:

- Understanding of their business arenas
- Limited number of competitors
- Understanding of the behaviour of their competitors
- Understanding of their customers (Available data)
    - Their location and limitations
    - Their shopping behaviour and options
    - Their needs and priorities
- Manage limited number of variables and objectives
    - Cost minimisation
    - Revenue maximisation
    - Maintain continuity of overall interdependent operations
    - Identify data based growth opportunities
- He wondered, what was more challenging:

Creative Management

- ○ Designing a self-driven car (SDC), or
- ○ Designing a self-managed business organisation (SMBO). Why?
- Could the limits or challenges be identified and defined?

Rishi decided to present his thoughts in his business class. His tentative approach to SMBO included:

- To ask each worker and manager in the organisation to:
  - ○ List his or her officially defined job activities
  - ○ Give source of their *inputs* of
    - ◊ Data and information
    - ◊ Instructions for processing of inputs
  - ○ List out how they *process* their inputs
    - ◊ Logic and skills used
  - ○ List out what they do with the *output* of their work
    - ◊ Who uses the output
    - ◊ Output distribution practices
- With this information, he felt an indicative *framework* of work-process of the organisation could be developed.
- He wondered:
  - ○ Which areas were the problem HI areas for generating data or information for AI systems?
  - ○ What would be the optimal mix of AI and HI in corporate management?
  - ○ If we cannot design SMBOs, is it due to the limitation of our human imagination or of digital technologies?
  - ○ Do we need new principles, processes and practices of management?
  - ○ Do we need new management mindset?
  - ○ Are there future business consultancy start-up opportunities in this idea?

  He requested his class to share their views.

*****

Aware, Mindful and Customer-Focused Creative Management

In VUCA business environment, to manage turmoil one requires an analytical, tranquil and focused mind. How can one be tranquil in turmoil? How can one be comfortable in uncomfortable situations? How can a manager be meditative as well as creative in a dynamic and disruptive business environment?

While discussing this topic, an artist said:

> Creativity is meditation in action. Take a critical look at the players in a football field. Closely watch the goal keeper and the penalty shooter. You will see their very calm, meditative postures in their most competitive, vibrant and creative acts. This is a dynamic mix of thoughtful reflections and cold-blooded actions.

Management is the art and science of finding solutions in disruptive situations. Business solutions require data based analysis, synthesis and integrative thinking. Being calm, creative and meditative is essential. Corporations need dialogue with themselves.

With increasing uncertainties as well as turbulences in the commercial arena, imperatives of on-the-move reflective, meditative and creative management cannot be over emphasised. It is frequently said that solutions evolve from problems. Creative design-thinking helps business units collectively analyse problems and design creative solutions. This is especially important during times of failures.

Discussing this topic, the CEO of a leading retail company said:

> I remember reading once about a famous scientist, perhaps Albert Einstein. He was asked how he would approach to solve a problem on which his life depended, in the given timeframe of one hour. His reply was that he would spend fifty minutes to understand the problem, five minutes to solve it and five minutes to review the solution. Perhaps this is what we have to do in the current VUCA situations.

Explaining the need for meditative, multi-focal decision making in a fast changing business environment, a senior business consultant said:

> To understand the need to incorporate meditative multi-focal thinking in quick decision making, ask a person who has experienced rafting in turbulent waters. Or ask a football goal keeper.
>
> There is no contradiction in being meditative and operating under compulsions of on-the-go, speedy, decision making. Or, being multi-focal in a disruptive fast changing business environment. If customers can make decisions while on-the-move, why can't managers who have to meet their requirements?

As discussed in the earlier chapters, to be of value, creativity in business has to add value at the speed of business operations. The new high speed business game requires new high speed critical and creative design-thinking. Managing disruptions, adding value and reinforcing continuity is the essence of creative management. This designs roadmap to sustainable competitiveness and excellence.

A Short Story

Experiencing Integrative Creative Process

Discussing the role of integrative creativity in management, a senior executive, sharing her personal experience said:

> Some years ago, as a high school student in India, I had the opportunity to accompany my father to attend the commencement programme of a new batch of 120 MBA students at a business school. My father was a visiting faculty there. A large, blank canvas was placed on the stage with many different oil colours on the side. In one of the events, each student was asked to walk up to the stage and make just one stroke of colour on the canvas. Each student was free to choose the colour, the point of initiating their line and

the shape and size of their inputs on the canvas. One by one each new MBA student came on the stage and added their bit. It was a fairly long, but very interesting, process to see the canvas developing, alive with collaborative vibrant colours.

In his welcome speech, the director of the institute, besides various other things, referred to the "cooperative and integrative creation" on the canvas. He advised the students to think of their future career as a proactive, continuous, creative and integrative process. He said that time and again, they will be required to add their creative bit to the overall operations of their organisations. They should try and do it proactively. Whatever the context, they should do their best, as they did today. He advised them that the painting they had created had some value at that time and will increase in value with time. He hoped that, with the learning from this cooperative experience, they would keep adding new value in their learning at the school as well as their future careers and lives.

He advised the students to think of themselves as creative future business managers. Wherever they worked, they should not be afraid to do their proactive creative bit to add value to the corporate processes or to improve of products and services as they had done that day.

With passage of time, I realise his words were full of wisdom and value. No matter how one looks at it, management is a very creative activity, if not the most creative activity—be it in planning, organising, directing or controlling, as well as development of people, products and services. I feel every business activity, every product, is a creative product, just as that painting created by students at the business school. Producing replicas of prototypes is another form of creativity and selling them yet another. Every move in business is creative, just like the stroke of a brush on the canvas. At times I see myself as one of those students walking up on the stage, picking up the brush, dipping it in paint and adding colour on the canvas. I really do.

At times I strongly feel that if business is not creative and innovative, nothing else is. Creativity is the essence of competitive advantage. Business units remain competitive by creatively maintaining their competitive advantages and sharpening their competitive edges. Just like painters, musicians, sculptors or play writers, they do creative work. Creativity is the soul of the business process.

You know, another interesting thing about the teaching methods in that school — teaching started with students being asked to take up a research project on the very first day in the very first class. The students were asked to "go out and discover the mind, heart and soul of a business". They were not given any guidelines and they were free to make teams, if they wanted.

I have often recalled her words. What she had described seemed to be an effective way to make managers aware of the role of creativity in their professional lives — by discovering creativity and innovation in management.

*****

Change and Creative Management Imperatives

Change is omnipresent and impacts everything. It creates multi-faceted challenges. Changes in business environment as well as acts of competitors create various kinds of fault-lines, gaps and frictions in business processes as well as market operations. Each competitor has a different strategic perspective of customers. Competitors use their creative talents to outsmart one another. The objective of every business organisation is to convert the purchasing power of customers into their business revenue streams. An aware, learning and creative organisation is aware of change, understands risks and is prepared to transform opportunities into commercial advantages.

Managers need to be aware of possible emergence of disconnect between their organisations and their customers. Customers constitute the life-line of business units. The bonds with customers may develop weaknesses, flaws and faults due to various reasons, such as:

Inability to understand and keep pace with change: Change is universal. Organisations often fail to keep pace with change. Weaknesses, fault-lines and frictions develop in organisations and business processes. It is not uncommon for business units to experience boiling-frog syndrome.

Change impacts life-span of products, services and business models: It is important to remember that everything — products, services and policies — have a life-span. Change impacts all.

Customer fatigue: Customer requirements, the other side of organisation's life-line, keep changing. Products and services need to keep pace with changing requirements of their customers. With globalisation and mobile global connectivity, customers have many more options. Customers may tend to feel stressed, fatigued and disconnected with their current options sooner than expected.

Changes in relative position: Organisations often fail to notice changes in their relative positions. Even if the rankings remain the same, the distances between competitors may change.

Differences in speeds of learning, unlearning and relearning: Different organisations have different speeds of learning, unlearning and relearning. Different people have different perceptions of change. All this impacts internal relationships in organisations.

Failure to understand customer dynamics: Customers are influenced by their families and friends. Business organisations often fail to keep track of the ways how customers source and use information about their products and services.

With change in the nature of change, business organisations have to adopt new, appropriate, contextual policies toward creative-creation, as well as creative-destruction of their existing offerings. Purposefulness of business purpose must be creatively and contextually enhanced to sustain customer bonding. Change initiates curiosity, questioning and creativity. Solution focused creative management is essential for a business organisation to keep pace with disruptive changes of the digital-era.

*****

Caselet 10.3

Any-Time, Any-Where and Any-Age Entrepreneurship

Aging populations in different parts of the world was an often discussed topic in his business school. Rishu envisioned synergy between digital technologies and senior citizens.

While chatting with his *nani* (grandmother) and other family members, Rishu suggested the possibilities of her venturing out as an entrepreneur. *Nani* and others laughed. He was serious. He was aware of the academic achievements of his *nani* and also the high positions she had held in academics. He asked, "Why not *nani*? Why not?"

He said, "*Nani*, you are a writer and a poet. You have written more than ten books. You know how to use iPad, mobile phone and computer. You have all the basic resources you need."

Nani asked, with a smile, "What business can I do, Rishu?"

Rishu replied with confidence, "Whatever business you want to do. Would you like to be a publisher?"

Nani asked him with a surprised look, "At my age?"

"What has age got to do with it?" he asked.

"I do not have any business degree or background in business," she said.

"Entrepreneurs do not need degrees. Also, there is no age bar for them. Steve Jobs never graduated. Which college did Dhirubhai Ambani go to? Bill Gates does not have a *real* degree. He is a college dropout. And he hasn't written a single poem like you." All laughed. *Nani* hugged Rishu.

Rishu decided to make this into his business class project.

He visualised senior citizens and digital technologies as synergistic business partners.

He visualised senior-citizens as:

- A reservoir of experience, ideas, data and information.
- They had lived as customers and are experienced customers who would know:

- Shortcomings and "irritants" in customer-product relationships.
  - They can suggest product and service improvement ideas.
  - They would know *why* and *what* of business ideas and objectives.
- They had worked in organisations and knew the working of organisations.

He visualised digital technologies along with internet as:

- User friendly, problem solving services and facilities
- Near zero marginal-cost facility for gathering, storing, processing and transmitting information.

He also visualised possibilities of collaborations:

- Between students and grandparents, like he and his *nani*
  - Grandparents and grandchildren (GPGC)
- Collaborations between senior-citizens and junior-citizens (SCJC)
  - Senior-citizens may require inputs of *how*, that is the technology of operations.
- Also, in this context, low-cost and low-risk ventures would be created.

He wondered, was he wrong in visualising synergy between digital technologies and senior-citizens?

He thought that all that was needed was seeding the seeds of curiosity and creativity. Why could his *nani* not become a publisher? What was the missing link?

He visualised a "near zero marginal cost economic zone" consisting of:

- User friendliness of digital technologies
- Knowledge and experience base of senior citizens, and
- Kindled creativity — desire for self-expression or self-actualisation.

He wondered how to go about the whole process. He was keen to crowd-source ideas from his class.

*****

Digital Technologies and Creative Management Synergies

The new era is also known as the digital-era. Information and communication technologies (ICT) facilitate and synergise creative management. Computers and creative thinking form synergistic support systems for business managers. Also, as discussed in earlier chapters, digital business models have introduced many disruptions and new unknowns in the business arenas. Besides new, creative thinking, managers require new attitudes, skills and knowledge (ASK).

Understanding the nature and appropriate use of digital technologies is essential for creative managers. In an uncertain, complex environment, where business is conducted at the speed-of-thought, contextual use of ICT and creative decision making are of critical importance. Artificial intelligence, self-learning machines and predictive analytics are being increasingly used in business processes.

Technology supported organisational systems and creative management thinking are essential for the traditional industrial-era organisations for transitioning to the information-era. Depending on the nature, scope and scale of a business unit, the reasons and need for new technology supported creative management include:

New life-styles, landscapes, cyberscapes and mindscapes: Digital technologies and globalisation have transformed the mind-sets, social and commercial landscapes and life-styles of citizens, customers and voters. New situations require new creative management thinking.

Bonds with customers: Mobile connectivity has transformed product-customer and service-customer bonding. Customers are globally connected and information empowered. Smart systems based dynamic bonds are developing between business organisations and their customers.

Digital technologies based customer bonds: Creative use of artificial intelligence and real-time, big-data analytics is emerging as an integral part of the sales promotion strategy. To enhance customer experience, managers have to learn to make contextual and creative use of new technology options. Many creative methods are being used to *lock-in* customers. To stay *customer-fit* as well as *customer-connected*, insightful understanding of each touch-point of the customers' purchase journey is essential.

Speed of operations: On-the-move customers do their shopping by clicking buttons of their mobile phones. Real-time monitoring of customer shopping behaviour is crucial. Creative management response must match expectations of customers.

All competitive advantages are temporary: Digital technologies have reduced the life-span of competitive advantages. Being customer, future and creativity focused is a strategic imperative for business organisations.

Digital technologies and business operations: Digital technologies are inextricably intertwined with all aspects of business operations. New digital-technology savvy creative management thinking is essential.

New business economics: Cyberspace, disruptive business innovations, new business models, near zero marginal-cost transactions, e-commerce, possibilities of working from home and creating various kinds of real-virtual teams have introduced various kinds new business economic possibilities. Contextual, critical and creative design-thinking and creative management approach are essential.

Globalisation: Globalisation has created new dynamic local-global and global-local sentiments. Cross-cultural and trans-national diversity management is an integral part of creative management.

Real-virtual and local-global business operations: Many organisations operate with multinational, local-global, real-virtual, multi-disciplinary teams. Multi-cultural, integrative and creative management approaches facilitate navigation of business in global business arenas.

Product and service designs: In multi-cultural, local-global operations, business organisations have to ensure appropriateness of their products, services and packaging designs vis-à-vis local needs. To navigate business through dynamic, multi-cultural, business arenas, creative use of business diplomacy is an integral part of global creative management.

New sharing economy: Digital technologies have introduced various new elements in the traditional economic systems as well as economic thinking. Besides e-commerce, technology platforms such as Uber, Airbnb, LendingClubs and Library-of-things, where people can share or lease resources, products, machines and real estate facilities have come up. These economic activities are known by various names such as peer economy, people economy or collaborative economy. All this creates new situations and need for contextual, creative management.

Low marginal cost economy: Internet and digital technologies have reduced the cost of communication, commercial transactions, sourcing, storage, processing and delivery of information, coordination of local and global activities, as well as producing additional units of data, information or software to almost zero. To benefit from new opportunities, new, contextual, creative management thinking is essential.

Multi-cultural global inter-dependence: With global connectivity, global interdependence has increased. New uncertainties keep emerging in cyberspace as well as real physical space due to geo-economic and geo-political dynamics. New continuous awareness and learning approaches are essential.

Era of cyber uncertainties and conflicts: At times, the digital-era seems to be emerging as an era of cyber conflicts. Cyber hacking and cyber security are often discussed topics. It is an era of many unknown risks.

New situations require new thinking, new theories and new paradigms along with new skills and mindset. Machine-driven industrial-era has given way to brain-driven knowledge-era. Managers need to develop insightful understanding of change. New contextual, creative management thinking is an imperative.

Caselet 10.4

Creative Business Fiction

Science fiction includes imagined future science and technical advances as well as socio-economic scenarios. Rishi had read some science fiction stories and also seen some science fiction movies. As a student of business, he wondered — just as science fiction presents various future scenarios of science and technology, could business-technology (bus-tech) fiction be used to present future options for business organisations?

He wondered whether imaginative stories of business organisations making creative use of artificial intelligence in various business activities could be used to sow seeds of innovation, create future business scenarios, visualise future products, services and business models, nudge curiosity and generate ideas?

To test his thoughts, he requested permission to discuss his ideas in class. He made a small presentation to initiate discussions. His class presentation included the following observations:

- Digital technologies and cyberspace offer many creative options for entrepreneurs. Can bus-tech fiction stories be created to show innovative use of digital technologies in areas and activities such as:
  - Artificial intelligence, automation, robotics and Internet-of-Things?
  - Space journeys, future life-styles, work-life and local-global social connects and disconnects?

- Business models, e-commerce and bitcoin options?
- New perceptions of cost, revenue and profits?
- Alternate political, economic, social and technological (PEST) scenarios, including volatility, uncertainty, complexity and ambiguity (VUCA) challenges for creative managers?
- Physical and cyberspace dynamics in the world of business?
- Imaginative start-ups in different industries?
- Future business-war like situations and challenges for creative managers?
- Business organisational architecture and customer-business relations?
- Develop realistic and futuristic business games?
- Competition, big-data, predictive analysis, 3D printing, business-wars in physical and cyberspace?

• Rishi was of the opinion that the creative business fiction would help in:
- Creating curiosity in all employees of the organisation
- Bring all employees of the organisation on the same page
- Help provide future focus with questions:
  ◊ What we can be?
  ◊ What should we want to be?

• Rishi was keen to explore and test the limits of imagination in designing products, services and business models, as well as the use of digital technology in the world of business — both physical and virtual.
- Explore limits of creativity in transforming business fiction into viable business ventures.

Rishi invited feedback from his class. He was also keen to explore the possibilities of developing "creative bus-tech fiction" that could be used in business schools.

*****

Looking Ahead: A Creative Management Perspective

What will be the future scenarios? For managers? For business organisations? What roles will the different digital technologies such as artificial intelligence, virtual reality, Internet-of-Things, predictive analytics and so on, play in business operations?

Will the future business arenas be more level? Fair or unfair? Ethical or unethical? How will the success-failure ratio tilt for business organisations? What will be the dynamics of roles and relationships between artificial-intelligence and human-intelligence? What will be the new challenges-risks-opportunities mix for creative business managers?

Whatever the future, business operations will continue to be networks of creative value adding relationships.

Creativity is future focused. As discussed in the earlier chapters, for sustainable competitiveness in the digital-era, creativity must be nurtured as a core-competency. Creativity in business is a proactive awareness that assimilates learnings from customers as well as competitors. It is an approach that creates a network of creative corporate teams, an ability to find value adding solutions, a desire to enhance competitive advantage and aim for excellence, and a contextual, customer focused, creative approach to enhance customer satisfaction. It is also a solution seeking, creative mindset that is an integral part of the corporate and business culture.

Awareness, curiosity and questioning (ACQ) sustain creativity. To avoid corporate creativity fatigue and enhance sustainability, creativity should be cultivated as an integral part of the work culture. Also, for empathetic understanding of customers as well as competitors, business team members may also be asked to do role plays as customers and competitors. They can act out being their own customers as well as competitors. Organisation team members should be asked to shop and share their experiences as customers and consumers of the products produced and marketed by them. Business may be viewed as a game and enjoyed as a game. It is a continuous, innovative and creative game.

To enhance customer empathy, customers should be invited to be a part of the information sharing process.

Occasionally *mystery-shopping* techniques may be used to evaluate competitive effectiveness of marketing operations. This would facilitate collaborative creativity, institutionalise learning and also help in upward movement on the corporate learning curve.

Development of contextual, creative, business capabilities and competencies must be a cooperative learning process. Mutual trust and respect is essential for professional information sharing. It requires credible creativity promotion policies and a policy framework that provides for respect for ideas, experimentation, failures and re-experimentation.

Business units have networks of business partners and stakeholders. For effective teamwork, cooperation of the business partners and confidence of the stakeholders is essential. Synergising as well as harmonising business partnerships is essential. With an integrative, creative, design-thinking corporate culture, a transformed dynamic partnership framework in the organisation would evolve over time. This may also happen at various corporate-public interface points. All this would require commitment to customer focus and creative management.

To navigate corporations through disruptive VUCA times, managers would have to judiciously and creatively merge hard facts with soft science of meditation. Along with big-data and high-speed computers, business is also a game of head, heart and emotions. It is also a game of mind and mindfulness. A meditative, creative and customer focused mind is an integral part of creative management.

A creative corporation would be a socially aware, good corporate citizen. Creative organisations systematically create new sources of value for their products, services and business processes. Learning and creativity are futuristic activities. Hence, a creative organisation may also be seen as an integrated organisational team trying to craft its own future.

Creative management is a multi-layer, multi-dimensional and multi-faceted management operation. It requires focused, integrative design-thinking. Creative managers have to seed, nurture and harvest creativity in the overall business process.

They have to enhance creative capabilities of each activity and synergise relationships between different activities. This involves analysis as well as synthesis, while being customer focused.

Creativity by itself is of no significance. Only when it is creatively managed and contextualised that it acquires an existence, significance and a meaning. In a way, management gives creativity its life. Simply stated, creative management may also be seen as a proactive, holistic, value-adding, solution focused, management.

Creativity and innovation are processes to create wealth in the world of art as well as business. Management has to constantly rethink its own role and consider creative management options. Creativity, the greatest resource of corporate success, lies within the corporation. It is a matter of initiating it, nurturing it and harvesting it with a creative management mindset. In the disruptive, fast changing, VUCA business environment, creative management is essential to transform visions of future into reality. New situations require new thinking, theories and mindsets. The proposed creative management paradigm is an effort in that direction.

*****

Creative Management: *A Role Play*

Select a business unit of your choice. Give its business profile — physical and cyberspace. State your assumptions regarding its PEST environment and SWOT outline. Give your approach to seed, nurture and harvest creativity in the organisation to make it:

- Competition aware, creative and competitive.
- Excellence focused for long-term sustainability.
- How would you nurture, mentor and monitor sustainability?
- Present some alternate scenarios of:
    - What can be the *ultimate* use of digital technology in your selected business area?

○ What creative challenges would the creative managers face in the fast-changing digital-age in your selected business area?

- Develop a professional profile—attitude, skill-set and knowledge-base (ASK)—you feel would be most appropriate for the creative managers in your selected business area.

*****

Epilogue

I started this learning journey with a few questions. Many more questions cropped up as I moved on. I have tried to include some of them in this book. Many remain unexplored, to be used for future learning.

How does one navigate in a multi-cultural scenario where everything is changing in erratic ways, at varying speeds and in different directions, towards a fuzzy future? Added to this, business itself is a complex, multi-variable game. My learning process was full of contradictory experiences.

Many people from different industries and countries have contributed to my learning. Some helped me in designing answers, others enhanced curiosity and raised more questions and indicated future learning options. I am grateful to all of them for sharing their experiences, observations and perceptions.

I often found myself at the crossroads of learning. The world of business is becoming more turbulent. More VUCA. Within the scope of my enquiry, I have tried to examine the new digital-era contexts and also understand impact of new business models. Like the movement of a paint brush on a canvas, creative management may be seen as a search for contextual and futuristic solutions. I often experienced similar situations as I have presented this book.

Now, as I conclude the current phase of my learning adventure, I feel some of the initial queries raised by the participants at the executive seminar may have remain unanswered. In some ways it feels like a work-in-progress situation. During my learning journey, some of the questions which initiated my learning venture acquired new perspectives and still remain in the forefront include:

Epilogue

- As we transition from industrial-era to the knowledge-era, how should we *unlearn* the industrial-era learnings? This challenge will have to be faced by many Fortune 500 companies.
- How will or should the creativity priorities in business organisations be divided between artificial intelligence embedded self-driven systems, and business leaders?
- What will or should be the role of creativity in the future job profiles?
- How different will or should the business schools be in the knowledge-era?
- Will the business arenas be more or less volatile, uncertain, complex and ambiguous (VUCA) in the knowledge-era?
- As the knowledge-era matures, how different will be the bonds between customers and business organisations?

As I present my reasons and thinking on the need for Creative Management in the knowledge-era, I welcome suggestions from readers to enhance the relevance and utility of the concepts discussed in the book.

Also, I would appreciate suggestions from the readers for further research on related subjects to make Creative Management proposition more comprehensive as well as my learning venture a continuous life-long learning venture.

Thank you!